AS TAIWAN APPROACHES THE NEW MILLENNIUM

Essays on Politics and Foreign Affairs

John F. Copper

University Press of America,® Inc.
Lanham • New York • Oxford

Copyright © 1999 by
University Press of America,® Inc.
4720 Boston Way
Lanham, Maryland 20706

12 Hid's Copse Rd.
Cumnor Hill, Oxford OX2 9JJ

Library of Congress Cataloging-in-Publication Data

Copper, John, F.
Taiwan approaches the new millennium: essays on politics and
foreign affairs/John F. Copper.
p.   cm.
Includes bibliographical references and index.
l. Taiwan—Politics and government—1988- 2. Taiwan—Foreign
relations—1945- 3. Chinese reunification question, 1949-
I. Title. II. Title: Essays on politics and foreign affairs.
DS799.847C65   1999   951.14'905—dc21   99—30463 CIP

ISBN 0-7618-1432-9 (pbk: alk. ppr.)

⊖™ The paper used in this publication meets the minimum
requirements of American National Standard for Information
Sciences—Permanence of Paper for Printed Library Materials,
ANSI Z39.48—1984

To Yuan-li Wu, Scholar and Friend

Contents

Preface

As the twentieth century comes to a close, Taiwan (or the Republic of China, its official name) remains a "front-line" nation in international affairs—something not too different from the position it played during the hot days of the Cold War. In fact, in 1996, as a result of an escalation of the conflict between Taipei and Beijing, the Taiwan Strait was viewed as the number one flashpoint (place where a major war might be ignited) in the world.

When the Republic of China was about to hold its first direct presidential election (the first ever such election in a Chinese political entity in its long 5,000 years of history), China's People's Liberation Army reacted in anger: To disrupt the election it fired missiles at targets close to Taiwan's two biggest ports, closing ship and air traffic and virtually quarantining the island. Beijing's leaders subsequently ordered military exercises that were said to be a mock up to an invasion. The United States responded in kind. President Clinton dispatched aircraft carriers to the scene, and a face-off, including nuclear threats, followed.

One of the root causes of the conflict was Beijing's vastly expanded influence in international affairs as a consequence of a booming economy. China's economic growth had transformed it into an economic giant, and, with the rapidly growing military budget this made possible, it became a military force in the region. That happened while a virulent nationalism supplanted communism in China and a leadership or succession crisis festered.

The second cause was Taiwan's political modernization. Political change had transformed Taiwan from authoritarianism to democracy. This meant that both the leaders and population of Taiwan perceived that their "nation" deserved to choose their own future and that other countries and the world community would agree.

The author hopes that the following chapters will provide the reader with a better understanding of the conflict between Beijing and Taipei, which ultimately will likely involve the United States and the rest of the world. Taiwan's role in the world as the 21st Century approaches will certainly not be a minor one.

John F. Copper

Publisher's Note

The publisher wishes to acknowledge that the essays in chapter 2,3 4 and 5 were published in the following courses.

Chapter 1 was published in the *Journal of Contemporary China* (1997) 6 (15) by Carfax Publishing Ltd.

Chapter 2 was published in John F. Copper, *Taiwan's Mid-1990s Elections: Taking the Final Steps to Democracy* (Westport, CT: Praeger Publisher, 1998).

Chapter 3 was published in *Occasional Papers/Reprints Series in Contemporary Asian Studies*, School of Law, University of Maryland, Number 1—1996.

Chapter 4 was published in the *Journal of East Asian Affairs* (by the Research Institute for International Affairs) Volume XII, Number 2 Summer/Fall 1998.

Chapter One
Introduction

As Taiwan (officially known as the Republic of China or the ROC) approaches the 21st century, the conflict between Taipei and Beijing has become the most salient factor defining its future. Some say Taipei will win the fight and will remain separate. Some say Beijing will win and incorporate Taiwan into the People's Republic of China (PRC). Others suggest a compromise is likely. The United States and the international community favor the latter solution—a compromise. But will their view prevail? The PRC's growing nationalism (and irredentism) and its rapidly increasing military capabilities seem to say no. Political trends in Taiwan, especially the fact that Taiwan has democratized and the population (which does not favor unification, at least in the short run) has much more influence on foreign policy decision making than in the past likewise argues against a moderate solution. The situation in both China and Taiwan indeed seems to indicate that successful negotiations are not likely and that confrontation will continue.

This struggle is not new; it has a long history. The standoff between Beijing and Taipei, in fact, was at center stage in the arena of international politics during the Cold War. And, on at least two occasions their confrontations portended igniting a global war involving the use of nuclear weapons.

In 1954, Beijing attacked Quemoy, one of several islands just off the China coast controlled by the Republic of China known collectively as the Offshore Islands—land that the Nationalist Chinese held after China was "liberated" in 1949 by the Communists. In September the bombardment commenced. In December, in response to the crisis, the United States signed a mutual defense treaty with Taipei. In January 1955, President Eisenhower asked Congress to broaden the scope of the treaty; the Formosa Resolution was passed forthwith authorizing the President to also defend the Offshore Islands if he deemed this necessary to protect Taiwan. By late February, the Chinese People's Liberation Army had seized a number of the Nationalist-held islands. The United States, determined to help Taipei hold Quemoy, prepared tactical nuclear weapons (which it was estimated might kill ten to twelve million people in China).[1] Beijing de-escalated the conflict.

Another confrontation occurred in 1958. Mao was emboldened by the Soviet Union seemingly lurching ahead of the United States in strategic military power after the launching of Sputnik in October 1957; alternatively he want to test China's defense relationship with the Kremlin. That the United States was preoccupied with conflict in the Middle East was possibly also part of China's calculation. In July, Mao ordered another attack on Quemoy and for forty-four days and nights artillery shells rained on the island. This time the Chinese air force and navy joined the attack. The result was an even stronger U.S. response than in 1954. Washington moved seven aircraft carriers and accompanying ships to the Taiwan Strait and sent 3,800 marines and a number of fighter planes to Taiwan. The Seventh Fleet ferried weapons and supplies to Nationalist forces on Quemoy through ocean space claimed by China as its national waters and within range of its artillery. With even greater adamancy than in 1954-55, the United States government made nuclear threats. The conflict ended with China continuing to fire on Quemoy, but only every other day—on odd number days.

In 1962, there were ominous signs that another conflagration was about to occur. Aware of domestic political instability in Taiwan, or perhaps perceiving his leadership to be in trouble due to his masterminding the disastrous Great Leap Forward, after which China experienced widespread famine, Mao planned another siege. He readied one-half million troops, 150 ships, 600 aircraft and other weapons of war. He intended to urge North Korea to attack South Korea as part of the battle plan and even considered sending 100,000 troops to Africa to create a diversion there. The People's Liberation Army deployed long range guns near Quemoy to destroy U.S. ships entering the conflict to supply Nationalist forces on the island. The Chief of Staff of China's military voiced his support for Mao's plan.[2] In the end, however, for reasons unknown, the plan was not implemented.

In 1975, Deng Xiaoping, then Chief-of-Staff of the People's Liberation Army, ordered the PLA to draft contingency plans for resolving the "Taiwan issue." Deng may have perceived that in the wake of its defeat in Vietnam the United States did not have the will to defend Taiwan. Another possibility is that Mao issued the order because of a concern over popular dissatisfaction with his government following the bitterly divisive Cultural Revolution and various Communist Party intrigues such as the Lin Biao affair (when Mao's heir apparent, who was also China's defense minister, allegedly attempted to assassinate Mao and was killed himself while trying to flee to the Soviet Union). In any case, the United States, at this juncture, reaffirmed its support for Taiwan and the plan was canceled.[3]

During the two Offshore Islands crises and the two occasions when Beijing drew up plans to "liberate" Taiwan, charges were made that the United States sought to create two Chinas or an independent Taiwan. Mention of China's "lost territory" in every instance served as a call to action. Internal political instability also appeared to be an influencing factor in most if not all of these cases. Problems elsewhere that diverted the attention of the United States were also a common factor. Cold War hostilities and the bipolar system constituted the backdrop.

One might think that the end of the Cold War would have ended the Beijing-Taipei feud, or at least dampened it and made it easier to revolve. After all their conflict was part of the bipolar struggle between Communism and democracy/capitalism. However, the end of the Cold War saw instead the intensification of hostilities across the Taiwan Strait and Taipei faced a dramatically increased external threat. There were several reasons for this.

As a product of the end of the Cold War, Sino-Soviet relations saw a quick and marked improvement. This had at least two, and perhaps three, serious implications for Taiwan.

First, during the Cold War the People's Republic of China maintained a high level of military forces on the Sino-Soviet border. In fact, more People's Liberation Army manpower and more strategic weapons were positioned on the northern border than anywhere else in China. After all, China's main enemy was the Soviet Union. When the Soviet bloc began to dissolve, signals of which became apparent in 1989, a thaw in relations followed. This made it possible for Beijing to transfer military forces away from the border and relocate them to other places in China. Across the Taiwan Strait in Fujian Province was the favored place where military units and weapons were sent. Thus, the level of military forces Taiwan faced, unlike most other nations which benefited from the decline in global military spending and the fading of the threat of armed attack after the Cold War, vastly increased.

Second, the collapse of the former Soviet Union was accompanied by serious economic travail in what then became Russia. A shortage of foreign exchange was soon a serious problem. Russia had little it could sell abroad except arms. Because of this situation the Kremlin changed its arms exports policies and almost anyone with money could buy whatever weapons Russia produced. Beijing had money—after over a decade of phenomenal economic growth. It not only bought weapons, but plants to build them and scientists to improve upon them.

Third, for years observers had speculated that the Soviet Union preferred Taiwan to remain independent. Soviet ships had signaled bases in Taiwan and military and diplomatic officials made contacts with Taiwan from time to time. Taiwan was a convenient diversion when Beijing brought up the issue of territory it claimed in the Soviet Union. Taipei thus seemed to have a possible supporter in coping with Beijing's intimidation. With Sino-Soviet relations warming after the Cold War and Moscow's military-industrial complex becoming dependent upon China's buying its products, this situation changed.

Also, coinciding with the end of the Cold War, internal politics in China changed dramatically. After the Tiananmen "turmoil, China's political leadership took a sharp turn to the left and hard-liners, who opposed Deng's capitalist reforms and intensely disliked Taiwan, plus the military, which also did not like Taiwan's independent status, now had much more political clout. They had distinctly shorter fuses when it came to Taiwan talking about or moving toward independence.

Because the military "rescued" the Chinese Communist Party and the government (according to Deng Xiaoping at least), it was, moreover, favored in ensuing years with steady increases in its budgets. In fact, in the next eight years it probably tripled.[4] Of special poignancy: many of the weapons purchased with the new funds were earmarked for military action against Taiwan. Making matters even worse, new military procurements have generally favored the navy. If Beijing were to boycott, quarantine, invade or take almost any action against the island, its navy would play a leading role. China's naval buildup was thus especially ominous for Taiwan.

The military situation for Taiwan thus became critical. The balance of power across the Taiwan Strait, in fact, became so seriously out-of-balance that in 1992 President Bush, who was generally known for his pro-Beijing views, acceded to Taiwan's request to purchase 150 F-16 fighter aircraft from the United States. Bill Clinton, who became president the next year, agreed with Bush's decision and delivered the planes. This, of course, angered Chinese leaders in Beijing, who accused the United States of arming Taiwan so that it could resist its offers to negotiate and "return to the fatherland."

Another part of the equation is that Deng Xiaoping gradually supplanted communism with Chinese nationalism after he came to power in 1978. By the 1990s, nationalist feelings had become very strident and a potent force in Chinese politics. It also became a major factor influencing Sino-American relations and Beijing-Taipei relations. Nationalism, moreover, engendered irredentism, which made "lost territory" an even more important issue. Beijing demanded the return of Hong Kong and Macao, and got both (Hong Kong in July 1997; Macao will be returned in December 1999). Taiwan remained "outside the fold."

Deng, to use a Chinese expression, was "riding on the back of a tiger"—meaning that he had unleashed a force that he himself was not able to control. Chinese nationalism, in fact, was used against Deng by the military and hard-line leftists in the party and government who demanded that Deng take a stronger position on the issue of Taiwan's reunification and press the United States to help. Deng did not want to endanger China's economic development by straining relations with the United States over Taiwan, but at times he was compelled to take a hard line on Taiwan. Jiang Zemin, his successor, has been compelled to do so also.

Since the United States provided arms to Taiwan and supported democracy there, hard-line Chinese leaders saw Washington as seeking to keep China divided and "colluding" with independence advocates in Taiwan to accomplish that. Further suspicion and anti-Americanism in China were engendered by U.S. policies on human rights, Washington's opposition to Beijing's arms sales, accusations about Beijing's alleged nuclear proliferation, and complaints about the trade imbalance. However, among areas of disagreement the "Taiwan issue" seemed to be the only one impossible to resolve by negotiations.

The big question then for the United States was, and is, how to manage the stand-off between Beijing and Taipei and prevent it from damaging U.S.-China relations or escalating into a conflict that might draw the United States into a war with China.

To better understand the current situation some background is helpful. The recent crisis finds its origins in 1989, when China's image was very seriously, perhaps irreversibly, sullied by the Tiananmen Massacre. This event not only drew attention to China's human rights abuses, but increased the political influence of the left and the military (both of whom as noted above disliked Taiwan and advocated stronger measures to resolve the "Taiwan issue.") At the same time, Taiwan held a watershed election: one that pushed the democratization process ahead by a giant leap. It was also an election that saw the opposition party, the Democratic Progressive Party, which has long advocated the independence of Taiwan and its permanent separation from China, make significant gains in the legislative branch of government. Following the election speculation was rife that the DPP would be in power within a few years or perhaps after the next election—if the

opposition party could simply persuade or force the "senior
parliamentarians" (those delegates to the Republic of China's elected
bodies of government who were elected when the ROC ruled all of
China or who were appointed to replace those who died and whose
presence sustained the Nationalist Party's claim to a one-China policy)
to give up their positions.[5]

The senior parliamentarians, in fact, resigned in 1991, and forthwith
there was a plenary election for the National Assembly. The next year,
in 1992, there was also a plenary election of the Legislative Yuan (the
lawmaking body of government). The DPP performed well in the latter
election, again leading to speculation that it would control that branch
of government very soon—probably in the next election in 1995. Leaders in Beijing viewed these development with grave concern.[6]

Beijing hence launched a new offensive. It sought to both intimidate
Taipei and to diplomatically isolate Taiwan and thus force it to accept
China's demands to discuss reunification. President Lee Teng-hui
countered with pragmatic diplomacy (pursuing foreign relations
without concern about formal diplomatic ties or a said nation's position
on whether there was one China or two). Taipei also began to promote
the argument that Taiwan had democratized (as opposed to China, a
dictatorship, which had not) and that unification was thus a decision to
be made by the populace (knowing that numerous public opinion polls
reflected that the public did not favor unification, but rather the status
quo). Lee and other top leaders also talked of Taiwan's right as a
democratic nation to determine its own future and the plight of its
citizens and human rights abuses in Taiwan, not to mention a likely
exodus of people, if Taiwan were forced into unification with the communist People's Republic of China. Beijing perceived all of this with
extreme displeasure.

Americans and the United States Congress were convinced that
Taipei had a valid argument and that it deserved better treatment.
Underscoring Taiwan's shabby treatment by the United States, in 1994
President Lee sought to get off his plane during a transit stop in the
United States while in route to Central America and on to South Africa
to attend Nelson Mandela's inauguration and was refused. President
Clinton subsequently met Gerry Adams (whom many labeled a terror-
ist). The contrast prompted the press to criticize the Clinton Adminis-
tration for shunning the leader of the most successful democratizing
nation in the world while 'wining and dining" a terrorist leader in the
White House. Congress was also upset and put pressure on the
Administration to revamp U.S. policy toward Taiwan. A few months

later the Taiwan Policy Review allowed a name change for Taiwan's representative offices in the United States and more access for its diplomats.

The next year, when President Lee sought to make a trip to the United States to attend a graduation ceremony at his alma matter, Cornell University (where he got his Ph.D in agricultural economics), the State Department promised Chinese leaders in Beijing that Lee would not be granted a visa and hence would not visit the United States. The promise was made by Assistant Secretary for Asia and the Pacific Winston Lord and Secretary Warren Christopher. An angry Congress forthwith voted on a sense of the Congress resolution—with an overwhelming majority favoring it—saying that Lee should be given a visa. Worried about relations with Congress, President Clinton ordered that President Lee be given a visa.

Hard-liners in Beijing went ballistic and made their views felt within the leadership. China terminated on-going talks with Taipei. A barrage of anti-Americanism followed. In this context and amidst a succession problem (Deng was ill and was not expected to live long), the military assumed greater decision making authority and ordered missile tests near Taiwan's shores. The tests frightened the population of Taiwan and impacted the election—incidentally just as Beijing hoped inasmuch as the opposition Democratic Progressive Party did not do as well as expected and the Nationalist Party (led by President Lee whom Beijing labeled a splittist and a traitor, among other pejoratives) also lost seats. The pro-unification New Party performed very well.[7]

The United States reacted post facto by sending the aircraft carrier *Nimitz* through the Taiwan Strait as an apparent warning to Beijing. It was the first time for a U.S. carrier to pass through the Strait in almost two decades. The Department of State said the *Nimitz* took the course it did because of bad weather. Many observers thought differently.

Thus, the stage was set for more serious confrontations...

Chapter 2 assesses the different views of the "Taiwan issue" as espoused by the governments, scholars and people on the two sides of the Taiwan Strait. The issues of history, Taiwan's legal status, differences in perception by both sides, current relations, and the global context of the dispute are analyzed.

The two sides, Beijing and Taipei, as this chapter explains, differ markedly on whether a study of Taiwan's history indicates it is part of China or not. The government of the People's Republic of China, and scholars representing the government, have written several treatises in recent years arguing Taiwan is a part of China based on early exploration and contacts. Contrariwise, Taiwan scholars argue these were too intermittent and no territorial claim was ever made. The two sides also give a different slant to Taiwan's more recent history when it was ruled by China (under the Manchu Dynasty) and Japan (from 1895 to 1945). Taiwanese say they were ruled by the Manchus as a colony and less efficiently and with much worse cruelty than the Dutch earlier or the Japanese later. Chinese historians in Beijing must contend with the fact that most officials sent to Taiwan were neither competent nor benevolent. Still, they refute the notion that Taiwan was ruled like a colony by a foreign regime, that it did not prosper at this time, or that it lost its Chinese identity. Finally, it is worth noting that Taiwanese generally applaud Japanese rule; Mainland Chinese (both in China and in Taiwan) have or espouse considerable antipathy toward Japan and do not like this interpretation.

Beijing claims it is the successor government to the Republic of China. Therefore the transfer of Taiwan to the ROC after WWII meant Taiwan legally became part of the People's Republic of China in 1949. Officials as well as legal scholars in Taiwan have a good riposte: The Republic of China still exists; so there is no successor government. The two sides also disagree about the relevant declarations and treaties and about how other governments, especially the United States, interpret both past treaties and the present legal status of the two governments. The argument about Taiwan's legal status is obviously a divisive one.

Fundamental perceptions of the "Taiwan issue" espoused by the governments, scholars and population on the two sides of the Taiwan Strait also differ markedly. In the People's Republic of China, the view is that the population of Taiwan is Chinese. In Taiwan, many Taiwanese (Chinese whose parents were born in Taiwan) consider themselves Taiwanese rather than Chinese, or think of themselves as Chinese only in the sense that caucasian Americans consider themselves European. In fact, one recent poll, incidentally, indicates that only 15 percent of the residents of Taiwan view themselves as Chinese.[8]

Both leaders and the populations on both sides similarly hold very different views on whether or not China should be united. Chinese leaders in Beijing feel very strongly that it should be. They are acutely aware that history has treated leaders who have united China as heros; historians see leaders who have allowed China to break up as poor leaders, or even as traitors. In Taiwan, on the other hand, scholars have pointed out that a united China is not the norm in Chinese history; it has been divided at least half of the time. Moreover, they say, human rights fared better when China was divided. They might also note that the government of the People's Republic of China has decentralized power and that this has contributed to its economic prosperity and expanded civil and political liberties. Some in Taiwan also point out that unification is proceeding inasmuch as economic ties across the Strait have intensified and this is enough for now.

It follows that there are big disparities between the two sides in terms of views about their current relations. And that is the case. Beijing claims that Taiwan is a province of China and that the Republic of China does not possess sovereignty; Taipei contends the Republic of China is a sovereign nation-state. Beijing promotes the "one country, two systems" formula for bringing Taiwan "back into the fold"; officials and scholars in Taiwan say this formula, which was created for the reversion of Hong Kong, doesn't apply to Taiwan since Taiwan is a nation, not a colony, and can defend itself. They say also that Taiwan is being offered a special status when it becomes part of China, something like Tibet, which has been grossly mistreated by Beijing. More recently, they point to problems in Hong Kong itself.

Clearly the "one country, two systems" formula has no appeal in Taiwan.[9] Leaders in Taipei instead suggest a "one China, two governments" formula, or the "German Formula." The two Germanies did not obstruct the other's formal diplomatic ties and both gained membership in the United Nations; only then they were able to successfully negotiate reunification. How can the two sides negotiate, Taiwan asks, when the word negotiation, and its practice as well, assumes the sovereign equality of the negotiators? Taipei demands that Beijing repudiate the use of force; Beijing, seeing the matter as a domestic dispute, of course, refuses.

Talks between the two antagonists, called the Koo-Wang in Taiwan and the Wang-Koo talks in Beijing, in 1993 brought the two sides together for the first time to resolve some of these problems. Little of real substance was accomplished, but it was a significant beginning. However, President Lee Teng-hui's visit to the United States in 1995 prompted Beijing to cancel these talks. The two "negotiators" met again in mid-1998. Talks were thus renewed, even though again little was accomplished except that a further deterioration in relations seemed to have been stopped. On both sides, the view prevails that cross-Taiwan Strait relations are not friendly.[10] Thus, the situation of bad relations remains basically unaltered.

Beijing and Taipei, last but not least, hold opposing views about the global context of their dispute. Officials in Beijing assert that Taiwan is being more and more diplomatically isolated. It is true that Taipei has formal diplomatic ties with no important nation in the world. In 1998, it lost ties with four countries. It has diplomatic ties with only twenty-some countries. But, it contends it maintains meaningful economic, cultural and other ties with more than 140 countries. It says the international community favors Taipei (which almost everyone recognizes is a genuine democracy) over Beijing (which is a pariah nation as a product of the Tiananmen Massacre and its authoritarian political system). Thus, time may be on Taiwan's side. On both sides there are vastly different views about the global context of their dispute. This complicates the matter still further. In the People's Republic of China, many in the military, plus hard-line leftists, advocate disregarding the international community and using force to deal with Taiwan; civilian leaders, especially reformists, do not agree. In the ROC, a number of opposition leaders call for Taiwan to join the North American Free Trade Association and maintain trade and other ties with the West or try to become the "Switzerland of the East" (implying neutrality). Others say this is unrealistic; they predict that Taiwan's future is with the Pacific Rim bloc or "Greater China." They think Taiwan's future will be decided by economic forces and, in the long run, its future will be with China.

Chapter 3 concerns the watershed election held in Taiwan in March 1996. This election was the capstone on Taiwan's nearly two-decade long process of democratization. It brought Taipei-Beijing differences to a head. It brought the United States into the conflict, and for a time it appeared that a "shooting war" between the U.S. and the People's Republic of China might result.

This election was preceded by two others in 1994 and 1995 that help explain its salience in terms of the democratization process and cross Strait relations. In 1994, Taiwan held elections for the Taiwan provincial governor for the first time. This had previously been an appointed position; a recent constitutional amendment changed this. It was the first-ever national election in the sense that the political parties had to campaign island-wide for a provincial chief executive. They compete only in electoral districts in national elections. Elections were also held for the mayorships of Taiwan's two metropolitan cities (Taipei and Kaohsiung); these positions had been appointed jobs for some time. Voters, in addition, chose a new provincial assembly and two metropolitan city councils.

The campaign for provincial governor evoked a debate about foreign policy issues and Taiwan's relationship with China not seen before. The "ethnic" issue (actually a sub-ethnic matter) of Taiwanese versus Mainland Chinese also pervaded the campaigning since the incumbent and winner, James Soong, a Mainlander, was the Nationalist Party's stalwart, yet the government was becoming dominated by "native" Taiwanese and the opposition party had long campaigned successfully for more "Taiwanization" of the political system. Finally, the opposition Democratic Progressive Party's candidate, Chen Shui-bian, won the Taipei mayorship. Chen was known as a strong advocate of independence (even within the DPP, which had put a tenet of its basic policy, one calling for an independent Taiwan, in its party platform) and reflected that during the campaign. Finally, Beijing's People's Liberation Army (PLA) held military exercises during the campaigning. Taiwan replied by holding its own military games.[11]

In 1995, Beijing-Taipei relations headed quickly southward. In February, newspapers in Taiwan published reports of Beijing redeploying surface-to-surface missiles to a location putting Taiwan within their range of fire. China's military having just seized an island in the South China Sea claimed by the Philippines and President Jiang Zemin having just warned Taiwan about talk of independence in his New Year's address, Taiwan became jittery. Relations worsened even more dramatically when President Lee visited the United States in June, the first visit by a high official from Taiwan since the United States and the Republic of China broke diplomatic relations in 1979 and the first ever by a president of the Republic of China. Lee, while at his alma mater, Cornell University, made a splash with the media and promoted the case for Taiwan's sovereignty and better treatment by the international community. U.S. Congressmen went to see him. As noted above, leaders in Beijing were incensed. They felt they had been not only lied to by the Department of State but also that the United States had reneged on its promises about keeping Taiwan at arms length and dealing with Taipei only informally (which meant not allowing Taiwan's leader to visit the United States). In anger the PLA conducted missile tests in the Taiwan Strait just days after Lee's visit. Beijing made other threats and even talked of using "fresh blood and lives" to prevent Taiwan from rejecting reunification. Looking at the results of the election (the pro-unification party did well; the Nationalist Party did poorly and the opposition DPP was disappointed by its performance and many of its top candidates lost), Beijing won.

The election in March 1996 constituted the biggest challenge yet to Beijing. And its leaders became even angrier. The Republic of China, which Beijing denied was a country, held a direct election for its chief executive officer, the president. It was the first such election of a national leader in 5,000 years of Chinese history, so the Western media noted. Taiwan was said to be the most democratic country in East Asia, with the exception of Japan. Others said it was the best example of democratization among Third World countries. No one said anymore that Taiwan was not democratic. Autocracy or dictatorship, as words used to describe Taiwan, were a thing of the past. Taiwan's image in the international community and in the United States was much improved as a result of the election.

In the minds of leaders in China, Taiwan's democratization was nothing more than the product of a foreign plot to keep Taiwan from re-unifying with China and thus keep China divided. Democracy and "splitism," an emotion-laden term Beijing used now with great frequency, became synonymous. Beijing also viewed the United States as plotting to keep China weak and saw Washington's encouragement of democracy as part of this effort. On America's part protecting Taiwan became viewed as part of America's "responsibility" and linked to its "destiny" to promote democracy throughout the world. Thus Taiwan's 1996 election was a watershed event in terms of both democratization and a new strain in United States-People's Republic of China relations.

In addition, the election, precipitating as it did an ominous confrontation between Washington and Beijing when the Clinton Administration sent two aircraft carriers and a flotilla of ships with each to the area, transformed the "China threat" idea from a minority position to the majority view. The next year, Richard Bernstein and Ross Monro published the book *The Coming Struggle with China* which created an intense policy debate in Washington that has still not ended. Profound questions arose: Is China America's enemy? Is the system reverting to a bipolar one, with China replacing the Soviet Union as the other pole? Does failing to see China's intentions correctly and acting on the premise that China will be, if it is not already, America's antagonist, constitute dangerous appeasement? Or will labeling China such make an enemy of China, which it is not now, and the China threat become a self-fulfilling prophesy?

Meanwhile, other East Asian countries, most of whom, including Japan, were very concerned about China's expansionism as reflected in its "aggressive" actions in the South China Sea (such as seizing an island there claimed by the Philippines in early 1995 after taking some other islands claimed by Vietnam earlier) and making territorial claims to the Senkaku Islands, islands north of Taiwan returned to Japan by the United States in the 1970s.

What is more, going into the election it looked as if Beijing's nemesis, Lee Teng-hui, whom China accused of being a closet supporter of Taiwan independence, seemed a sure winner. Thus, the dispute between Beijing and Taipei took on a personal character, something like the one between Mao and Chiang Kai-shek which lasted until the mid-1970s and added to the bitter nature of the conflict across the Taiwan Strait.

This election was also important, as noted above, because it constituted in the minds of many observers a turning point or a "final-Isetan" of the democratization process in Taiwan. Afterwards few observers, including the Western media, talked about Taiwan becoming a democracy. It was now a genuine or "full-fledged" democracy.

In terms of its impact on domestic politics in Taiwan, the election seemed to mark the transition to a presidential system. This also had implications. Having a direct election for the president certainly gave President Lee, and presumably this applies to all future presidents, a very strong democratic mandate that Taiwan's chief executives did not have before.

Drawing even more attention to the democratic nature of the election, President Lee was challenged by three other candidates during the campaign. One was Peng Ming-min, a strong advocate of independence. He represented the opposition Democratic Progressive Party. He had been imprisoned in the 1960s for promoting independence and later lived in the United States for many years. Peng was known in Taiwan as the "father of Taiwan independence." Two other candidates, or sets of candidates (since the contestants were teams of presidential and vice presidential candidates), ran as independents, though one set was favored by the New Party, which advanced unification. All of the candidates were well known locally. One vice presidential candidate was a woman.

There were thus clear choices for the electorate. This and the lively nature of the campaign and Beijing's intimidation engendered intense voter interest.

President Lee and the ruling Nationalist Party won the election with more than half of the popular vote in a four-way contest, a clear victory. He was aided, some said, by a backlash caused by Beijing's missile tests and intimidation. Beijing influenced the 1995 election as it wanted with such tactics; this time it had the opposite effect.

As noted in the concluding part of Chapter 3, this election had significance that would last for some time. Indeed it has.

Chapter 4 assesses the situation in the ruling Nationalist Party at the time of it 15th party congress, held in August 1997, and what the party accomplished and failed to accomplish in terms of internal reform, choosing new leaders, etc. It was a critical time for the KMT. Since the 1996 election when it won a major victory and President Lee was given a new and special mandate many serious problems beset the ruling party. Clearly, all was not well.

After the 1996 election President Lee became the target of blame for increasing crime and corruption. There had been a sharp increase in some categories of crime, notably kidnapping. Political corruption had gotten much worse in the eyes of the public and gangs were seen to be involved in politics much more and were making their influence felt through elected officials who were venal or afraid. Crime had also been sensationalized by the media aided by some vicious and highly publicized incidents.

Three months before the Party Congress, one of Taiwan's, and the Nationalist Party's, "best and brightest," Ma Ying-jeou, who earlier had served as Minister of Justice and in that job had with great determination cracked down on vote-buying, political corruption and crime in general, resigned in protest. This discredited the party's efforts to crack down on corruption and hurt the party's image

Causing the ruling party considerable travail also was the fact that it had not done well enough in the 1995 Legislative Yuan election to have a solid majority and it was having to play coalition politics in legislative sessions. Meanwhile the Legislative Yuan had increased its powers as a result of democracy and the new talent recent elections had brought into this organ of government. The legislature thus challenged the executive branch on many important issues. In some cases, the "leftist" Democratic Progressive Party and the "rightist" New Party co-operated. The DPP also controlled the mayorship of Taipei, its standard bearing having won that job in 1994. He was popular and did his best (or worst) at times to torment the ruling party in the capital city. In many respects politics was now a "new ball game" in Taiwan and KMT leaders found it difficult to adjust.

Democracy and the direct election of the president also changed the way the political system operated putting it out at variance with the way it was supposed to work according to the Constitution. This necessitated basic political reform. This was a big task and required the ruling party to get support from the opposition.

In December 1996, President Lee convened the National Development Conference to debate various systemic problems and other fundamental and important political issues. Lee called for consensus building, but this was difficult. He won the Democratic Progressive Party's support in dealing with the most controversial issue: downsizing or eliminating the provincial government. The issue, for Lee, was overlap and the cost of government. Yet the provincial government was popular, generally effective, and its governor elected for the first time in 1994. Eliminating a lower level of government was also divisive.

Provincial Governor James Soong tendered his resignation. He and President Lee subsequently became in the words of the press "bitter enemies." Clearly the ruling Nationalist Party's two most popular leaders were at odds and this was hurting party unity. It also brought to question the party's future leadership since Lee was presumably not going to be a candidate for the presidency again and did not want Soong to succeed him.

Governor Soong did not attend the meeting. His friends did though and represented him. Soong received a resounding vote of support when it came time to pick new party leaders. Lee, however, ignored Soong and made Vice President Lien Chan the top vice chairman of the party. This put Lien in line to be the next party chairman and its presidential candidate in 2000. Yet Lien did not have Soong's popularity. The party is still plagued by this dilemma.

The issue of Hong Kong was also on everyone's mind in Taiwan. It had reverted to the People's Republic of China's jurisdiction on July 1, 1997. Hong Kong was important to Taiwan. Trade with China flowed through Hong Kong. Beijing said that the "one country, two systems" formula used to incorporate Hong Kong would be employed also to "bring Taiwan back into the fold." President Lee and others said otherwise. Not only did Hong Kong's fate create apprehension in Taiwan, it also reignited the controversy about Taiwan's future and the independence versus reunification argument.

Finally, the ruling party hoped to build unity and get ready for local elections in November. As it turned out it did not do this very well. The opposition Democratic Progressive Party won an overwhelming victory in that election, giving it control over local executives that have jurisdiction over more than 70 percent of the population.

Chapter 5 assesses the changing role of the United States in Beijing-Taipei relations. For years the United States has skirted the problem by saying that the "Taiwan issue," or problems across the Taiwan Strait, or between Beijing and Taipei, were for "the Chinese to resolve themselves." The United States would play no direct role. This meant, in short, that it was too difficult a problem for the United States to resolve and/or it was a problem Washington saw no hope and no gain in trying to negotiate.

Thus when the Nixon Administration sought a rapprochement with China, it dealt with the Taiwan problem by obfuscation. Chinese on both sides of the Taiwan Strait, said the Shanghai Communiqué signed at the end of the Nixon visit, agree that there is but one China. Since no one had done an opinion poll asking this question, no one knows whether this was true or not. Presumably, in Taiwan at least, it was not true. In any case, the statement depended upon what is meant by one China. China is a term that has never been clearly defined. Is China a country or a culture? Are we to assume that Taiwan or the Republic of China does not have sovereignty? More nations of the world had diplomatic ties with Taipei than with Beijing at the time, including the United States.

President Jimmy Carter, who sought a more clear and forthright U.S. foreign policy, created even more ambiguity when he established formal diplomatic relations with the People's Republic of China and "abandoned" Taiwan in 1979. The Normalization Agreement was woefully short on explanations. Subsequently the Congress passed the Taiwan Relations Act into law—the only time in U.S. history when the legislative branch of government set the parameters for United States policy vis-a-vis a foreign country. This created what some called "two China policies": one made by the executive branch and another made by the legislative branch. Clearly the two were at odds about relations with both Beijing and Taipei after that, making it difficult to design coherent policies.

But maybe this was all for the better. It was at times certainly convenient. In fact, it led to the use of the term "strategic ambiguity" when talking about the "Taiwan issue" and as well to Washington's relationship with Taipei. Washington-Taipei relations could hardly be completely unofficial in view of the Taiwan Relations Act. Yet the United States had promised Beijing it would have only unofficial relations with Taiwan. Whether the United States was Taiwan's protector or not was also a question. The TRA suggests so; a communiqué concluded (but not signed) in 1982 between Washington and Beijing, in which the United States pledged (but assumed a promise of a peaceful settlement of the dispute by Beijing, which

Chinese leaders forthwith said they did not make) to reduce arms sales to Taiwan, hinted otherwise.

If Taiwan cannot buy weapons from the United States, and it has had serious difficulties trying to purchase them elsewhere, it will presumably be forced to negotiate reunification with Beijing on the latter's terms. Or at least Beijing presumes this, explaining why it has so strenuously opposed such sales. Yet, in view of Taiwan being a democracy and China not, should the United States withhold sales? China's rapid military buildup after 1989 which threatened other East Asian countries and seemed to challenge the United States as well as threaten Taiwan became a factor influencing this debate. In 1992, President Bush decided in favor of Taiwan and agreed to the sale of F-16 fighter planes to Taipei, seemingly putting the question to rest.

Since Chinese leaders in Beijing at the time faced a host of other problems and considered George Bush their friend, they could forgive him for this and not make major trouble over the U.S. decision. But this did not end the matter.

The face-off in 1996 after China's missile tests in the Taiwan Strait and the Clinton Administration's sending aircraft carriers, led to a re-appraisal of the U.S. position of not trying to negotiate Beijing-Taipei differences. So did the big election victory of the Democratic Progressive Party in 1997 and the more serious talk in Taiwan about declaring independence the opposition party's win evoked. And while the White House sought to dampen the conflict with China and responded to the opposition's election win by warning against talk and any action toward independence or separation, Congress became more and more sympathetic toward Taiwan. The Clinton Administration did not have a good reputation in making foreign policy anyway and Republicans liked Taiwan better than Democrats. So Congress made its views known.

President Clinton sent a number of former high ranking officials to Taiwan to get opposition leaders there to cool the talk of independence and to influence public opinion. Some hinted that the United States would not come to Taiwan's rescue if it provoked an attack by Beijing by declaring independence. The White House also made its support of talks between Beijing and Taipei known. It even seemed to offer to do more. When talks were held in October 1998, the United States expressed its approval.

Meanwhile, the Clinton Administration announced the termination of the policy of strategic ambiguity as Congress complained about lack of clarity contributing to uncertainty and even being the possible cause of confrontation. In its place the Administration talked about "engagement" and "comprehensive engagement" with China while delivering more arms to Taiwan and even mentioning, or allowing mention of, anti-missile defense with Taiwan or at least upgrading Taipei's capabilities in this realm.

The chapters that follow provide more details on these three topics, topics which are critical to Taiwan's future and to understanding Taiwan's role in the world as it approaches a new century.

1. See "Draft Policy Statement Prepared in the Department of State," April 8, 1955, in John P. Glennon and Harriet D. Schwar (eds.), *Foreign Relations of the United States, 1955-57, Volume 2* (Washington, DC: U.S. Government Printing Office, 1988), p. 459.

2. Weiqun Gu, *Conflicts of Divided Nations: The Cases of China and Korea* (Westport, CT: Praeger Publisher, 1995), pp. 26–27.

3. Ibid, pp. 28–29.

4. The amount of military budget increases in China is a subject of much debate. It is clear that Taiwan has perceived that vastly increased military spending by China has increased the level of military threat it faces. For details, see Dennis VanVranken Hickey, *Taiwan's Security in a Changing International System* (Boulder, CO: Lynne Rienner Press, 1997), chapter 8.

5. See John F. Copper, *Taiwan's Recent Elections: Fulfilling the Democratic Promise* (Baltimore: University of Maryland School of Law, 1990), chapter 4.

6. See John F. Copper, *Taiwan's 1991 and 1992 Non-Supplemental Elections: Reaching a Higher State of Democracy* (Lanham, MD: University Press of America, 1994), chapters 2 and 3.

7. See John F. Copper, *Taiwan's Mid-1990s Elections: Taking the Final Steps to Democracy* (Westport, CT: Praeger Publisher, 1998), chapter 3.

8. See "Taiwan Briefs," *Topics,* November 1988.

9. According to a recent poll (June 1998), more than 70 percent of Taiwan's population disapprove of the formula; less than 10 percent approve. See ibid.

10. Only 21 percent of those polled recently call relations "friendly." See ibid. The writer has seen no such poll conducted in the People's Republic of China. Increased hostility by the government toward Taiwan indicates that a poll would not reflect "friendly" relations.

11. For details on this election, see John F. Copper, *Taiwan's Mid-1990s Elections: Taking the Final Steps to Democracy* (Westport, CT: Praeger, 1998), chapter 2.

Chapter Two
The Origins of Conflict Across the Taiwan Strait: The Problem of Differences in Perceptions

Introduction

In February 1995, officials in the Republic of China (ROC) announced that they had learned that the military of the People's Republic of China (PRC), the People's Liberation Army (PLA), had just redeployed surface-to-surface missiles from elsewhere in China to Fujian Province just across the Taiwan Strait, putting Taiwan within their range of fire.[1] Giving this incident greater salience, if indeed it needed it, the revelation came just a short time after the PLA seized an island (Mischief Reef) in the South China Sea near to and claimed by the Philippines.[2] Both events occurred in the wake of PRC President Jiang Zemin's New Year's speech in which he accused Taipei of insincerity regarding talks leading to the reunification of Taiwan with the People's Republic of China.[3]

All of this signaled a more aggressive PRC policy vis-a-vis Taiwan and an end to a several-year period of steadily improving relations between Taipei and Beijing during which time successful negotiations resolved a number of thorny issues between them.[4] In fact, it reversed what some observers had called a period of significant rapprochement between Beijing and Taipei.

Worse still the crisis escalated. On April 1, Beijing declined Taipei's offer to host a meeting of "negotiating groups" to talk about cross Strait issues. PRC officials cited President Lee Teng-hui's "Six Point" speech (given in response to President Jiang's "Eight Point" address on Beijing-Taipei relations earlier in the year) as the reason. Lee suggested Taipei possessed sovereignty, proposed that both the ROC and the PRC participate in international organizations, and asked Beijing to renounce the use of force to resolve the "Taiwan issue." These points, at first blush, seemed quite reasonable, but were very unwelcome to PRC leaders for reasons which will be discussed in further detail below. Lee subsequently blamed Beijing for "stagnating the pace of reunification" and for failing to recognize the sovereignty of the ROC.[5]

In June, Chinese leaders in Beijing were enraged when President Lee visited the United States and addressed a graduation ceremony at Cornell University, his alma mater, in what became a public relations coup for the ROC and an event which focused U.S. and global attention in a very positive and sympathetic way on Taiwan.[6] Beijing's policy makers, who had sought to isolate Taiwan and reduce its nation-state status to that of a province of the PRC, seemed at this juncture to have failed. Lee's visit also promoted Lee's position that Taiwan deserved a more legitimate place in the world community because the Cold War was over and the new world order was suppose to be inclusive.

In a slightly delayed response, in July, the PLA—conducted missile tests in the Taiwan Strait less than 100 miles from Taiwan. Coinciding with the tests, Beijing accused President Lee of "wrongdoing" and of "seriously damaging" relations across the Taiwan Strait. Xinhua News Agency went even further saying that China should "use fresh blood and lives" to prevent Taiwan from rejecting reunification.[7]

According to many observers, Beijing's actions could be interpreted as Chinese leaders needing to vent their anger over Taiwan's President Lee Teng-hui's U.S. visit and Taipei's efforts to join, or rejoin (depending on one's perspective), the United Nations. But, the PRC's hostility toward Taiwan also seemed immediately and closely related to a power struggle in Beijing evoked by Deng Xiaoping's ill health and strong prospects he was about die.[8] This "leadership crisis" was intimately connected to the "Taiwan issue" and U.S.-ROC relations since Deng and his reformist supporters had built close relations with the United States (in large part to facilitate economic growth) and had all but scrapped communism (for the same reasons), supplanting it with Chinese nationalism. Deng and his supporters, and his likely successors, hence were vulnerable to charges of sacrificing the recovery of Taiwan for better Sino-American ties.[9]

The timing also suggests that Chinese leaders in Beijing may have wanted to pressure President Lee not to run for president in the first direct presidential election in the ROC's history or, alternatively, persuade Taipei to cancel the election. This election, in addition to representing a big step forward in the democratization process, strongly implied Taiwan possessed national sovereignty apart from China and therefore represented a two China or one Taiwan, one China policy—

anathema to some Chinese leaders. In any event, President Lee forth-with declared that he would be a candidate. Making matters worse, he spoke of building a "great Taiwan" (meaning, to some, he was pro-moting Taiwanese nationalism). He also mentioned "developing the Taiwan political miracle" (flaunting the fact that the ROC was demo-cratic and the PRC was not).[10]

Beijing responded with genuine wrath. The *People's Daily* quickly lashed out—calling Lee a "schemer" and "double-dealer" while blam-ing him personally for strained relations between Beijing and Taipei. A few days later the paper went even further: saying his father was a "100 percent traitor" for having served in the Japanese colonial government. Xinhua was still harsher, saying: "To sweep Lee Teng-hui into the trashbin of history is the common, historical responsibility of Chinese on both sides of the Taiwan Strait."[11]

President Lee reacted with obvious pique, charging the PRC with slandering him. He repeated his pledge to build a "great Taiwan" and recast his earlier statement that the ROC is a democratic country, adding that the PLA's missile tests "increased opposition from the people of Taiwan." Then, in what appeared to be a counter-challenge, Taipei's military organized a parade of 11,000 troops and put some of the ROC's newly purchased and recently built weapons on display for the public to view. The Ministry of Defense also proposed a 20 percent increase in defense spending—the largest in many years.[12]

The crisis passed, but not before Beijing announced that it would do more missile tests at the time of Taiwan's first direct presidential election to be held in March 1996. PRC leaders said that this decision was made because of Lee visiting the United States and his attempt to create two Chinas.[13]

Come February, just before the missiles were to be launched, the PRC Ministry of Foreign Affairs said the tests were going to be conducted to "safeguard China's sovereignty and territorial integrity." The ROC's Minister of Defense responded by declaring that Taiwan's military was prepared to defend the island and would be compelled to counter-attack if missiles fell within the country's territorial waters. While on the campaign trail, President Lee said that the provocative actions were the product of a power struggle in the PRC which "had no system for picking leaders" and because of Beijing's "fear of democra-tization in Taiwan which might cause its people to rise up against the government." Peng Ming-min, the presidential candidate representing

Taiwan's largest opposition party, the Democratic Progressive Party, declared that Taipei should immediately stop any cooperation with Beijing and suggested that Taiwan hold war games off the coast of Shanghai or Guangdong Province.[14]

On March 8, the day of the tests (of three M-9 surface-to-surface missiles, two west of Kaohsiung and one east of Keelung), PRC Defense Minister Chi Haotien accused President Lee of trying to create two Chinas. Chi quoted from one of the founders of the Red Army who said that "Chinese will suffer humiliation until Taiwan is liberated."[15] PRC President and General Secretary of the Chinese Communist Party Jiang Zemin asserted that Beijing would not abandon the struggle "until Taiwan gives up."[16]

The next day, Beijing escalated the conflict another notch. The PLA announced it would conduct live ammunition tests 55 kilometers from the Pescadore Islands (off Taiwan's west coast) and that ships should not enter the waters in that area from March 12 to 20. Shortly thereafter it was reported that the People's Liberation Army would do exercises near Taiwan involving 150,000 troops, 300 planes, guided missile destroyers and frigates as well as submarines and fighter planes. Taipei, in reply, announced that it was opening a missile base on the Pescadore Islands ahead of schedule.[17]

Four days before the election Beijing lowered the level of its threats. Taipei followed suit, issuing less provocative statements than usual. The war of words and threats subsequently diminished further and the crisis passed. But there appeared to be permanent scars. Months later, efforts to restore relations to their 1994 level seemed to be going nowhere.

The United States, which got involved in the conflict, sending two aircraft carriers and other naval ships to the Taiwan Strait, could take credit for dampening the crisis by forcing Beijing to back down. But, given America's military drawdown in the region and the PRC's huge military buildup many observers wondered if it might be different the next time.[18] And it seemed there would certainly to be a next time.

The fact that recent Chinese history is replete with violent disagreements between the two regimes underscored the belief the issue had not been laid to rest and Beijing-Taipei relations were permanently strained. The two engaged in military conflict over the Offshore Islands of Quemoy and Matsu in 1954–55 and 1958. In 1962 and 1975 Beijing formulated detailed plans to invade Taiwan. All of these confrontations threatened to escalate into a full-scale war.[19] In addition, both Taipei and Beijing on a number of other occasions discussed launching an invasion of the other while Taipei once attempted to assassinate a PRC prime minister.[20]

Thus, whereas relations had improved for several years before 1995, causes for friction between the two sides remain and various nettlesome issues seemed unlikely to be resolved. In fact, the reasons for their mutual hostility appeared to be even stronger and the conflict less amenable to reconciliation than perceived two or three years earlier.

In order to understand the across the Taiwan Strait problems, and commensurately to know where it may lead, it is necessary to comprehend the reasons for and the nature of the disagreement between Beijing and Taipei. The main factors in the dispute are: (1) the disparate views between the two sides of Taiwan's history as it relates to its ownership or sovereignty over the island; (2) disagreements about Taiwan's legal status; (3 variances in the perceptions of the two governments about the "Taiwan issue"; (4) current relations between the two sides; and finally (5) the global context of the dispute. It is also instructive to talk about some scenarios that may suggest where the conflict may lead. Due to the constraint of space, however, only the most important and most frequently heard arguments will be discussed.

Different Historical Views

Different historical views espoused by scholars and officials on the two sides of the Taiwan Strait about Taiwan and in particular regarding ties between China and Taiwan are fundamental to their conflict. This is especially so because historical data and historical writings provide evidence for disparate arguments regarding Taiwan's legal status, and therefore Beijing's rightful, or not, claim to sovereignty over the island. An analysis of these different views thus facilitates a better understanding of the nature of and the reasons for the dispute between the two antagonists.

Historians in the People's Republic of China have shown little interest in Taiwan's pre-history. The main reason for this: geology, archaeology, and anthropology have garnered little interest in China. They are disciplines that have developed only recently and are still not very advanced fields of study. Another problem, of course, is that it has not been possible for scholars from the People's Republic of China to do excavations or even library research *in situ* in Taiwan. As a consequence of this situation, PRC scholars do not give much weight to pre-historical evidence in assessing Taiwan's status or in debating the question whether the island was historically part of China or not.

PRC historians, when writing about Taiwan's past, rather focus on early historical ties or links between China (or the mainland) and Taiwan. They cite expeditions and visits by Chinese government "representatives" to Taiwan over the centuries. They note that Taiwan is mentioned in historical records nowhere else and that Chinese visits to Taiwan occurred earlier than visits by others and over a period of many centuries. They, almost unanimously, suggest then that these visits and the "administrative organizations" set up on the island substantiate a Chinese historical claim to the island.[21] Filling the gaps, PRC scholars assume that Taiwan had significant pre-historic ties with the mainland or China based on geological evidence and state as much.[22]

In contrast, Republic of China anthropologists and geologists have diligently studied Taiwan's early origins and have debated often and in detail whether or not Taiwan was originally part of the mainland. Its volcanic soil, most note, indicates that Taiwan's origins are the same as Japan and the Philippines, and thus Taiwan is not geologically part of the mainland. Others, however, point out that other evidence, such as rock formations and the structure of the coastlines, means the island was torn away from the mainland during a geological cataclysm in the distant past. In other words, to historians in Taiwan, the case is one of conflicting evidence or it is still an open case.[23]

The origins of the Aborigines have also been the focus of Taiwan's historians' interests which, they think, is important. From where they hail, like the physical origins of the island, is considered uncertain and open to debate, and in need of further study. The Aboriginal languages, they note, are closely related in both structure and vocabulary to Malay or Bahasa (the language spoken in Malaysia and Indonesia). Most Taiwan historians (and linguists too) thus argue for a Southeast Asia or South China point of origin of the earliest inhabitants of the island (though they point out that Chinese people or Han Chinese did not yet inhabit the part of South China in question). Cultural similarities also speak for a southern origin. On the other hand, some recently discovered geological and anthropological evidence suggests multiple origins.

In fact, one or two Aboriginal tribes may have come to Taiwan from North China or Japan.[24]

Taiwan's historians, when studying the early history of the island, focus on the arrival of Chinese migrants (explaining why they came, etc.), the presence of some Japanese on the island, and other events. Discussing the arriving Chinese, they note their different provincial origins, the fact that most did not plan to return to China and the unique social system they built on Taiwan. They also cite their hard life and suffering when they moved to Taiwan, fighting with the aborigines, their different (from China) political organizations, and trade and commerce with other areas in East Asia.[25] Some write about the different geography from the mainland (such as no large rivers) and the effect this had on the society and culture, changes in the social class system (the lesser importance of formal education to high social class and the higher position of the soldier) of Chinese who migrated to Taiwan and the different political system (more feudal in nature than bureaucratic) that evolved in Taiwan.[26]

In stark contrast to early accounts of visits by Chinese missions to Taiwan that are viewed as significant by PRC historians, Taiwan's historians do not generally believe that contacts Chinese from the mainland had with Taiwan were very important.[27] Part of the reason for this, of course, is that they have many other things to write about. However, ROC historians also suggest that these historical contacts were intermittent, each were of very short duration, and they do not reflect any effort to colonize, occupy, or lay legal claim to Taiwan. They consequently feel that historical links do not provide the basis for a strong territorial claim by Beijing to Taiwan. It should be noted, however, that there is a marked difference among historians in Taiwan in terms of perceptions about these historical ties and whether they might provide the basis for arguing that Taiwan is part of China depending on whether the writer is Taiwanese or Mainland Chinese. Mainland Chinese historians (those Chinese residents who migrated to Taiwan after World War II) take a position much closer to historians in the PRC than Taiwanese (Chinese who moved to Taiwan several centuries ago) historians.[28]

PRC historians also approach Taiwan's more recent history very differently from ROC historians in some important ways. They write little about Taiwan under foreign rule in the 1600s. For example, they do not say much about the Western colonial period and generally ignore or play down the change, mostly progress, brought to the island by Western nations, notably the Dutch who colonized the island in the early 1600s. They likewise say little about Cheng Cheng-kung's (known in the West as Koxinga) rule of Taiwan.[29] When queried about this, PRC scholars point out that both were of very short duration and neither had lasting influence. The real reason, however, seems to be that the former suggests an important difference between Taiwan and China: Taiwan was colonized; China was not. The latter constituted a period of local self-rule and is not something PRC historians care to discuss for obvious reasons. (It is worthy of note that the Nationalist government has long made a comparison between Cheng's opposition to foreign Manchu rule and the Nationalists' condemnation of "foreign" communist rule. When asked, PRC historians say that this has little significance other than underscoring the Nationalist government's failure in ruling China before 1949.)[30]

PRC historians write more about China establishing jurisdiction over the island in the late 1600s—which lasted to the end of the 19th century. They say little specifically about Manchu rule of Taiwan (China being under the political control of the Manchus at that time). They, in fact, do not distinguish Manchu rule from Chinese rule or note in this context that the Manchus were subsequently overthrown by Chinese who called for the end of "foreign rule" and a republican form of government. Nor do they talk about the rebellious nature of the people in Taiwan, the difficulties Beijing had in pacifying the island, or the endemic corruption and cruelty associated with their governance of Taiwan. The reason, they say, is this was not unique to Taiwan and therefore is not something of special interest.[31] They instead emphasize the fact that Taiwan was part of China for more than two centuries, a much longer time by several-fold than the period Taiwan was controlled by Western nations or was self-governing under the Cheng family. They also note that Chinese culture prevailed and took root there during that time. PRC historians emphasize that Taiwan's status during the period was one of being liberated from Western colonization and returned rightfully to China. They also point out that Beijing ruled Taiwan in cooperation with local Chinese and that during that period there was considerable trade and Taiwan's economy grew and progressed.[32]

PRC historians see the subsequent period of Japanese rule in Taiwan as resulting from a treaty made under force or duress, and therefore not legitimate. In short, it was another of the "unequal treaties" imposed upon China by foreign predatory and imperialist nations during this time. PRC leaders have been quite consistent, in fact, in saying this and also that the agreement was made during the period of imperialism and for both reasons should also be seen as both bad and illegitimate.[33] They also point out that China was weak and divided at the time and that it suffered from feudalism. They conclude that China needs to "settle accounts" (meaning get even) about this period and note that when China is strong it will do that.[34]

In contrast, Taiwan's historians say that Manchu rule of Taiwan (1663 to 1895) was cruel, uncaring, corrupt and incompetent and that the population opposed the government and frequently revolted against it. Some Taiwanese historians even speak of Manchu (some say Chinese, since most of the officials sent to Taiwan were, in fact, Chinese, not Manchu) rule of Taiwan during this period as "colonial rule" and assert, moreover, that it was one of the worst examples of colonial rule in the world at the time.[35]

Regarding subsequent Japanese rule (1895 to 1945), Taiwan historians aver that Japan ruled Taiwan legitimately (the Treaty of Shimonoseki having been a legal transfer by the government of China to Japan). They also point out that China abandoned Taiwan at this time even though there was a local effort to resist Japanese control and that the only alternative to Japanese rule (if there was an alternative) was self-rule. Most speak of the benefits brought to the island by Japanese, especially economic progress and political and social stability.[36] Ethnic Taiwanese, of course, see more legitimacy in Japanese rule than Mainland Chinese in Taiwan, but both generally see Japanese rule as legal.

Different interpretations of past events by historians in the PRC and the ROC engender (since they influence what is taught in the educational systems, the perceptions of the populations on each side of the Taiwan Strait and ultimately official policy) are important. Clearly differences in historical perspectives explain other differences.

Varying Views on Taiwan's Legal Status

The governments of the PRC and the ROC as well as legal scholars on both sides take very different positions on Taiwan's legal standing or its status under international law. These disparate views are a source of discord between officials on the two sides of the Taiwan Strait and contribute to or reinforce disagreements in other areas.

The government of the People's Republic of China espouses the view that Taiwan was transferred to China *de facto* and *de jure* at the end of World War II. It admits, of course, that it was transferred to the Republic of China, not the People's Republic of China, since the latter did not yet exist. PRC officials argue, however, that the People's Republic of China, in 1949, became the successor government to the Republic of China. Thus, the PRC assumed legal jurisdiction over Taiwan as is the right of successor governments under international law.[37] They add that the government of the Republic of China was not, and is not, a legal or legitimate government, it having been repudiated by the Chinese masses during the 1930s and 1940s proven by its defeat by the Communists in 1949.[38]

In Beijing's eyes, owing to American imperialism, Taiwan did not *de facto* revert to the People's Republic. Specifically, U.S. forces, in collusion with Chiang Kai-shek and the Nationalist Chinese government and military, prevented the PRC from assuming jurisdiction over this "Chinese territory" as PRC leaders intended in 1949. PRC military forces were, they point out, poised to invade Taiwan in early 1950 and thus put an end to the Chinese civil war.[39] This plan, in fact, was about to be put into operation when the Korean War began and the United States sent the 7th Fleet into the Taiwan Strait to bloc the invasion.

The "American occupation" of Taiwan subsequently sustained and perpetuated the "illegal and illegitimate Nationalist government's jurisdiction over Taiwan."[40] This is evidenced, say PRC officials, by the fact the United States gave large amounts of military and economic aid to Taiwan, stationed U.S. troops there, and in 1954 signed a defense treaty with the ROC. They argue, and Western historians almost unanimously agree, that had the United States not "propped up" the Nationalist regime it could not have survived even for a short time.[41]

Beijing, its scholars note, on four occasions formulated plans to wrest Taiwan from Nationalist Chinese (and American) control: in 1954–55 and 1958 (during what became known as the Offshore Islands crises), and in 1962 and again in 1975 (on both occasions Beijing made detailed plans to liberate Taiwan but never operationalized them).[42] These efforts were stymied, except the latter, by the fact that the United States was a nuclear power and China was not and by the fact the

Soviet Union failed to come to the PRC's rescue when it was intimidated by the U.S. or otherwise help the PRC recover its lost territory.[43]

During the 1970s, PRC leaders began to perceive that they did not need to employ force to bring Taiwan back into the fold. In 1971, Beijing was given the China seat in the United Nations. The ROC was "expelled" after which Taipei lost diplomatic support and Beijing won formal recognition from most nations of the world. In the eyes of both PRC historians and officials this unequivocally proved that the PRC legally represented "all of China." Furthermore, they argue, other countries recognized this (having blindly taken another position in the past due to their allegiance with the West or U.S. pressure or economic help). This means, to most countries of the world, Taiwan was regarded as territory of the People's Republic of China.[44] At this time, PRC officials are quick to point out, whenever a nation wanted to establish formal diplomatic relations, Beijing demanded that the said nation break ties with Taipei—and they did.[45]

In Beijing's view, the Shanghai Communiqué signed in 1972 by official representatives of the United States and the People's Republic of China, finally corrected this "wrongful" situation in terms of U.S. policy. The People's Republic of China should have, and presumably soon would have, assumed jurisdiction over Taiwan inasmuch as the U.S. government reiterated its one-China policy (this time, meaning the People's Republic of China). PRC negotiators also, they are quick to point out, wrote in the Shanghai Communiqué that the People's Republic of China opposes any activities aimed at the creation of "one China, one Taiwan," "two Chinese governments," "the view that Taiwan's status remains to be determined." (Otherwise, say PRC officials, Beijing would not have pursued or accepted formal diplomatic relations with Washington.)[46] Hence, from Beijing's point of view, Taipei had no alternative but to negotiate unification in the face of America withdrawing its military and diplomatic support.

PRC officials also note that in a second agreement concluded in 1978, at which time the United States and the People's Republic of China established formal diplomatic relations, the U.S. recognized that "the government of the People's Republic of China is the sole legal government of China." Beijing therefore made generous offers on the conditions and means of reunification which it expected Taipei to accept.[47] Whereas this did not happen, it should have and it will, say leaders in Beijing. The PRC, contend its spokespersons, has been patient because it understands the difficulties faced by the American government in "abandoning" Taiwan. They also say Beijing seeks to avoid using military force against Taiwan. However, PRC representatives suggest the United States reneged on promises regarding Taiwan and has not pressured Taipei as it should have to bring about reunification talks.[48]

The view of legal experts in Taiwan and officials of the government of the Republic of China, generally speaking, is that the Cairo and Potsdam declarations promised the return of territory "stolen" by Japan. Though these declarations did not specify the rightful owner of Taiwan or say to whom the territory should be transferred (because the United States tentatively planned to invade Taiwan and took the position that its fate would be decided later) the presumption can be made that it was the Republic of China. The reason: the People's Republic did not exist at that time and the ROC constituted the only legal government of the Chinese people, and the island had been originally taken from China by Japan.[49]

Taipei's sovereignty over Taiwan, however, is better justified in terms of legal reasoning, according to both ROC officials and scholars, based on the concept of prescription, a term used by international legal experts that means rule without challenge. In other words, the ROC and its legal experts contend that the PRC has made no serious or sustained efforts to make Taiwan a part of the PRC after 1949 and that the jurisdiction of the government of the Republic of China has been undisturbed and that, furthermore, the latter has expressed consistently and often its claim of sovereignty and jurisdiction over its territory.[50]

More specifically they argue the PRC's military assaults on the offshore island of Quemoy and Matsu in 1954-55 and in 1958 did not constitute a sufficient threat to the territory of the Republic of China to be considered a serious or genuine challenge. Some ROC territory (the Tachen and Nanchi islands and some other small islands) was lost during the first crisis, but this did not have a significant impact on Taiwan's territorial integrity. The islands were, in fact, sacrificed, say authorities in Taiwan, by Taipei for military reasons (meaning it could not be defended) and because of U.S. pressure. In any event, the said islands are very small and the civilian populations of each (just over 17 thousand in the case of the Tachens, the largest) were evacuated to Taiwan.[51] More important, the PRC made no effort to seize the island of Taiwan (most of the territory governed by the ROC) or the Pescadores or other islands close to Taiwan under the ROC's juris- diction at this time.[52]

During the second Offshore Islands crisis in 1958, the PRC again failed to directly threaten Taiwan or the Pescadores; only islands held by the ROC very close to the coast of the PRC were attacked. The fact Beijing did not threaten or assault other ROC territory, particularly the island of Taiwan, exposes the fact that Beijing had no immediate plan to change the legal status of the ROC.[53] Thus Taiwan's argument for territorial ownership based on prescription was strengthened.

The argument for ROC ownership of Taiwan and other territory under its jurisdiction based on prescription was strengthened in ensuing years because Beijing made no further attacks on any ROC territory. In fact, they note, considerable time passed and Beijing made only vague threats against which over time grew less credible.[54] Taiwan officials and scholars say little or nothing about subsequent PRC plans to attack Taiwan in 1962 and 1975 and regard the reports about this as little more than speculation.

Taipei also mentions the fact that Japan signed a peace treaty with the Republic of China in 1952 (Japan having formal diplomatic relations with Taipei at the time). This action hence may be seen as formalizing Tokyo's abandonment of sovereignty over Taiwan and transferring it to the Republic of China at a time when the People's Republic of China existed, indicating that Japan took the position that Taiwan and adjacent islands (though not the Offshore Islands) belonged legally to the ROC thereby undermining Beijing's successor govern- ment argument. They also point out that other nations that had been involved with Taiwan and that may have been qualified to register an opinion about its legal status, particularly those favoring Beijing, did not object.[55]

Officials in the Republic of China also observe that whereas the U.S. recognized that Taiwan is "part of China" in the Shanghai Com- muniqué, this document was not binding on other parties and did not affect Taiwan's legal status since the United States did not own Taiwan: Washington never said so or even hinted this and its aid and military help cannot be construed to impact Taiwan's legal status. The U.S., in fact, treated the ROC at all times as having nation-state status and as having sovereignty over Taiwan. It did this in treaties and agreements and in numerous official statements.[56] This lasted until 1978.

Furthermore, as some Western scholars have observed and ROC scholars have duly noted, the United States wrote in the Shanghai Communiqué that (rather than citing its own view): "All Chinese on either (sic) side of the Taiwan Strait maintain there is but one China and that Taiwan is part of China. The United States Government does not challenge this position." The phrase "does not challenge" can, in fact, be taken to mean that the U.S. did not agree, but did not choose (because of wanting to pursue better relations with the PRC for stra- tegic reasons) to make issue of the matter.[57] Clearly the United States subsequently took no steps to see that China was reunified or that the ROC was rendered illegitimate.

In addition, say officials and scholars in Taiwan, the argument that because the United States recognized the PRC as the sole government of China (in the Normalization Agreement) and therefore repudiated the Republic of China's sovereignty is foolish. The U.S. patently did not say this. Furthermore, the provisions of the Normalization Agreement were, moreover, contradicted by the "more legal" Taiwan Relations Act of 1979 (which was a law passed by the U.S. Congress and thus gave it superior legal status to the communiqués which simply formalized the results of negotiations between Washington and Beijing in 1972 and 1978).[58]

Taiwan scholars and officials also state that the Republic of China meets the traditional criteria for nation-statehood status: territory, population, government and diplomatic recognition. They point out that its territory and population are comparable to member nations of the United Nations (in fact, its population is larger than three-fourths of U.N. members), that its government is stable (and democratic) and that Taipei has diplomatic relations (though many ties are informal) equal in number to most Third World countries. Moreover, Taipei has other relations with many countries making its informal diplomacy broader and more extensive.[59] Finally they observe that the criteria for nation- state status have been diluted by United Nations practice.[60]

Disparate Views about the "Taiwan Issue"

Differences between PRC and ROC officials, scholars and even the populations on the two sides of the Taiwan Strait concerning Taiwan's political status or its status other than simply its legal standing constitute another area of disagreement between Beijing and Taipei. There are, in other words, troublesome disparities of views on a range of issues that relate to Taiwan's place in the world and how the "Taiwan issue" (if it indeed can be called an "issue") can be resolved.

Political leaders in the People's Republic of China say that it is their "sacred duty" to recover Taiwan. They assert Taiwan is a part of China, not simply for legal reasons, but also due to the fact Taiwan's population is predominantly Chinese. They say that the Chinese civil war can not be considered over until Taiwan is "brought back into the fold," that its remaining apart is "humiliating to all Chinese," and that China cannot play a legitimate place in the world until its "lost territory" is recovered. Finally, they contend that the Chinese people favor this and that there is virtually no opposition in Taiwan or among Chinese anywhere to Taiwan's returning to the fatherland.[61]

In Taiwan, there are a variety of views about whether the island and other territory under the ROC's jurisdiction are part of China (beyond the legal arguments already discussed) or not. This reflects both the pluralistic nature of Taiwan's society and differences in "ethnic" views espoused by people in the ROC.[62] The bottom line, however, is that the issue of Taiwan's status (usually discussed as Taiwan's future) is a question that has not been resolved as far as the population, much less scholars and officials of the ROC, is concerned.

For the sake of an orderly presentation of the views of both sides, it is convenient to first examine Taiwan's viewpoint. The PRC's position (at least as reflected in their public statements) on the "Taiwan question" is in large part a reaction to Taiwan's arguments or statements.

A decision concerning the most basic question—whether or not citizens of the ROC are Chinese—to scholars in Taiwan, especially the native-born Chinese or Taiwanese—is murky to say the least. That most of the population of Taiwan trace their ancestry to China and are Chinese (or Han people to be more precise) is not in dispute. On the other hand, many Taiwanese say they are Taiwanese first and Chinese second, or that they are Chinese in the same sense as Americans of European descent are Europeans.[63] They suggest that, like Europeans who went to America, their ancestors left China centuries ago with little or no desire to return to China. Almost all came from southern China and few had any ties with the government which was located in North China. Their new home was much different from the one they left. They were a minority for a long time after their arrival on the island. They developed a different view of the world. And for fifty years prior to World War II they were ruled by Japan, were educated in Japanese and spoke Japanese, and had little contact with China or Chinese culture. Thus they are unique; they are not the same as Chinese in China.[64] Mainland Chinese in Taiwan (those Chinese who migrated there after World War II) and who constitute less than 15 percent of the population, do not agree with this view; but they do understand it. Moreover, many young Mainlanders sympathize with this "Taiwanese" view to some degree.

PRC historians and officials alike point out, in contraposition, that China is a very large country (the largest in the world by population) and that its population is not homogeneous. The Constitution, in fact, recognizes fifty-five minority nationalities, some of them different races, as well as different "national" customs among the PRC's population.[65] Thus, what so-called "native" Taiwanese (a meaningless term in any case, since only the Aborigines are "native") say about their uniqueness is exaggerated if not vacuous rubbish. They are not, in the context of a large and heterogeneous China, either very unique or very different. The Chinese living in Taiwan are, they declare, less different from the "ordinary" Chinese (whatever that is, PRC historians might ask) than Chinese in the PRC.[66] PRC officials also point out that few nations are homogeneous and if such differences as Taiwanese note are important were duly taken into consideration the United States as well as many other nations should be split into a number of parts (certainly a point about which Western scholars will agree).[67]

Regarding the Chinese civil war, Taiwanese contend they know very little about its origins and have had no direct experience that would help them understand it. Furthermore, it has little or no relevance to Taiwan's history, its legal status, or its future. It started, they observe, when Taiwan was under Japanese rule and Taiwan had almost no contact with China. They learned about it in detail only in 1945 when Taiwan became part of China and, incidentally, suffered from it because the Nationalist government did not pay adequate attention to Taiwan and misgoverned it, and the economy and social stability deteriorated as a result. They thus feel they were victimized by something they know little about and certainly had no place in starting or ending. In 1949, when Chiang Kai-shek and the Nationalist Party plus between a million and two million people fled the mainland to take up residence in Taiwan after the Nationalists were defeated by Mao's armies, the population of Taiwan again suffered.[68]

Chinese historians and officials in the People's Republic of China, in contrast, say the Chinese civil war was a continuation of the revolt against and liberation from the Manchu Dynasty and the forces of colonialism and imperialism that began in the 19th century when Taiwan was ruled by Beijing and was part of China. Sun Yat-sen's revolution (which incidentally had support in Taiwan even after Taiwan became part of the Japanese Empire) did not go far enough; the Communist revolution, which expanded on Sun's, went further and succeeded. They assert, furthermore, that they fought against Japan and helped liberate Taiwan from colonial rule and that Taiwan should have done more and at minimum should be grateful for what their "brothers and sisters" on the mainland did.[69]

Concerning the matter of Chinese suffering humiliation because China is not a unified country, scholars in Taiwan have presented a variety of opinions. One scholar has observed that China has been divided or fragmented for long periods of time during its history, and, in fact, has been divided more of the time in its recorded history than it was together.[70] Thus not being unified is not unusual. Other scholars have noted that China has survived over a long expanse of time because it is a culture rather than a nation that has a fixed territory and that this is its most admirable characteristic. In Taiwan, academics have also observed that by the standards of human freedoms and human rights and in some other important ways, a divided China was historically better than a unified one.[71]

It should be noted, however, that these observations represent the academic community more than the government. Officials in Taiwan speak more often about rash or premature plans by Beijing to unite the country that would result in horrendous loss of "Chinese" lives when the passage of time can resolve the problem without bloodshed. Some say that the present PRC government is overcome (drunk, some say) with nationalism and its insecure and aging leaders are too concerned about how history will view them—thinking that heroes unify China, villains allow it to break up or remain in pieces. Thus they are irrational about the fact Taiwan is ruled by a different Chinese government.[72]

About Taiwan being "lost territory," scholars in Taiwan suggest that China's territory was never well defined since Chinese rulers did not understand or espouse the nation-state concept until very recently in its history and because China was a cultural idea rather than a territorial one.[73] Furthermore, making China now strictly a territorial concept is wrong. It ignores the Overseas Chinese. Those who espouse it are, furthermore, oblivious to the possibilities of an economic federation or other such kind of arrangement.[74] In any event, China has other "lost territory" to worry about and as long as Taiwan is not taken (and it won't be) by someone else, why should Beijing worry about it? It might, instead, focus on territory in Russia that Beijing claims, territory "taken" by Japan recently (the Diao Yu Tai or, in Japanese, the Senkaku Islands) and territory in the South China Sea (that both sides agree is Chinese).[75]

Leaders as well as academics and the population in Taiwan see the unification of Taiwan with China occurring, if it does happen, because of economic integration via trade and investment ties rather than politics providing the impetus or justification. In fact, they see unification as already having happened to a considerable extent through trade and investment connections. In short, efforts to unify China, to both scholars and officials in Taiwan, should put economics first and politics second. Some in Taiwan even point out that reform in China has put economic change ahead of political change and this has been successful.[76] So, why not apply the same reasoning to the "Taiwan issue"?

Chinese leaders in Beijing see the logic in economic ties and perceive that they will indeed bring the two sides together. In fact, they chide Taiwan for not making economic links easier (by allowing direct trade, mail, etc., which the PRC has proposed for some time) and suggest hypocrisy in Taiwan's comments about promoting business ties to facilitate reunification. They cite Taipei's "Three Nos" (no contact, no negotiations, no compromises) policy as contradicting their claims about economic "bridge building" and as representing a hard-line Cold War mentality.[77]

PRC leaders also point out, however, that political and military relations are important. So is territory. How, they ask, could it be otherwise? They point out that the nation-state system is still very much alive and the rules about territory and sovereignty are basic to international relations. They also relate territory to their economic health, especially because China needs energy and the South China Sea is seen as a source of oil.[78]

On the matter of Chinese leaders in Beijing saying that all Chinese want Taiwan returned to China immediately, many in Taiwan wonder if such statements are really serious. Indeed, how important, many in Taiwan ask, is this to the average person in the PRC? Since the PRC is not a democracy and opinion polls have not been taken on this issue there, it is virtually impossible to say anything for certain about this.[79] It is even more difficult to know what the millions of Overseas Chinese think about this matter. That most Chinese wish to see China united is probably accurate both officials and scholars in Taiwan say. But, at what cost? And how? Could not a federation accomplish this? Does not the concept of "Greater China" (the PRC, the ROC, Hong Kong, Macao and Singapore linked by economic ties, by Chinese culture and in other ways) already do it?

PRC leaders speak regularly and compassionately, almost with a preoccupation, about the importance of restoring China's greatness and its place in the world. They clearly do not feel that a loose confederation of Chinese "entities" can accomplish this. They contend that because the nation-state is still the main actor in international politics only Beijing can effectively promote China's interests. They also feel strongly that the fate of countries that were not unified or did not pursue common goals (such as the former Soviet Union) are portentous examples that must be duly heeded.[80]

Finally, ROC leaders and scholars alike suggest that Taiwan has been, and remains, a model for China. When China modernizes (vis. democratizes) its political system as Taiwan has done, unification will be easy, most in Taiwan say—including almost all government officials (since this is official policy in Taipei). If unification is attempted before that, they argue, the PRC will not have a model. Worse, democracy, which should be in China's future, may be sacrificed. Human rights will also suffer. And China's hope to be a great nation will be diminished.[81]

Both scholars and government officials are usually reluctant to discuss the issue of the Taiwan model. When they do it is usually for domestic consumption. Rightist reformers like the model and hard-liner leftists do not. It is obvious there are strong disagreements between the two. Reformers sometimes praise Taiwan's economic and political modernization, only to be criticized because Taiwan remains separate. Hence, when models are broached, Beijing more often cites Singapore, even though it is only a city state and is less Chinese in population or culture than Taiwan.[82] Clearly, the matter of the Taiwan model is a sensitive one in the PRC and may in the future be an issue that brings them together or causes the gulf to widen.

Relations Between Beijing and Taipei

From 1949 to the 1970s, Beijing and Taipei were extremely hostile toward each other. Relations then improved. Taipei allowed its residents to visit the mainland, trade flourished and investment flowed. The ROC abandoned its position that the Beijing government was an illegitimate one and ended the state of war between the two. Beijing ended the shelling of the offshore islands, toned down, and in some areas practically ended, its propaganda aimed at Taiwan, and, contrary to previous statements that it would never do this, engaged in talks or negotiations with ROC counterparts.

Notwithstanding this progress, there are still serious differences between the two sides regarding the status of their relationship and how they should deal with each other. Moreover, some of these points of disagreement seem difficult, perhaps impossible, to resolve and are formidable obstacles to future better relations.

The most salient issue of divergence of opinion is whether the Republic of China has sovereignty or not. The PRC's long-held position is that it does not (adamantly opposing the use of the appellation ROC) and that "Taiwan" (its correct name) is a part of China and more specifically is a province of the People's Republic of China. By claiming nation-state status, say PRC officials, "certain people in Taiwan are trying to alter the status of Chinese sovereignty."[83] Beijing, therefore, refuses government-to-government ties or negotiations in the formal sense since that would, or might, indirectly constitute recognition of the ROC as a legitimate and sovereign nation-state.

Taipei's stance is (as discussed earlier in connection with the legal arguments) that it has sovereignty and qualifies for nation-state status. Taipei thus proposes that the two sides negotiate and that negotiations imply the mutual recognition of the others' sovereignty. Furthermore, Beijing must accept these parameters for such talks if progress is to be made and peace preserved in the Taiwan Strait area. ROC leaders also insist that the equality of nations (even if Beijing does not accept the ROC's sovereignty it must accept diplomatic practices) is a basic principle in both international law and diplomacy and that only on this basis can anything be accomplished.[84]

To break this impasse, Beijing has proffered what it calls the "One Country, Two Systems" formula. According to this formula, which was first cited, say Chinese scholars, by Deng Xiaoping in 1978, Taiwan can maintain its non-socialist economic system and its social and other systems, and its lifestyle, even its military–though it can not have a separate foreign or defense policy or use its flag.[85] The PRC, to formalize its guarantees to Taipei, put the provisions of this formula in a Nine-Point Proposal made by President Ye Jianying to "Taiwan compatriots" in 1981 and in its Constitution the next year.[86]

The "One Country, Two Systems" formula, note PRC leaders, was applied when negotiating the return of Hong Kong with the U.K. in 1984 and when incorporating Hong Kong in July 1997 and governing it after that. Hong Kong, according to the provisions of the formula, will become an "special administrative region" of the PRC. Its economic and social systems will remain intact after reunification. PRC officials and its scholars alike express the opinion that this is a reasonable approach and that it will work. They cite the current prosperity Hong Kong is enjoying as evidence. They furthermore see the model of applying the "one country, two systems" formula as flexible and as definitely applying to negotiations with Taipei and to the final step in reunifying China.[87]

Most people in Taiwan, on the other hand, do not believe the formula is reasonable. Scholars in Taiwan point out that the document is the second longest "treaty" (that term applying since it has been placed on the record with the United Nations) ever signed by Beijing and is complicated, difficult to interpret, and vague. It cannot be understood much less made the basis of a working relationship between two governments or political entities, say Taiwan scholars.[88] Further, ROC officials aver, it makes statements regarding separate branches of government, suggesting a separation of powers; yet the PRC's political system is not based on such a concept. Hong Kong will relate to or connect with the government of the PRC through the National People's Congress, which scholars and officials in Taipei (and Western scholars as well) regard as a rubber stamping organ of government controlled by and beholden to the Chinese Communist Party (CCP). Thus, Hong Kong has been ruled by the CCP since July 1, 1997—and Taiwan will be also if it accepts the One Country, Two Systems formula. Finally, note officials and scholars in Taiwan, the PRC's Constitution cites, as basic precepts, "Four Cardinal Principles": adherence to the socialist path, loyalty to the leadership of the Chinese Communist Party, support for the people's democratic dictatorship, and following Marxism-Leninism and Mao Zedong's Thought. These, they say are contradictory to free market capitalism, political pluralism, democracy, and respect for human rights.[89]

Officials and scholars in Taiwan also warn that Tibet and Inner Mongolia have the same status that will be given to Hong Kong and is promised to Taiwan. This does not inspire confidence in Taiwan in view of the fact human rights abuses abound in these areas (even worse than in other parts of China), not to mention the low standards of literacy, living conditions and other problems, in these places.[90]

Finally, observers in Taiwan note that Beijing has promised that Taiwan may keep its economic system and has spoken of maintaining Taiwan's prosperity, while at the same time the PRC has taken actions to isolate Taiwan diplomatically (which is obviously not good for Taiwan, it being a major trading entity). Similarly Beijing has promised Taiwan can keep its military; yet it opposes U.S. military sales to the ROC. These are obvious contradictions![91]

Political leaders in Taipei have instead proposed a "One China, Two Governments" and a "One China, Two Entities" formula.[92] (Though the main opposition party, the Democratic Progressive Party, and others advocating Taiwan independence do not agree with these formulas, the ruling Kuomintang and the New Party generally do.) According to this formula Taiwan is to be regarded as historically part of China and should eventually be reunited with China, but the ROC government should be viewed as legitimate in the meantime. More important, the procedure to accomplish unification should assume the ROC has sovereignty and can decide when and under what conditions it will become part of China.[93]

They also view Taiwan's situation as radically different from Hong Kong's. Hong Kong, they note, was a colony; therefore, there is no legal similarity between Hong Kong's status and the Republic of China's. In addition, they point out that Hong Kong is dependent on the People's Republic of China (even importing its water from China) economically and cannot defend itself. Taiwan is not economically dependent on the PRC and can and will defend itself if necessary. In short, Hong Kong is not, and cannot be, a model for Taiwan to use to relate to or negotiate with the PRC.[94]

The solution to this conundrum, say some officials and quite a number of scholars in Taiwan, is the German Formula.[95] The two German governments became more flexible on the issue of (dual) diplomatic recognition in the 1970s (incidentally at almost the same time that Taipei and Beijing began to pursue better relations) and were both granted formal recognition by important members of the global community. In 1973 both became members of the United Nations. Subsequently the two engaged in negotiations (meaning talks between two equal and sovereign nation-states), reconciled their differences, and agreed to unify.

Officials in Beijing do not agree with Taiwan's stance, though they have not specifically or directly addressed the first points made above. In other contexts, however, they have argued that Tibet and other autonomous regions are better off both economically and in human rights terms than they were in the past or would be if they ruled themselves. They have, however, addressed the German formula, saying it does not apply to the Taiwan problem and is not a model for Taiwan's reunification. They contend it would encourage dual recognition (which it no doubt might) and see it as a nefarious effort to create two Chinas. They suggest that China is different from Germany because China's unification threatens the United States and other powers who are trying to split China through spiritual pollution, etc. This was not the case of Germany they say.[96] Hence, because China was exploited in the past and is now a great power and because its economic and military expansion frightens other countries, it cannot be compared to Germany.

Leaders in Taipei also argue that Beijing should agree to a peaceful settlement only of the "Taiwan issue" and repudiate statements about using military force to revolve the problem in order to create an environment conducive to meaningful talks. They say that the unwillingness of Chinese leaders in Beijing to do this reflects the fact that they have not yet graduated from their Cold War mentality and are not really serious about talks with Taipei. (However, there is reason to doubt leaders in Taipei really want such a promise since the PRC could make such a commitment and there would be no way to know that it would be kept. Moreover, the PRC threat makes it easier to sustain large defense spending which enhances Taipei's bargaining position.)

The PRC's response to this is that Taiwan is a domestic issue and that promising not to use force to resolve it is unreasonable and something that no sovereign nation would do. In fact, they say it is ridiculous even to make such a request. On occasion they point out the position Abraham Lincoln took toward the South during the U.S. civil war. They parenthetically note that if they were to do this, it would encourage independence and separatist advocates in Taiwan. Anyway, say PRC leaders, Beijing's military power is not directed at "our Taiwanese compatriots," but at foreign forces (who are or might interfere in China's unification).[97]

Taipei argues just the opposite: that the right to threaten the use of force against Taiwan is not an issue of national sovereignty since China already has two legally constituted governments. Furthermore, as can be attested to by observing recent election campaigns and the actions of independence advocates, Beijing's threats abet their cause.[98] Finally, they note that considerable progress was made in improving relations in the 1970s when Beijing became less hostile and as Taiwan policy became less monopolized by Mao and a few other top leaders and when Beijing announced a policy (though not a promise) of a peaceful settlement of the Taiwan issue.[99]

Taipei also advances the argument that by pursuing a political or military solution, as opposed to an economic solution in the form of a "Greater China" economic federation of some sort, the PRC is in essence abandoning Singapore and the Overseas Chinese and turning its back on the best means possible to restore China's greatness: by capitalizing on the network of Chinese outside of the PRC (not just in Taiwan) that are linked by culture and economic interests. In so doing, they are thus relinquishing leadership of the Pacific Rim economic bloc to Japan.[100]

Chinese leaders in Beijing, while they do not disagree that economic ties are important (in fact, as noted above, they criticize Taipei for impeding them) also envision political and other ties as central to any future Chinese federation. They have often remarked that to restore China's greatness China must be genuinely unified, and a weak economic federation will not accomplish that. Furthermore, they assert, the PRC must become a great military power for China to play its rightful role in international affairs and this being the case its use of military intimidation is not only justified but is quite natural.[101]

The Global Dimension of Beijing-Taipei Relations

Another factor affecting Beijing-Taipei relations is the international community. Taipei feels it has the sympathy and support of most of the world. Beijing feels it does not, or at least does not accord this any consideration. Alternatively, PRC leaders perceive they can change the view of the international community. It is likewise evident that Beijing and Taipei have different views of the world, in particular the evolving structure of the international system, that complicate the situation even further.

More specifically, Taipei's perception of international community is this: The fact that twenty-nine or thirty nations officially recognize the Republic of China, over one hundred have some kind of meaningful unofficial ties with Taipei and most nations deal with Taiwan economically (though trade or investments) is significant.[102] Furthermore, Taiwan is not isolated and its citizens can travel easily to other nations. All of this reflects the general view that Taiwan is not simply a PRC domestic matter.[103] Finally, the international community treats Taiwan with respect and as different from Tibet, Inner Mongolia and other "autonomous regions" of the PRC.

Also, Taipei cites as evidence that the "Taiwan issue" is a global matter, not a PRC domestic matter, the fact that the United States, which is the foremost power in the world, intervened in the recent missile crisis by sending two aircraft carriers and a flotilla other ships to the Taiwan Strait in response to what Washington perceived was a threat to a friendly "nation" (Taiwan) and a domestic law that obligated the U.S. (the Taiwan Relations Act, which, incidentally treats Taiwan as a sovereign nation-state) to protect Taiwan. In addition, statements made by U.S. officials, the Western press, and to a great extent other nations of the world mirrored a view of cross-Strait relations that acknowledged Taipei's sovereignty. The international community, in short, generally agreed with the U.S. actions and did not support the PRC's stance that Taiwan is simply a domestic question.[104]

There are three fundamental reasons the international community takes the stance it does in Taipei's view, note officials and scholars in Taiwan. One, most nations believe, and take the position in terms of formulating their foreign policies, that national boundaries should be taken as fixed or at least not subject to change except by peaceful negotiations. This applies to divided nations as shown in the views about the two Germanys before reunification and the two Koreas currently. Since World War II this has been a dominant "rule" in international politics as witnessed by the fact that nations have not seized territory from other nations by force as was the practice in the past.[105]

Two, many smaller nations side with the ROC (also a small nation) saying that its sovereignty should be protected against a larger aggressive nation. More important, they support the idea of self-determination and apply that principle to Taiwan. In addition, future trends in this regard probably favor the ROC, particularly given the fact, among other reasons, the PRC's relations with the Third World are generally tenuous owing to Beijing's becoming a major recipient of aid and loans from international lending institutions while absorbing large quantities of private investment capital to the detriment of other developing nations.[106]

Three, the big naval powers and the large economies of the world do not want to see the Taiwan Strait changed from its present status —that of an international waterway that allows free and unimpeded use. The United States, as well as Russia and Japan, thus espouse the position that Taiwan should be regarded as separate from China at least as regards the status of the Taiwan Strait. The same goes for the South China Sea where the two have territorial claims and where one-quarter of the world's shipping passes. In short, there is concern that the PRC, in its present expansionist mode, will threaten sea and air traffic and the movement of air and naval forces and it must be dissuaded from this view.[107]

Clearly Taipei perceives that it is not isolated and can count on sympathy from the international community in general and help from both the major powers and from small or Third World countries specifically.[108] And it has. Over the last four years, Taipei has made a bid to be readmitted to the United Nations and has won the sympathy and the support of an increasing number of Third World nations in making its case. It has also won a vote of support for its position from the European Union and from the United States Congress.[109]

In contraposition, Beijing's point of view is that it has succeeded in reducing the ROC's formal diplomatic ties to a handful of small, unimportant nations in recent years and has kept Taipei out of almost all important international organizations. Beijing has, in fact, managed to pressure most nations and international governmental organizations not to internationalize the dispute in the sense of giving Taipei any formal diplomatic or legal status. Beijing thus sees Taipei as isolated, having no hope of becoming an international player or winning sufficient global support that matters. Chinese leaders in Beijing clearly do not see any trend favoring Taipei and they are determined (and feel the PRC has the capability) to counter whatever effort is taken by Taipei or any government on its behalf to grant Taiwan greater international status than it has at present.[110]

Given this standoff and in order to understand the views of the two sides and where Beijing and Taipei are coming from and where their differences might lead them, it is necessary to assess their disparate views of the world. Clearly they are different.

Beijing's view of the world system is a multipolar one. Five powers, the United States, Russia, Japan, the European Community, and last, but emphatically not least, the People's Republic of China, dominate world affairs at the present time. Furthermore, they will control world politics even more in coming years. Chinese leaders also perceive world politics as being characterized by power politics: as a game or contest involving the use of various form of power or influence, not least of which is military power.[111] Officials in Beijing perceive disagreements that the European countries and Japan have with the United States as evidence of this kind of system evolving. Moreover, their strategy of regional dominance is founded on this world view.[112]

Taipei, on the other hand, perceives the world order as being partly a universal one. Smaller nations or political actors should not, and can not, be excluded, especially one so important as the Republic of China. The future world is, to officials and scholars in Taiwan, also one in which political power plays a bigger role than military power. Further-more, since military might has proven unusable in the bipolar world, it will continue to drop in utility. Not only will political power to a considerable degree supplant military power, but so will moral power. Hence, Taipei's frequent mention of the human rights of its 21 million citizens has resonance. The ROC can, therefore, it thinks, enhance its position in the world and parry attempts by Beijing to isolate it or force it to negotiate its sovereignty against its will through active diplomacy and by making a case internationally for its right to sovereignty.[113]

Taipei also views the world as evolving toward tripolarity, with three huge economic blocs dominating world politics and a system founded on economic power. The Republic of China can, in this context, use its economic clout (ranking number one or two in the world in foreign exchange, one of the top ten in foreign investment, number fourteen in trade, and number twenty in gross national product) to preserve its nation-state status and to influence global affairs more than in the past.[114] Officials and scholars in Taiwan also point out that Taipei is a member in good standing in the Asian Development Bank and it is winning support to join or rejoin other global financial organizations.

These divergent views suggest that Beijing and Taipei would experience difficulties in negotiating with each other. And they have. On the other hand, in some respects, the global perspectives of the PRC and the ROC are similar and may be converging. Beijing clearly views the world in economic terms and does not deny the existence of a Pacific Rim economic bloc. And Taiwan knows it is in the same bloc as the People's Republic of China and this should lead to a more intense and meaningful relationship in the future reducing the likelihood that the two can go separate ways. They both perceive that economic blocs are forming elsewhere that are protectionist on trade matters and that may thus be hostile, at least in competition with, the Pacific Rim bloc. To both, a Chinese economic federation is as much desirable as it is the wave of the future.

Related to the differences in perspectives between Beijing and Taipei are some other questions. One is, how have views about the international system evolved in recent years? Another is: How have views of the PRC and the ROC changed in recent years?

Some specific questions to address are these: Most nations view democracy as the wave of the future and see no reason to treat the ROC as a pariah state (as it was in the past) or to isolate Taiwan. Taiwan's democratic experience is too important and treating Taiwan badly would be sending the wrong signal. Most nations thus generally favor Taiwan's participating in world affairs.

Of course, whether the international community would be willing to fight for Taiwan's sovereignty is another matter and something Taipei has to ponder. There are many indications they will do little if anything to help Taiwan in the final analysis or in a real crunch. America's willingness to protect Taiwan in the next decade is likewise not certain. Most nations of the world community have trade and other commercial interests in Taiwan and thus see Taiwan as an economic player, and one without which the international economy will function less well. Thus, there is broad and rather strong support for Taiwan not being excluded from international economic relations or institutions. Taiwan hence has support and will probably garner increasing votes for membership in such organizations.[115]

However, another fact of life is that Beijing is a bigger economic actor and has much more potential to be a trading partner for most nations than Taiwan and will ultimately be a much bigger force in the international economy. In fact, the PRC and its supporters more and more send the message that it is the foremost world economic actor of the future (based on projections that it will be the number one trading nation in the world in just four years and will be the largest in gross national product in little more than a decade).[116]

Finally, many see the PRC as having become a pariah nation due to its human rights record (since the Tiananmen Massacre in 1989). In fact, some countries support Taiwan playing a bigger and more important international role in order to punish Beijing for its human rights abuses.[117]

Yet this stance applies almost exclusively to Western countries; former communist countries and Third World nations do not espouse such a view. The Western negative view of the PRC on the human rights issue is, moreover, offset by the rather effective campaign China has made to promote its own position on human rights among Asian and Third World countries.[118] Even in the West, Beijing has convinced the business community that as a rapidly growing economic power the PRC constitutes a market opportunity that should not be missed and therefore human rights and trade should not be linked.

Conclusions

Both Beijing's and Taipei's future depends upon their relations with each other. This may present a less than rosy future. As the author has suggested in the above pages, the PRC and the ROC have many reasons for not understanding each other. And, as world history tells us, misunderstanding often leads to conflict. It could well lead to a war in the Taiwan Strait. Certainly to most observers this is considered a real possibility. In fact, for this reason the Taiwan Strait is considered one of the world's most serious flashpoints.

Yet there seems to be hope that each will comprehend the others' viewpoint and even empathize and sympathize with the other. Reconciliation is not only possible, it is very much to the advantage of both. And both seem to realize this. Yet reason will not necessarily prevail. It is, therefore, instructive to consider what the consequences of a lack of understanding might be. Taking a look at some scenarios is a first step.

The worst case scenario, but probably the least likely, is for Beijing to launch a nuclear attack on Taiwan. Beijing has said many times it will never use nuclear weapons first. Such an act would, moreover, be counterproductive since Beijing would garner a terrible reputation worldwide for using nuclear weapons, especially against its own people (something that has never been done) and would probably be disdained by the world community for years to come. It would also have possession of an island in ruin and an economic burden (instead of a source of valuable investment and trade as Taiwan is now).

A variation on this scenario would be a conventional attack on Taiwan in combination with or following a quarantine or blockade. However, since a quarantine would have to be supported by control of the air to work and would probably escalate, this is probably best seen as one scenario rather than two. A conventional attack would very destructive since Taiwan is prepared to defend itself and no doubt would. Clearly it not something either side can take lightly.

Inasmuch as a conventional invasion of Taiwan could not be undertaken without preparations that could be observed by other nations, namely the United States, and the U.S. could be expected to take diplomatic actions to stop or prevent either a quarantine or an attack on Taiwan by Beijing or interdict an attack, an invasion of Taiwan also seems fairly unlikely for yet another reason. There are, however, doubts about Washington's willingness to protect Taiwan. But the U.S. did intervene in March 1996 as a result of the PRC's missile tests. In this connection one should bear in mind the favorable opinion of Taiwan in the U.S., much more than Beijing. This situation will likely obtain in the near future given the present state of Sino-American relations and predictions of future problems.

Of course, if Taiwan provokes an attack in some way, and declaring independence would surely be one of these (being probably both the only sufficient provocation and the most likely one), Washington might react differently since public opinion may not in this instance favor

Taiwan. This situation appears more dangerous if radical forces on the left of the political spectrum in Taiwan (namely independence advocates) and in the PRC (mostly in the military, but also in the Communist Party) increase in influence. The main question this evokes is: Will the United States continue to espouse a positive policy aimed at reducing the influence of both. Or, will the U.S. succumb to isolationist sentiment resulting from its inability to compete economically with East Asia or prove unwilling to sustain its military strength in the region at current levels. Both are legitimate concerns.

Another scenario might be the Republic of China, in response to the fear of an attack and/or continued threats by Beijing, seeking and joins an alliance with the U.S., Japan or the Association of Southeast Asian Nations or any combination (perhaps even all of them) against the PRC. Beijing has certainly created serious security concerns among leaders, scholars and the local populations in Japan and the nations of Southeast Asia because of its rapid and perceived unjustified (while the other major powers in the world are cutting their defense spending) military buildup. All three see Beijing's military growth as mirroring anti-status quo intentions. And its actions in the area as witnessed by its recent military incursions in the South China Sea are seen as aggressive if not expansionist behavior.

The problem with such a scenario is that both Japan and the Association of Southeast Asian Nations (which represents the nations of Southeast Asia) are not exactly friends. Both exhibit noticeable military weaknesses and without U.S. leadership are not likely to align against the PRC. Furthermore, for Taipei to align against China would present a domestic political dilemma and certainly a split along ethnic and other lines that would be difficult to handle.

Still another scenario is for China to experience internal problems leading to the breakup of the People's Republic of China. Leaders in Beijing transparently fear this, though they often say they do not. There are strong centrifugal tendencies in China and Beijing faces a dilemma in finding it necessary to maintain a decentralized economic system in order to promote continued economic growth, yet seeing that as a threat to the nation's integrity and even its survival. Western scholars also see the breakup of China as a genuine possibility.

If this were to happen Taiwan might remain as is. Or it might link up in some ways, economically and/or politically, with South China or one or more province (most likely Fujian and perhaps also Guangdong) in South China. Taiwan's investments are for the most part there. Also, democracy is much further advanced in South China than in North China. Alternatively China could fragment or split along north-south lines. This might lead to civil war; or it may be a something that no one opposes seriously and becomes a fact of life. Probably it would be the former.

Another possibility is for Taiwan to remain separate from the mainland or the People's Republic of China indefinitely. In other words, keep the status quo. After all, their mutual differences and problems did not begin yesterday and in many ways defy easy or quick solutions. A variance on this scenario might be for Taipei to adopt policies of distancing itself from the PRC. Taipei, in fact, has recently announced some policies (promoting more investment in Southeast Asia as opposed to the PRC, for example) that suggest it is moving in this direction. Many members of the opposition Democratic Progressive Party advocate this and say Taiwan's future is that of "the Switzerland of East Asia." Another variance on this scenario might be for the PRC to accept a separate Taiwan as better for China in terms of investment (since any effort to change the status quo quickly or by force would result in capital flight) or agree to it temporarily (the "German formula with a time limit.")

This, however, assumes a rather static world and seems to run counter to economic, not to mention global political and military, trends. Also Taiwan is not Switzerland. Finally, PRC leaders have gone on record many times opposing the German formula; changing their position may be very difficult for domestic political reasons.

Last, there is the scenario of a Greater China. Some say a Chinese community or federation is evolving simply because of expanded economic relations between the two sides. Others contend the power of Chinese culture will bring them together at a time when the world is dividing along ethnic lines. Still others cite networking and other factors. The reality is that relations across the Taiwan Strait have improved over the past seven years rather dramatically and recent difficulties seem to be the exception rather than the rule and was provoked by unusual circumstances and/or a small group of people.

1. In the interest of fairness and in an effort to avoid bias or the appearance of bias, the author will use various terms for the two sides or antagonists. The official names are used first and most frequently. The PRC, of course, objects to the use of the term Republic of China. The term Taiwan will be used frequently both because it is widely employed in writings in English and because it is the term used by Beijing. ROC and PRC are used for convenience and Beijing and Taipei for variety.

2. See Julian Baum, "Idle Threat," *Far Eastern Economic Review*, April 13, 1995, p. 29.

3. This speech was given on January 30, 1995. It was published as a pamphlet by the Taiwan Affairs Office of the State Council on this date.

4. For details, see Hungdah Chiu, *Koo-Wang Talks and the Prospect of Building Constructive and Stable Relations Across the Taiwan Straits* (Baltimore: University of Maryland School of Law, 1993). These talks resolved a number of legal and other matters between Beijing and Taipei.

5. President Lee set forth these points in an address to the National Unification Council on April 8, 1995. For details, see "ROC President Makes Six-Point Speech on Relations with the Mainland," *Asian Bulletin,* June 1995, p. 25.

6. For the PRC's response to Lee's visit, see Ren Xin, "Speech Expresses Lee's Real Aim," *Beijing Review*, July 3–9, 1995, p. 27 and "Lee's Cornell Speech Rapped in Chinese Press," *Beijing Review,* August 14–20, 1995, pp. 12–13. Part of the reason PRC officials were so displeased was that both Secretary of State Warren Christopher and Assistant Secretary Winston Lord had promised that President Lee would not be given a visa and would therefore not visit the United States. They definitely felt they had been lied to.

7. See Julian Baum, "A Case of Nerves," *Far Eastern Economic Review*, July 20, 1995, p. 26. For details concerning the context of these remarks, namely the ROC's legislative election, see John F. Copper, *Taiwan's 1995 Legislative Yuan Election* (Baltimore: University of Maryland School of Law, 1995), p. 8.

8. See William Overholt, "China After Deng," *Foreign Affairs,* May/June 1996. It is also worthy of note that Taiwan policy during the Mao period was made personally by him. This has not been so true of the Deng era. For further details, see Qingguo Jia, "The Making of Beijing's Taiwan Policy," in Tun-jen Cheng, Chi Huang, Samuel S.G. Wu (eds), *Inherited Rivalry: Conflict Across the Taiwan Strait* (Boulder, CO: Lynne Rienner Publishers, 1995)

9. See Nicholas Kristof and Sheryl WuDunn, *China Wakes* (New York: Times Books, 1994) for further details on this point. Also see Thomas Christensen, "Chinese Realpolitik," *Foreign Affairs*, September/October 1996.

10. See "President Lee Announces Intention to Stand for Re-Election in 1996," *Asian Bulletin*, October 1995, p. 37.

11. Julian Baum, "Up and Running," Far Eastern Economic Review, September 7, 1995, p. 14.

12. See John F. Copper, "Taiwan's March 1996 Presidential, Vice-Presidential and National Assembly Elections," (forthcoming).

13. See "Beijing admits motives behind tests," China Post (domestic edition), March 8, 1996, p. 1.

14. See Christopher Bodeen, "Presidential candidates differ on handling crisis," China Post (domestic edition), March 4, 1996, p. 1.

15. "China Continues War of Words with Lee," China News (domestic edition), March 9, 1996, p.1.

16. Ibid.

17. "New Missile base opening moved up," China News (domestic edition), March 10, 1996, p. 1.

18. This view was evoked by several books published in the PRC reflecting the growing of Chinese nationalism and anti-American sentiments, such as The China That Can Say No, China Megatrends, Why China Said No. For further details see John Chen's review in the newsletter China 2000, December 1996. Also relevant to this perception is the fact that China's defense budget was increasing at a rapid rate and there were projections putting its military spending ahead of the United States by the year 2010. See, for example, David Shambaugh, "The Security of Insecurity: The PLA's Evolving Doctrine and Threat Perceptions Toward 2000," Journal of Northeast Asian Studies.

19. For details, see Weiqun Gu, Conflicts of Divided Nations: the Cases of China and Korea (Westport, CT: Praeger, 1995), p, 1.

20. Ibid.

21. See The Taiwan Question and the Reunification of China (Beijing: Taiwan Affairs Office and Information Office, State Council, 1993), Section 1. Also see Bai Liang, "Taiwan Issue Brooks No Foreign Interference," Beijing Review, November 6–12, 1995, p. 22. The latter author states that as early as the 12th century the Chinese government had established "administrative organizations" on the island.

22. See The Taiwan Question and the Reunification of China, Section 1.

23. For details, see John F. Copper, Taiwan: Nation-State or Province? (second edition) (Boulder: Westview Press, 1996), pp. 21–22. Cited in the footnotes are a number of authors that have done research on this subject.

24. Ibid.

25. Ibid.

26. Ibid.

27. See, for example, Christine Vertente, Hsu Hsueh-chi and Wu Mi-cha, The Authentic Story of Taiwan (Knokke, Belgium: Mappamundi Publishers, 1991).

28. See, for example, Yu-ming Shaw, "The Modern History of Taiwan: An Interpretative Account," in Hungdah Chiu (ed.), China and the Taiwan Issue (New York: Praeger, 1979).

29. See *The Taiwan Question and the Reunification of China,* Section 1.

30. The author has never seen this point in print, but has heard it from PRC officials and scholars.

31. See The Taiwan Question and the Reunification of China, Section.

32. See Yu-ming Shaw, "Modern History of Taiwan," p. 14.

33. The Common Program, the PRC's provisional constitution written in September 1949, cites abolishing imperialist prerogatives and the goal of liberating "all of the territory of China and accomplish the cause of unifying the country." This theme was mentioned many times after that.

34. The notion of settling accounts is cited in *The China That Can Say No* and in a number other articles in such places as *Beijing Review* in recent months.

35. See Vertente, Hsu and Wu, *The Authentic Story of Taiwan,* p. 130. The authors note that the Manchus wanted to rule Taiwan only to prevent the revival of anti-Manchu Ming loyalists.

36. See George H. Kerr, *Formosa: Licensed Revolution and the Home Rule Movement, 1895-1945* (Honolulu: University of Hawaii Press, 1974), chapter 2.

37. This view is presented in *Taiwan and the Reunification of China.* Also see Hungdah Chiu, "The Question of Taiwan in Sino-American Relations" in Hungdah Chiu (ed.), *China and the Taiwan Issue* (New York: Praeger Publisher, 1979) for further details.

38. See *The Taiwan Question and the Reunification of China,* Section 1. This view has been stated by PRC scholars and officials for some time, in fact, since 1949.

39. The Chinese Communist Party drafted plans to use eight armies of the Third Field Army under Su Yu to assault Taiwan. After allegedly hearing that the Nationalists might hire mercenaries and after the Nationalists withdrew troops from Hainan and Zhoushan Islands in May 1950 to Taiwan, the PRC had to assemble a larger force. See Gu, *Conflicts of Divided Nations,* p. 22.

40. In September 1958, Mao, at a Supreme State Conference, said: "U.S. imperialism invaded Taiwan and has occupied it for nine years." In 1962, Zhou Enlai said that Chinese "firmly opposed the forcible occupation of Taiwan by U.S. imperialism and its scheme of creating two Chinas." See Dan N. Jacobs and Hans H. Bearwald (eds), *Chinese Communist: Selected Documents* (New York: Harper and Row,1963), p. 156 and p. 226.

41. See Peter VanNess, "Taiwan and Sino-American Relations," in Michael Oksenberg and Robert B. Oxnam (eds.), *Dragon and Eagle* (New York: Basic Books, 1978), p. 265.

42. Gu, *Conflicts of Divided Nations,* pp. 26–28.

43. Ibid. The author, however, states that the PRC agreed in talks with the Soviet Union earlier not to invade Taiwan.

44. This position has been stated repeatedly by PRC leaders and appears often in official publications. See, for example, "Taiwan's Return to the UN Out of the Question," *Beijing Review,* August 30–September 5, 1993, p. 4. The writer

states that China's representation "has been settled in the political, legal and procedural terms."

45. In short, the PRC's policy was not to accept dual recognition. This was also Taipei's policy for a long time, but it changed its policy in this regard.

46. Gu, *Conflicts of Divided Nations.*, p. 28. Some authors also suggest the existence of secret agreements that Beijing interpreted as committing the U.S. to help the PRC recover Taiwan.

47. In a letter from the Standing Committee of the National People's Congress in January 1979, the PRC government promised that it would "respect the status quo" in Taiwan after reunification. On September 21, 1981, National People's Congress Chairman Ye Jianying (or head of state of the PRC) issued a declaration stating Taiwan, after unification, would be a special administrative zone and could retain its armed forces and maintain its current socioeconomic system as well as its way of life. Ye's nine-point policy was published in *Beijing Review*, October 5, 1981, pp. 10–11.

48. This was especially true in the early 1980s and gave rise to a reassessment of China's foreign policy and the establishment of an "independent" foreign policy line in 1982. For further details, see Carol Lee Hamrin, "Emergence of an 'Independent' Foreign Policy and Shifts in Sino-U.S. Relations," in James C. Hsiung (ed.), *U.S.-Asian Relations: The National Security Paradox* (New York: Praeger, 1983). The author cites a number of PRC sources to make this point.

49. For a detailed analysis of Taiwan's legal position see Chiu, "The Question of Taiwan in Sino-American Relations" and various chapters in Jean-Marie Henckaerts (ed.), *The International Status of Taiwan and the New World Order: Legal and Political Considerations* (London: Kluwer Law International).

50. Ibid. See especially Hungdah Chiu, "The International Legal Status of Taiwan," in Henckaerts (ed.), *The International Status of Taiwan and the New World Order,* p. 6.

51. See A. Doak Barnett, *Communist China and Asia: A Challenge to American Foreign Policy* (New York: Vintage Press, 1960), p. 103.

52. Ibid.

53. The PRC, in fact, stated that it would not again invade the Offshore Islands separate from invading Taiwan.

54. See Chiu, "The Question of Taiwan in Sino-American Relations," pp. 173–175.

55. Ibid.

56. For details, see Stephen P. Gilbert and William M. Carpenter, *American and Island China: A Documentary History* (Lanham, MD: University Press of American, 1989)

57. For further details, see Copper, *China Diplomacy,* p. 37.

58. Ibid., pp. 58–60.

59. See Hungdah Chiu, *The International Legal Status of the Republic of China (Revised Version)* (Baltimore: University of Maryland School of Law, 1992) and Tao-tai Hsia, "Taiwan and Its Return to the United Nations," *Asian American Review*, Winter 1996, p. 21.

60. See John F. Copper, "Taiwan's Legal Status: A Multilevel Perspective," *Journal of Northeast Asian Studies*, December 1982.

61 . This view has been put forth on numerous occasions by the PRC. See, for example, various statements in *The Taiwan Question and the Reunification of China*. For a more recent statement of this view, see "Premier Reaffirms Policy Toward Taiwan," *Beijing Review*, February 19–25, 1996, pp. 13–15. In this latter article, Premier Li Peng is quoted as saying, "The Chinese people, who have been bullied by foreign invasion, value the national sovereignty and territorial integrity greatly and are obliged to accomplish the cause of reunification."

62. "Ethnic" here refers to two groups of Taiwanese (the Hakka and those from Fukien (or Fujian) Province and the Mainland Chinese or later arrival Chinese who came from various parts of China after World War II. There is a fourth group: the Aborigines. The first three groups espouse quite different views on Taiwan's relationship to the mainland or to China.

63. See Peng Ming-min, *A Taste of Freedom* (New York: Holt, Rinehart and Winston, 1972), p. 2 and 3. Also see W.G. Goddard, *Formosa: A Study in Chinese History* (Lansing: Michigan State University Press, 1966), p. xii.

64. Ibid.; Goddard, *Formosa*, p. xiv.

65. See June Teufel Dreyer, *China's Political System: Modernization and Tradition* second edition (Boston: Allyn and Bacon, 1995), p. 279

66. See, for example, Leo J. Moser, *The Chinese Mosaic: The Peoples and Provinces of China* (Boulder, Co: Westview Press, 1985) for further details.

67. Nations that have a "good match" in terms of having a homogeneous population are less than thirty percent of the nations on the planet. Almost thirty percent, a larger number, have populations that are less than half comprised of one nationality. See John T. Rourke, *International Politics on the World Stage* (Guilford, CT: Dushkin Publishing Group, 1995), p. 190. The problem of ethnic conflict has been widely discussed among Western scholars, especially since the breakup of the Soviet Union and the publication by Samuel Huntington of the widely read piece "The Clash of Civilizations."

68. See George H. Kerr, *Formosa Betrayed* (Boston: Houghton Mifflin Co., 1965), Chapter 17.

69. This view is presented in a host of PRC writings. It is suggested in *The Taiwan Question and the Reunification of China.*

70. The exact amount of time that China was unified or fragmented is, of course, a matter of interpretation. A number of Western scholars have noted that China was not unified during a considerable time in its history. The scholar

in Taiwan who talked about this in connection with Taiwan being separate was Wei Yung.

71. When China was unified the political system was more a unitary one and generally more authoritarian and tyrannical. One can, of course, note the fact that the era of producing great ideas, including Confucianism, came before China was united. When China was unified, the government was very oppressive.

72. Such statements have been heard often during election campaigns, especially in the most recent campaigns. President Lee Teng-hui has also made these points either directly or indirectly in his public speeches and replies to criticism from the PRC.

73. This position was originally made by Western historians. Historians in Taiwan have picked it up and have talked about it in this context.

74. This is a position taken especially by the New Party.

75. It is interesting to note that Taipei has supported Beijing's territorial claims to the Diao Yu Tai Islands and generally to islands and ocean space in the South China Sea.

76. See, for example, Ren Xin, "Hong Kong 's Stability and Prosperity Depend on Ourselves," *Beijing Review*, August 8–14, 1994, p. 20.

77. See Ren Xin, "Direct Cross-Straits Exchanges Urged," *Beijing Review*, September 16-22, 1996, p. 9. The author states, referring to the policy of "no contact, no negotiations and no compromise," that Taiwan has refused the PRC's proposal of "three direct exchanges" and "continually put many obstacles in the path."

78. For details on this connection , see Kent Calder, *Pacific Defense: Arms, Energy and America's Future in Asia* (New York: William Morrow Company, 1996).

79. For a more detailed discussion of this point, see John F. Copper, *Words Across the Taiwan Strait* (Lanham, MD: University Press of America, 1995), p. 33.

80. Chinese leaders are very familiar with the analysis made in Zbigniew Brzezinski's book *The Grand Failure* in which the author predicted the demise of the Soviet Union because of lack of unity and botched attempts to decentralize economic and political power yet retain power at the center to preclude centrifugal tendencies.

81. See for example, several articles in Jason C. Hu (ed.), *Quiet Revolutions on Taiwan, Republic of China* (Taipei: Kuang Hua Publishing Co., 1994), Section V.

82. See Nicholas D. Kristof and Sheryl WuDunn, *China Wakes* (New York: Times Books, 1994), pp. 235–36.

83. "Premier Reaffirms Policy Toward Taiwan," *Beijing Review*, February 19–25, 1996, p. 15.

84. See, for example, President Lee's inauguration speech of May 1990.

85. For details, see John F. Copper, *China Diplomacy: The Washington-Taipei-Beijing Triangle* (Boulder, CO: Westview Press, 1992), pp. 82–83.

86. See Ralph N. Clough, *Reaching Across the Taiwan Strait* (Boulder, CO: Westview Press, 1993), p. 12.

87. Deng Xiaoping and other PRC leaders have made such statements. For details, see Enbao Wang, *Hong Kong, 1997: The Politics of Transition* (Boulder, CO: Lynne Rienner Publishers, 1995), p. 51.

88. See Copper, *China Diplomacy*, pp. 81–88,

89. Copper, China Diplomacy, pp. 83–84.

90. Ibid., pp. 84–85.

91. Clough, *Reaching Across the Taiwan Strait*, p. 15.

92. A government publication, *The Republic of China Yearbook 1996* (Taipei: Government Printing Office, 1996), states: "Taipei's fundamental policies toward Peking can be summed up as "one China, two political entities." (p. 109) This position was earlier set forth in the "White Paper on Cross Strait Relations." See Tao-tai Hsia, "Taiwan and Its Return to the United Nations," *Asian American Review*, Winter 1996, p. 26.

93. Ibid.

94. Ibid., pp. 113–115.

95. See, for example, Cal Clark and Steven Chan, "ROC -PRC (Non) Relations: Groping Toward the German Model, " in Bih-jaw Lin and James T. Myers (eds.), *Forces for Change in Contemporary China* (Taipei: Institute for International Relations, 1992).

96. Clough, *Reaching Across the Taiwan Strait*, p. 146.

97. This is one of General Secretary Jiang Zemin's points in his Eight-Point speech in early 1995.

98. This can be attested to by the actions of a number of Democratic Progressive Party candidates during recent election campaigns. They responded to threats by leaders in Beijing by burning PRC flags and referring to top PRC leaders as blowhards after they did not follow up their threats with actions or respond to the flag burnings and other insults. For details, see John F. Copper, *Taiwan's Recent Elections: Fulling the Democratic Promise* (Baltimore: University of Maryland School of Law, 1990)

99. Beijing, in negotiations with the United States, stated that its "fundamental policy" was a peaceful solution of the Taiwan problem. However, it never made a specific promise in this regard, except possibly orally. Regarding the decentralization of decision making on Taiwan policy, see Qingguo Jia, "The Making of Beijing"s Taiwan Policy," in Tun-jen Cheng, Chi Huang, Samuel S.G. Wu (eds.), *Inherited Rivalry: Conflict Across the Taiwan Straits* (Boulder, CO: Lynne Rienner Publishers, 1995).

100. See John Naisbitt, *Megatrends Asia* (New York: Simon and Schuster, 1996) pp. 35–36 and 243–44 regarding the Chinese ability to network. In this connection, it is interesting to note that there have been reports of DPP leaders

asking Japan to serve as a check on the PRC and that Beijing has accused President Lee Teng-hui of this. See Hsia, "Taiwan and Its Return to the United Nations," p. 29 and 30.

101. These views are propounded in a number of "nationalistic" books published in the PRC in recent months, such as *The China that Can Say No* and *Megatrends China*. The military has openly expressed a hostile attitude toward Taiwan. See, for example, Lowell Dittmer, "China's Taiwan Policy," *Asian American Review*, Winter 1996, p. 88. Dittmer notes that Liu Huaqing and Zhang Zhen, in particular, forced a hardening of policy toward Taiwan.

102. This is the gist of a number of ROC official publications. See, for example, "Why the ROC Belongs in the UN: Separating Fact & Fiction," and "Pragmatic Diplomacy and China's Reunification," both published by the Government Information Office (in 1996 and 1990 respectively).

103. For a discussion of the legal aspects of this issue, see Hungdah Chiu, *The International Legal Status of the Republic of China (Revised Version)* (Baltimore: University of Maryland School of Law, 1992). For information on Taipei's recent foreign contacts, see *The Republic of China 1996 Yearbook* (Taipei: Government Information Office, 1996), Chapter 9.

104. This is evident from reading various newspapers and magazines at the time of the missile tests in March 1996.

105. It is worthy of note that this has, in fact, not happened since 1945 except for Israel's seizure of territory and it appears that even this is not permanent. The cases of Vietnam invading and occupying Cambodia and Iraq invading and occupying Kuwait and the final results of each are quite instructive.

106. See John F. Copper, "The PRC and the Third World: Rhetoric Versus Reality," in David Chou (ed.), *Peking's Foreign Policy in the 1980s* (Taipei: Institute of International Relations, 1990).

107. See Calder, *Pacific Defense*, chapter 6.

108. See Frederick Chien, "A View from Taipei," *Foreign Affairs*, Winter 1991/92.

109. In July 1996, the European Union passed a joint resolution in support of Taipei's bid to participate in the United Nations. The U.S. House of Representatives also passed such a resolution.

110. In late 1995, a PRC writer noted that 159 nations have formal diplomatic ties with Beijing and that they have recognized that there is only one China and that Taiwan is part of China., He also observed that in response to Taiwan's effort to gain admission to the United Nations, the U.N. General Assembly dismissed the proposal and decided to adhere to Resolution 2758 (which admitted the PRC and gave it the China seat). See Bai Liang, "Taiwan Issue Brooks No Foreign Interference," *Beijing Review*, November 6–12, 1995, p. 22.

111. See, for example, Wang Shuzbong, "The Post-War International System," in Harish Kapur (ed), *As China Sees the World* (New York: St. Martin's Press, 1987) and Samuel S. Kim, "China and the World in Theory and Practice," in

Samuel S. Kim (ed.), *China and the World* (Boulder, CO: Westview Press, 1994).

112. See David Shambaugh, "Containment or Engagement of China? Calculating Beijing's Responses," *International Security*, Fall 1996, p. 187.

113. For further details, see John F. Copper, "Taiwan and the New World Order," *Journal of East Asian Affairs*, Winter/Spring 1995.

114. See Hsia, "Taiwan and Its Return to the United Nations," p. 21 and *The Republic of China Yearbook 1996* (Taipei: Government Information Office, 1996), Chapter 9.

115. The best example is the World Trade Organization which Taiwan is likely to be a member of soon.

116. Predictions about China's growth can be found in many current popular articles and in newspaper reports. For a more serious analysis, see *The East Asian Miracle: Economic Growth and Public Policy* (New York: Oxford University Press, 1993). This study was done by the World Bank.

117. Some nations seem to reflect this view when debating Beijing's membership in the World Trade Organization. Clearly human rights organizations espouse this view to a considerable extent.

118. See John F. Copper, "Peking's Post-Tiananmen Foreign Policy: The Human Rights Factor," *Issues and Studies*, October 1994.

Chapter Three
Taiwan's First Direct Presidential Election: The 1996 Presidential, Vice Presidential, and National Assembly Elections

Introduction

On March 23, 1996, Taiwan's voters went to the polls to pick the nation's president, vice president, and delegates to the National Assembly. The paramount significance of this election was the fact that it was the first time the electorate decided directly who would be the country's chief executive. Of lesser importance, it was the second nonsupplemental or plenary election of the National Assembly (a body of government that is responsible for amending the constitution and approving presidential appointments to the Control Yuan, the Examination Yuan, and the Judicial Yuan among other duties). It was also the Republic of China's ninth competitive national election, if one counts the gubernatorial election in 1994.[1]

Most observers regarded this as Taiwan's most important election to date—almost singularly because of the nature of the presidential race. Previously, presidents, including incumbent President Lee Teng-hui, were chosen through indirect election by National Assembly representatives. Many, especially opposition politicians, felt this method of electing the president and vice-president was neither democratic nor fair inasmuch as the National Assemblies that performed this duty were made up of mostly delegates who had been elected in the late 1940s when the government was located on the mainland. When the government moved to Taiwan these officials were frozen in office. Thus, the National Assembly had no fresh blood except for those who were appointed to replace members who died, although later non-supplemental elections provided for some new delegates to represent Taiwan only. The majority, however, still represented districts on the mainland, where Taipei had no jurisdiction, in fact where Taipei had abandoned legal claim. This situation, of course, changed with the nonsupplemental National Assembly election in 1991; however, at almost at the same time it was decided that Taiwan would have a direct presidential election.

To viewers outside of Taiwan, the election was important for another reason: it precipitated an international crisis when the People's Republic of China decided to conduct missile tests near two of Taiwan's major ports and other military exercises to intimidate the electorate and cause chaos. Chinese leaders in Beijing also engaged in diatribes against those they perceived were advocating independence, including and in particular, incumbent President Lee Teng-hui. The United States responded to the missile tests by sending ships to the area, including aircraft carriers. This move gave many observers the impression that Beijing's challenge might escalate into a full-blown war between the United States and the People's Republic of China.

Beijing's actions caused a decline in the stock market, a drop in housing and land prices, a deterioration in the rate of the N.T. dollar, and a rush on embassies and foreign representative offices to get visas. Clearly the population was apprehensive, if not possessed by fear, during the campaign. Yet Beijing had done something similar in the summer of 1995 and before the last election in December 1995; thus, although frightening voters, its actions also caused a backlash: the population of Taiwan was angry that Beijing used military threats to influence the election and did not want to see it succeed.

Four sets of candidates ran for president and vice president, making for a unique and complicated election. All were well known to the voters and each had his or her own following or constituency in some form. Three parties participated in the presidential election—though only two officially sponsored candidates. Three parties contested seats in the National Assembly.

Two of the presidential candidates were erstwhile high-ranking members of the ruling Nationalist Party, or Kuomintang (KMT). One resigned to run against President Lee. The other was expelled from the KMT. This gave the appearance the election contest would split the ruling party's voting constituency, resulting in a very split-ticket vote.

Public opinion polls conducted before the election anticipated a much closer race than the final vote tally reflected. Beijing's actions apparently caused serious anger among voters and helped incumbent Lee Teng-hui. The results, however, were difficult to predict for a variety of other reasons including the fact many voters were still undecided just before voting time.

The question of what constituted a mandate was at times hotly discussed during the election. Many predicted that incumbent President Lee would win but said he would not have a mandate unless he won 50 percent or more of the vote. There being no provision in the Republic of China Constitution for a run-off election, whoever wins the most votes wins the office. As it turned out this was less a matter of concern than it seemed it might be during the campaigning.

The National Assembly election was less of an attention-getter than the presidential race. Still it was important since there were a number of constitutional problems that had to be resolved in a coming National Assembly session. The parties also contested seats vigorously, even though the main opposition party advocated abolishing this body of government and the turnout at candidate forums was not good.

The usual charges of vote-buying, criminal influence in politics, and media unfairness were heard throughout the campaign. There were also many candidates who engaged in sensationalism and antics. And there was some campaign violence. All in all, however, the election campaign and the voting went smoothly, especially given the tense situation in the Taiwan Strait at the time.

The voter turnout was high, indicating continued voter interest in elections as well as proving that voters were not intimidated enough by Beijing's threats to stay away from the polls. Clearly the election contributed to the further democratization of Taiwan's polity; some, in fact, said it added the final touches to the democratization process. In other words, Taiwan had arrived.

The Election And Taiwan's Evolving Polity

Preparations for this election were both controversial and significant because of debate that had been going on for some years about the nature and structure of the Republic of China's political system and about the process of political modernization. The direct election of the president was viewed by most as an important, if not final, step in the process of democratizing the nation. Having a voter-elected president also strengthened the Office of the President and tilted the system away from a parliamentary one and toward a presidential one. In the case of the National Assembly, the main issues were the evolving role of that body and, commensurately, whether it should be disestablished. Constitutional changes were made to hold this election and more were needed as a result of it.

The Republic of China Constitution, which was written in 1946 and promulgated in January 1947, established a mixed presidential and parliamentary system of government, with the latter, according to most analysts, predominant. The supporters of a parliamentary system won when writing the constitution, though the presidentialists prevailed in 1948 during the civil war between the Communists and the Nationalists when the "Temporary Provisions," or the Provisional Amendments for the Period of Mobilization for the Suppression of Communist Rebellion, were passed. These articles gave the President expanded emergency powers (afforded originally in Articles 39 and 43 of the Constitution) and canceled the two-term limit on the president and vice president. The power of the presidency was again augmented by "amendments" to the Temporary Provisions, especially those added in 1966 when the National Assembly assigned further emergency powers to the president and made constitutional provisions for creating the National Security Council.[2] The expansion of the powers of the president, of course, increased the importance of the National Assembly, which was responsible for electing the president and vice president.

Early on, opposition politicians favored a parliamentary system, viewing the powers of the president as too extensive. One writer has even asserted that the constitutional power conferred on the president was "rarely conferred on any head of state in the world."[3] Oppositionists likewise viewed the extensive powers of the president as one of the main reasons, if not *the* reason, for making the system an authoritarian one while inhibiting the growth of democracy.

The Temporary Provisions similarly became viewed by opposition politicians and a large segment of the population alike as the paramount impediment to the practice of civil rights. They afforded the "legal" grounds for censorship, the use of arbitrary government power, and the continuation of martial law even into the 1980s. Furthermore, since the Temporary Provisions strengthened both the Office of the President and the National Assembly, the opposition viewed these entities as "colluding" bodies of government, strongly disliking both.[4]

Those who challenged the authoritarian nature of the Republic of China's polity and pushed for democratic change, however, did not generally focus much attention on changing the system so that the president would be directly elected by the people, even though they often complained about the undemocratic actions of the National Assembly. The main reason they did not strongly advocate a direct presidential election was that opposition politicians did not have a political party since forming new parties was prohibited by the

Temporary Provisions. In addition, the Nationalist Party commanded such resources and garnered such strong public support for having engineered Taiwan's miracle economic growth that it could have won a direct presidential election.[5]

Over time opposition politicians began to think more favorably about a presidential system, or at least became less enthusiastic about a parliamentary one. This shift in view was especially noticeable in the mid-1980s, when President Chiang Ching-kuo used the strength of the office to promote democratic reform. Patently, democratization would not have proceeded at such a rapid pace at that time had the president not held a great deal of power and authority. In fact, it was the strong presidential system that afforded him the means to make these changes.

When Lee Teng-hui assumed the presidency in 1988 following Chiang Ching-kuo's death, he announced that he favored returning to the constitutional limit on two presidential terms. He also stated that he wished to reduce the importance of the National Security Council and in other ways promote further democratic reform.[6] He did not, however, state a clear or unequivocal position on the issue of direct presidential elections. At the same time opposition politicians who had opposed a strong president, in part because former presidents had been Mainland Chinese (as opposed to locally born Chinese or Taiwanese), found the new "Taiwanese president" less objectionable and began to see the presidency as a "shortcut to power" for Taiwanese.[7] In short, the opposition's attitude toward a presidential system changed. Their hostility toward the National Assembly, however, remained and they more strongly than ever complained about the undemocratic means by which the president was chosen.

In March 1990 the opposition Democratic Progressive Party (DPP) organized demonstrations outside the National Assembly building protesting its authority to elect the president. A committee of the National Assembly responded by voting to expand the body's powers. This action engendered a public backlash such that, on March 14, 22,000 students demonstrated at Chiang Kai-shek Memorial in Taipei complaining about the slow pace of democratic reform. The National Assembly was the focus of their calls for change. By March 18 the number of protestors had increased to 30,000. President Lee met and spoke to the demonstrators and promised that a National Affairs Conference would be convened to look at various political issues, including the method of selecting the president, and that he would adopt strong measures to democratize Taiwan's political system.[8]

The National Affairs Conference opened June 28, with 150 noted individuals representing the government, various interest groups, academics, and others. The meeting had only an advisory capacity but was considered very important nevertheless. The consensus of the group was that a new National Assembly should be elected and that the constitution needed to be revised.[9] In the meantime the Council of Grand Justices (an organ of government made up of top justices and members of the Judicial Yuan and which interprets the constitution among other duties) ruled that by December 31, 1991, all senior members of the National Assembly and other elective bodies of government must step down.

There emerged no concrete recommendation about the election of the president, however. In fact, the majority of delegates sent to the National Affairs Conference did not favor a direct presidential election.[10] Nevertheless, James Soong, general secretary of the KMT, subsequently met with DPP leaders to discuss how a future president might be directly elected.[11]

In February 1991 President Lee ordered the National Assembly to call a provisional meeting in April. At that meeting, responding to Lee's request, the Assembly terminated the Temporary Provisions and approved articles regulating the election of a new National Assembly. The election of a second National Assembly followed in December. The DPP, during the campaign, called for a new constitution and a Republic of Taiwan—in other words, a new political system and a new nation. The DPP also put the issue of a publicly-elected president in its platform and tried to connect the issue of a voter-elected president to independence. Party leaders also said that whereas the people wanted a directly elected president, the KMT did not.[12] The KMT at this time declined to take a position on the matter, stating that the wishes of the populace were unclear and better proposals had to be worked out.[13]

In fact, the KMT leadership's position on this issue was unclear at this time. Whether President Lee favored a direct election was not known. Some say he did; others intimate that he did not.[14] Clearly the issue was a divisive one in the KMT, and President Lee probably did not want to push ahead on the matter when other problems were already causing a split in the party.

In any event, in March 1992 President Lee, at an important KMT meeting, came out in support of a direct election, startling members of his party and causing more friction in KMT ranks between the "Mainstream" (pro-Lee) and "Non-Mainstream" (anti-Lee) factions. Lee may have been influenced in the timing of his decision by a growing perception that the populace supported a direct election; also, he may have seen direct presidential elections as necessary to continuing Taiwan's rapid democratization.[15] Another possible explanation is that he long favored a direct election system but before this did not want to cause controversy over the issue by openly stating his position.

The new, second National Assembly met as a constitutional convention in May 1992 and added eight more amendments to the constitution. Included in these amendments were provisions whereby the president and vice president would be elected every four years instead of every six years (though details about how this would be done were not provided), and provisions for the National Assembly to likewise be elected every four years. Whether the president and vice president would be elected directly or by an electoral college as is done in the United States was not resolved and was still being debated.[16] The matter of whether Taiwan would have a U.S. presidential system or a European parliamentary one, an issue intimately linked to whether the president and vice president would be elected directly or indirectly, was being intensely debated as well. The KMT was split on both issues; the DPP favored a direct election of the president and a presidential system.

In early 1993, following the KMT's poor showing in the December 1992 Legislative Yuan election, there was pressure on Premier Hau Pei-tsun to take blame for the "defeat" and resign (as Premier Yu Kuo-hua and Premier Lee Huan had done in 1989 and 1990, respectively).[17] Hau resisted and was supported by demonstrators, but was forced out anyway, allowing President Lee to appoint Provincial Governor Lien Chan to the position. This appointment, plus Lee's further consolidation of power at the 14th KMT Party Congress in August (due to leading anti-Lee officials in the party leaving to form the New Party), gave Lee a stronger hand in pursuing changes in the system leading to a directly elected president.[18]

The National Assembly approved ten more amendments to the constitution (while consolidating within them the earlier amendments) in July 1994. The political system of the Republic of China was altered in some important ways by this process and provision was made for the direct election of the president and vice president. One amendment set forth the details for a direct election of the president and vice president beginning in 1996. Another strengthened the National Assembly by creating the position of speaker and institutionalizing yearly meetings. Still another restricted (in reality annulled) the power of the premier to countersign presidential appointments and dismissals, resolving one important issue relating to whether Taiwan's political system was presidential or parliamentary in favor of the former.

The provision for the direct election of the president and vice president led directly to the Presidential and Vice Presidential Election and Recall Law promulgated by the Legislative Yuan on August 9, 1995. Some of the controversial provisions of the new election law included: (1) requiring citizens of the Republic of China to return to Taiwan to cast ballots (canceling provisions for absentee voting), (2) restricting political parties' rights to nominate presidential and vice presidential candidates to those that received at least 5 percent of the valid votes in the most recent election above the provincial-municipal level (eliminating the influence of minor parties in presidential elections), (3) forcing independent candidates to acquire a petition signed by at least 1.5 percent of eligible voters in the most recent parliamentary election, (4) limiting campaign spending to an amount equal to 70 percent of the total population of the Republic of China multiplied by NT$15 plus an additional amount of NT$80 million (or NT$302.45 million in this campaign), (5) narrowing the campaign period to twenty-eight days, and (6) giving the Central Election Commission the authority to make television stations provide air time to candidates while allowing individuals or groups the right to sponsor televised debates using government funds.

A number of candidates complained about the Election and Recall Law rules regarding registering as a presidential candidate. One candidate, former Taipei Mayor Kao Yu-shu, dropped out of the race on January 5, saying that the requirement of getting a signature, a copy of the person's identity card, and a personal seal from at least 201,318 people was unfair and unconstitutional. The regulation, Kao charged, violated Article 129 of the constitution, which says that elections should be conducted "through universal, equal and direct suffrage." Kao also said that the US$550,000 deposit required of all candidates when registering was unreasonable and undermined the country's democracy. Chen Li-an supported Kao's complaints, stating that his volunteers felt the "white terror" of the 1950s suppression of free expression when they tried to get signatures of government employees (who felt that the information they provided might be misused).[19] Lin Yang-kang thought the qualifications required to run for president were too strict, saying they "contradict[ed] the spirit of the Constitution that grants people the right to elect and be elected."[20]

At the start of the campaign, it appeared that the measure requiring Overseas Chinese to return to Taiwan to vote would prove a major hindrance to them. The Overseas Chinese Affairs Commission originally estimated that 270,000 people would return to vote, but as of the end of February only 5,900 had come back. The commission noted that the expense of the trip and the fact that there are no holidays in most countries in March, was making the number of returnees low.[21]

The 5 percent rule did not become very controversial since similar provisions had been in effect during previous elections. The same was true of television time. Limiting campaign spending was not a big issue as there were too many ways around the legal limitations and opposition candidates found a good issue in criticizing KMT candidates for their "lavish" spending during the campaign. The short campaign period was also already a part of Taiwan's election system and for that reason it was not the subject of much debate.

Prelude To The Campaign

Candidates planning their campaigns had to move in sync with Taiwan's politics leading up to the election. In fact, a number of events set the political stage, affected campaign strategies for the campaign, and even decided the parties' platforms. The most noticeable factor in the weeks leading up to the campaign period was the "Beijing factor."

The hostile relationship between Taipei and Beijing, along with the PRC's anger at Taiwan in general and at President Lee Teng-hui in particular, goes back many years. Although the relationship seemed to be steadily improving at the end of the Cold War, the Tiananmen Massacre and Beijing's charges, authentic or not, that Taipei helped instigate the Democracy Movement caused relations to deteriorate temporarily. There were also other bumps along the way.[22]

Nevertheless, both Taipei and Beijing appeared to perceive that the bipolar system, which had kept the Chinese civil war alive long beyond its normal life expectancy, was now defunct and that a new system had replaced it. They did not perceive each other as remaining enemies in the new system, especially since that system was characterized by economic or cultural blocs.[23] Thus the two sides began to import from and export to the other, and this trade soon increased to very meaningful amounts. Taiwan businesses also began to invest heavily on the mainland. The two former antagonists even engaged in at least tentatively successful negotiations to resolve some of their legal and political difficulties—in the form of the Koo-Wang talks held in Singapore in 1993.[24]

However, the insecurity and its accompanying political maneuvering—or power struggle—in China evoked by the pending demise of strongman Deng Xiaoping reversed this process. Chinese leaders contending for power, or even those simply wanting to survive a post-Deng succession struggle, did not want to appear weak, especially on the "Taiwan issue." Similarly, the military, which has been traditionally more irredentist and less compromising toward Taiwan, saw its stock, and thus its political influence, soar. In Taipei, meanwhile, President Lee Teng-hui was under fire from the Democratic Progressive Party for a failed diplomacy. The opposition said it had caused Taiwan to become isolated and put in a position whereby it would eventually have to abandon its claim to sovereignty. The opposition, not being in power nor anticipating it would be soon, advocated an unrealistic policy (at least in terms of short-run hopes for success) saying Taiwan needed to join the United Nations and other international organizations. Lee, rather than suffer humiliation and perhaps even a deterioration of public (meaning voter) support, in large measure adopted the opposition's policy and made an overt effort to "participate" in the U.N.

Beijing, of course, successfully blocked Taipei's efforts, though at the cost of some embarrassment. Many in the international community believed the idea of a new world order encompassed the hope that the U.N. and other international organizations would become universal and that past bipolar feuds needed to be ended. Beijing's response was in this sense counterproductive. In August 1993 the Taiwan Affairs Office and the State Council in Beijing issued a White Paper entitled "The Taiwan Question and the Reunification of China." This apparently hastily written document reflected disagreements in the Chinese leadership over dealing with Taiwan. It thus became an issue that hardliners could use, particularly in the context of succession politics, against Deng and the reformist right, including Jiang Zemin, the Chinese Communist Party's general secretary and Deng's reputed successor.[25]

In January 1994, Jiang issued an eight-point statement on Taiwan's reunification that was patently less hawkish and appeared to set forth a serious design for negotiations. Foreign Minister Qian Qichen and even Premier Li Peng subsequently called on Taipei to give a positive response. Taipei, however, was slow in responding and was not as forthcoming as Beijing would have liked.[26]

In April President Lee Teng-hui issued a six-point proposal in response. Although generally friendly in tone and mostly in substance as well, Lee cited the "reality of the separation of China" and the fact that the Republic of China possessed sovereignty, meaning that negotiations between Beijing and Taipei had to be between equals. He called for Beijing to pledge a peaceful settlement only and repudiate the use of military force. Beijing, of course, could not do this in view of its long-held policy that Taiwan was a domestic issue, not to mention the hard-liners' and the military's view on the subject.[27] His reply, therefore, did not meet Beijing's expectations and evoked little positive response. In fact, it may well have strengthened the hand of the hard-liners.

This exchange set the stage for an explosive reaction when President Lee visited the United States that summer. Lee was highly visible before, during, and after the trip. He appeared determined to succeed with his flexible diplomacy lest the opposition have grist for labeling him a weak president and charging him with causing Taiwan to be isolated and allowing the PRC to undermine Taiwan's sovereignty and even its ability to engage in global trade.

To make matters worse, U.S. Secretary of State Warren Christopher and Assistant Secretary for Asia and the Pacific Winston Lord specifically and unequivocally promised Chinese leaders in Beijing that Lee would not be given a visa and would therefore not visit the United States. But President Clinton caved in to pressure from Congress and ordered that Lee be given permission to visit, incensing leaders in Beijing while playing into the hands of hard-liners. Adding to the insult was the fact that this was the first ever visit to the United States of a head-of-state from the Republic of China. Also Lee was given broad press coverage and made a hit with the public and the media on his U.S. tour. Beijing felt the visit set a very bad precedent and perceived that Taiwan's successful democratization had made the country popular in the United States.

Fearing that this popularity might spread, and that Lee, in making the trip, was promoting an independent Taiwan, on July 1 the Beijing media accused Lee of "wrongdoing" and said that he had "seriously damaged" relations across the Taiwan Strait. Xinhua News Agency was even more vitriolic and threatening, saying that China should use "fresh blood and lives" to prevent Taiwan from rejecting reunification. Taipei, to prevent panic, tried to get its news organizations to play down this unveiled and unexpected intimidation.[28]

Hard-liners in Beijing, obviously now exerting more political influence, wanted to pick a fight over Taiwan and attack those responsible for Taiwan relations at home and even challenge Jiang if he did not do something. Jiang, rather than risk his right of succession and perhaps more, joined the hard-liners in the military and the media, perfunctorily at least.[29] Voices of reason and moderation in Beijing were thus muffled.

Beijing conducted four separate military exercises in the Taiwan Strait—including two sets of missile tests near Taiwan from July to November 1995. And this had a prelude. In February Beijing had moved an artillery division equipped with M-9 missiles to Fukien Province adjacent to Taiwan (where they could hit targets on the island). Subsequently the People's Liberation Army demonstrated its aggressiveness in taking an island in the South China Sea by force from the Philippines.[30] Beijing's missile tests thus understandably had a deep and penetrating impact on Taiwan. The stock market plummeted, as did land and housing prices. Businesses were put up for sale, but there were no buyers, and a number of foreign embassies and representative organizations in Taipei were inundated with requests for visas.[31]

Just days before the December Legislative Yuan election, the People's Liberation Army announced that it had found many blind spots in Taiwan's radar network and that it planned large-scale practices for bombing in March leading up to Taiwan's presidential elections.[32] A Hong Kong paper subsequently reported that the PLA had "drawn up a strategy" for capturing Taiwan in the event it did not make major concessions.[33] Taiwan's stock market dropped even further.

Many assessing the impact of Beijing's actions on the Legislative Yuan election seemed to favor the view that the People's Republic of China had indeed influenced the election in the direction it wanted. The New Party, which strongly opposes Taiwan independence, did much better than expected, doubling its seats in the national lawmaking body, whereas the KMT lost a significant number of seats and the DPP did less well than expected while seeing its most famous advocates of independence go down in defeat.[34]

Meanwhile, turning to domestic politics in Taiwan, in March 1995 the DPP decided on a primary process to pick its presidential candidate. Four well-known DPP leaders entered the running: Hsu Hsin-liang, Lin Yi-hsiung, Peng Ming-min, and Yu Ching. Peng and Hsu survived the first round of the process and finally Peng won, but only after an exhaustive and divisive primary.[35] Peng, at age seventy-two, was considered by some to be too old; others said he was out of touch with Taiwan politics and unqualified for the job. He had spent two decades in exile in the United States and had been a member of the party only a year. Furthermore, he did not have much experience in government, and some called him emotional, idealistic, aloof, and fuzzy about both domestic and foreign policy issues. As the "father of Taiwan independence" and the DPP's single most famous personality, however, he had stature, and for that reason it was difficult, it was thought, for DPP voters not to give him their support. Peng also defeated Hsu in some part because of his hostile attitude toward China. For example, he even opposed investing in China because "China does not treat Taiwan as an equal and refuses to sign an investment protection agreement."[36] (China's saber rattling and missile tests incidentally coincided with the DPP primary race.) Peng then picked the younger and more experienced Hsieh Chang-ting as his running mate.

If the DPP's candidate selection process was divisive, the KMT's was worse, even though the ruling party was almost certain to nominate incumbent President Lee who had, by Western standards at least, stellar ratings in the polls. Some KMT leaders, using their ability to plant ideas in the press, recommended that President Lee live up to his promise of not running again (a promise he had made in 1990 and subsequently repeated several times) and yield to his protégé Premier Lien Chan. Some of them may have been serious; many no doubt sought to divide Lee and Lien. Beijing chimed in, assailing Lee as an advocate of independence while blaming him for the deterioration in Taipei-Beijing relations. Lee's supporters said that Beijing launched its attack on Lee thinking it could induce him not to run. After all, Beijing went on the offensive against Lee immediately after he visited the United States when it was still not certain that Lee would be a candidate. *People's Daily*, which generally represents the official view in Beijing, subsequently expressed hope that Lee would drop out of the race.[37] If officials in Beijing perceived they could dissuade Lee from running they were certainly wrong.

On August 17, just before the KMT was to convene a plenary meeting of the 14th Party Congress, Chen Li-an, president of the Control Yuan and a well-known KMT luminary, suddenly announced that he would run for the presidency. Chen, unhappy with Lee Teng-hui, said he wanted to offer "an alternative" to President Lee. Chen posed a serious challenge to Lee. His father, Chen Cheng, had been governor and premier and is widely credited for the success of

Taiwan's land reform policies (which President Lee was also involved with) and its early economic modernization. Chen Li-an himself had served as deputy secretary general of the KMT in the early 1980s at a remarkably young age and subsequently as chairman of the National Science Council and then minister of economic affairs from 1988 to 1990. He was appointed minister of defense in 1990 and president of the Control Yuan in 1993. He was known as a clean politician and a critic of corruption. He was also known to be a devout Buddhist and the lay leader of the Fo Kuang Shan Buddhist Order, which has a following of several million. Chen, at fifty-eight, also represented the younger generation.[38]

Chen's declaration brought to center stage the issues plaguing President Lee's leadership: trouble with Beijing, KMT vote-buying and money politics, and the current leadership's inability or unwillingness to do anything about it. Some also said that Chen would attract the "Buddhist vote," but many doubted whether there was such a thing. In any event, Chen's announcement froze the KMT leadership temporarily and caused further divisive strains in the party.

Chen's decision to run prompted Lin Yang-kang, vice chairman of the KMT, to make an announcement confirming earlier statements as well as widespread speculation that he would also be a candidate. Lin was commissioner of the Taiwan Provincial Department of Reconstruction from 1972 to 1976, Taipei mayor from 1976 to 1978, governor of Taiwan from 1978 through 1981, and minister of the interior after that. He was vice premier from 1984 to 1987 and president of the Judicial Yuan from 1987 to 1994. He had long been regarded as a very popular and charismatic Taiwanese politician. And he had the talent, experience, and ambition to be president, and had been considered likely to run in 1996. In 1990 Lin, together with Chiang Wego, Chiang Kai-shek's second son and the half-brother of Chiang Ching-kuo, made a bid (that was subsequently abandoned) for the presidency when the president was elected by the National Assembly and votes were controlled by the KMT.

Lin's declarations at this time may have pressured Lee Teng-hui to end speculation about whether he would run, though most people thought he would. In any event, at the second plenum of the 14th KMT Party Congress, Lee announced his candidacy. Lee's opponents, including Lin Yang-kang, argued for a closed primary, allowing all KMT members to vote for presidential candidates. This method would have made the process divisive and difficult to control, since the KMT has members all over the world. Lee's forces defeated this motion and he was nominated by the congress with 92 percent of the votes.[39] He selected Lien Chan as his running mate.

Lee had been involved in Taiwan's successful land reform program early in his career before getting a Ph.D. degree from Cornell University in 1968. He was mayor of Taipei from 1978 to 1981, governor of Taiwan Province from 1981 to 1984, vice president from 1984 to 1988, and president and chairman of the KMT from 1988 to the present.

The day after Lee was nominated to be the KMT's presidential candidate, Beijing again went on the offensive. Xinhua wrote: "To sweep Lee Teng-hui into the trash bin of history is the common, historical responsibility of Chinese on both sides of the Taiwan Strait." *People's Daily* called Lee a "schemer and a double dealer" and blamed him for strained relations across the Taiwan Strait. The paper even attacked his father, saying that he was a "100 percent traitor" for having served the Japanese colonial government on Taiwan.

Meanwhile a dozen KMT legislators refused to sign a petition endorsing Lee. Former Premier Hau Pei-tsun's son quit the KMT and joined the New Party to run for a seat in the Legislative Yuan.[40] Former Premier Hau voiced his opposition to Lee's decision, saying "people in power should not hold power too long." He added that it would be a "prouder contribution" if Lee were to step down and that "his term is up."[41]

Lee responded by repeating his promise to build a "Great Taiwan" while citing the "Taiwan political miracle" and "nurturing a new Chinese culture" (all of which sounded to some observers as supporting independence or at least berating Beijing). He further declared "power lies with the people," saying that Taiwan's democratic achievements warranted "equal and fair treatment of our nation in the international community."[42] Pro-Lee KMT officials were even harsher. One of Lee's supporters asserted that Beijing's comments sounded like the invectives against Hong Kong Governor Patten and Chinese democracy advocate Fang Lizhi. Another said that Beijing wanted to control Taiwan and needed a weak leader to do that, noting, "If we show signs of being influenced by China it would be very dangerous."[43]

On the heels of Lee's announcement, Chen Li-an and Lin Yang-kang met, leading to speculation that they would join forces against Lee. Talks, however, apparently broke down over who should be the presidential candidate.[44] Lin subsequently parlayed successfully with former premier Hau Pei-tsun to be his running mate.

On November 23, just as the campaign began for the Legislative Yuan election, a sizable number of KMT members protested Lin and Hau running for president and vice president without party approval (although they had not officially announced yet). They were also criticized for campaigning for New Party candidates. Many KMT loyalists felt that Lin and Hau should be expelled from the party. President Lee called on them to "behave themselves."[45] Lin and Hau responded by promising an "open letter" stating their position and criticizing President Lee, whom they said had "betrayed the nation and the party." They also said they would use Sun Yat-sen's thought to attack Lee.[46]

Chen Li-an officially registered as a presidential candidate on November 27, mid-way through the campaign. The next day Lin and Hau registered. The following day approximately 100 KMT members met in Taichung and threatened to quit the party unless Lin and Hau were punished.[47] Two days before the election, Hau, in a television interview, said that the KMT needed to experience being an opposition party if it was to "learn administrative impartiality." He also called on President Lee to resign from his position as chairman of the party because of "rampant corruption and money politics in Taiwan."[48] This attack provoked KMT members of the National Assembly from Taipei and Kaohsiung to demand that the party expel Lin and Hau.[49] The KMT subsequently "canceled" the party memberships of the two, an action short of expulsion.

The Legislative Yuan election in early December mirrored factionalism in the ranks of the KMT and Beijing's successful intimidation of voters, in addition to general concern about the economy and other important matters and disenchantment with incumbents. The New Party "won" the election, tripling its representation in the nation's lawmaking body. The KMT lost seven seats, winning only 46 percent of the popular vote, compared to 53 percent in the 1992 Legislative Yuan election. In fact, this was the first time its popular vote had fallen below 50 percent in a major election. The KMT did very poorly in the big cities and the major counties, which many view as a bellwether for future elections. The DPP gained four seats, but its most well-known candidates and a host of party leaders—particularly those known for their strong support of Taiwan's independence and hostility toward China—lost.[50] Clearly the election results indicated that voters were concerned about problems in Taipei-Beijing relations and that the KMT faced serious problems in the March election.

The Campaign

The campaign for the presidency began formally on February 24, twenty-eight days before the day of the election. Huang Kun-huei, chairman of the Central Election Commission, launched the campaign and at the same time announced a Commission decision to prohibit the publication of opinion polling data during the ten days prior to the election to keep polls from unfairly influencing the voters. As before, the Central Election Commission prepared a large number of officials to oversee the campaign and the voting. In most cities police officers were ordered not to take vacations and many worked overtime to prevent election violence.

Chen Li-an started an eighteen-day cross-island campaign trip on February 22 and the next day met with retired servicemen.[51] That same day Lee Teng-hui held a press conference, the first since just after he returned from his U.S. trip in the summer of 1995. He announced that he sought to sign a peace treaty with Beijing as a first step toward improving cross-strait relations.[52] Peng Ming-min, also on February 23, released an open letter he had written to Chinese Communist Party General Secretary Jiang Zemin calling on the People's Republic of China to recognize Taiwan's sovereignty and independent status. Simultaneously, he said that Taiwan should formally declare independence in the event of a Beijing missile strike against the island or an attack on Kinmen or Matsu.[53]

On Sunday, February 25th, in a Central Election Commission–sponsored nationally televised campaign forum, the candidates presented their views and summarized their political positions. Each candidate was allowed thirty minutes to introduce his platform. President Lee cited his achievements over the past six years and asserted that he would strive to improve relations with Beijing, though he also promised to continue his policy of pragmatic diplomacy to expand the Republic of China's international profile. Lee also talked about the future of the nation and about the historical strides it had made in democratization. Peng Ming-min spoke of injustices in Taiwan's past and called current national leaders "dishonest to history" and "lacking the moral courage to tell the truth." He said the people should elect him to show their disapproval of the current administration, which he called "irresponsible and gutless" and as having "corrupted the country." Lin Yang-kang criticized President Lee for causing tension with Beijing and promised to improve relations with the People's Republic of China.

He also blamed Lee for a recent series of financial crises. Lin further said that he would rebuild harmony among the four major ethnic groups in Taiwan and distribute power evenly between groups. Chen Li-an declared that the current government had turned "beautiful Taiwan" into a "place of filth and corruption" and a "place of greed and -." He said Taiwan was "no longer Formosa" (which means beautiful in Portuguese) and that if elected he would transform Taiwan into a place like Switzerland or Denmark.[54] The candidates clearly held very different views on most subjects, though all four promised to seek to improve relations with China (though with different slants).[55]

Simultaneously, the parties and campaign teams either announced policy statements or took some kind of action to draw attention to their candidate. The KMT promised a list of constitutional amendments, including proposals to lengthen Legislative Yuan terms to four years (from the present three), to redefine the relationship between president and premier, and to revise the electoral system into single-seat districts and a two-vote system (giving voters one ballot for candidates and another for a political party).[56] Whereas all of these ideas had been broached before, KMT leaders made more formal and specific proposals while taking up criticism about money politics (inasmuch as single-member districts would presumably alleviate this problem, since members of the same party would no longer compete) and party factionalism.[57] Lin Yang-kang proclaimed that if President Lee were ousted there would still be a chance of peace talks with Beijing. He also accused Lee of supporting Taiwan independence.[58] Meanwhile, fifty of Lin's backers organized a protest demonstration at the offices of China Television Company and complained of the KMT's domination of the broadcast media. The group threatened to storm the offices, but after attracting the attention of police, backed off. Elsewhere, a Lin campaign leader said one of Lee's campaign songs, "Taiwan Forward," came from a Japanese kamikaze song and mirrored Lee's "colonial subject" mentality.[59] A number of local DPP officeholders organized rallies, pledging their support to Peng Ming-min. They contradicted reports that some DPP mayors and county commissioners had appeared with President Lee on various occasions and had supported some of Lee's policies, leading many people to believe that the DPP had adopted a "drop Peng, protect Lee" mentality. DPP chairman Shih Ming-teh said that President Lee and his running mate, Lien Chan, were mere candidates and were the DPP's opponents. Taipei mayor Chen Shui-bian said that DPP officials "unconditionally supported Peng."[60] Chen Li-an, with 300 supporters, continued on a cross-island walk, on one occasion stopping at a garbage heap to put the trash into disposal cans. Chen used the occasion to talk about how he would improve the environment if elected.[61]

On February 27, three days into the campaign, President Lee declared that Beijing was using military exercises to interfere with the elections. "Don't be scared," he told an election rally audience. He also said there was nothing to fear even though the stock market had fallen due to the threats. Coinciding with Lee's comments, William Li, director of the Mainland Affairs Council, said that Beijing's military exercises were designed for psychological warfare purposes only and that Beijing was not planning to start a war.[62]

Meanwhile, Peng Ming-min attended a press conference where he warned of another 2-28 Incident (referring to February 28, 1947, when Nationalist troops killed a large number of Taiwanese who started an uprising against the government) if the government did not give up its one-China policy.[63] He subsequently visited Nantou County, the home of Lin Yang-kang. Lin attended election rallies in Chiayi and Tainan, while his running mate Hau Pei-tsun (a Mainland Chinese) attended a 2-28 Memorial in Chiayi to push the theme of ethnic reconciliation. Chen Li-an continued his cross-island trip.[64]

President Lee addressed a number of rallies in Taipei the next day, while his wife and daughter helped him campaign elsewhere. Minister of defense Chiang Chung-ling supported Lee's theme that the people should not worry about Beijing's military exercises, saying the reports about the exercises had been exaggerated.[65] Peng Ming-min campaigned in Hsinchu (where many Hakka live) and unveiled his Hakka policies. Chen Li-an at this time obtained support from a Hakka television station owner and for the first time ever made the arrangements to broadcast via satellite, to fifty stations in Taiwan, to promote his views.[66]

On February 28 all candidates did something to commemorate the 2-28 Incident. Peng Ming-min was undoubtedly the biggest winner from the events of the day which included renaming Taipei New Park. The new name was 2-28 Peace Memorial Park. Taipei Mayor Chen Shui-bian, who dedicated the park, condemned efforts to ignore the incident—echoing one of Peng's themes. Lee Teng-hui laid a wreath at the park in an official ceremony, while Lin Yang-kang spoke at Youth Park in front of a large list of names of victims.[67]

The front-page story in almost all of Taiwan's newspapers on March 1 was the nomination of President Lee for the Nobel Peace Prize. Lee's name was put in the running by former Swedish Prime

Minister Per Ahlmark. Ahlmark said, "Almost the entire transition by Taiwan to a democracy has occurred during Lee Teng-hui's presidency." He went on, "For the first time in several thousand years of Chinese civilization, part of the Chinese nation is today run through elections and an equal voice under political freedom."[68] Wu Poh-hsiung, secretary general to the president, was elated over the nomination and announced, "There wasn't any bloodshed during the entire process (of democratization)." He also declared, in a comment obviously aimed at Beijing, "It also means that Chinese people are well-suited to democracy."[69]

Peng Ming-min responded differently, saying that the nomination was "shameless." He pointed out that Lee was not the first person in Taiwan to be nominated: DPP chairman Shih Ming-teh had been nominated by Lech Walesa in 1983. Other DPP leaders argued that Taiwan democratized because of the DPP's "hard struggle" and that Lee and the KMT had put a spin on the democratization process to make it look like their fight.[70]

That day, while on the campaign trail, Peng issued a three-plank platform on welfare reform, saying that compared to other countries with similar income levels Taiwan's welfare system "hardly bears mentioning." The proposal included more spending for elderly benefits, gender equality, and social welfare (including labor). Peng said welfare had been disproportionately given to the military, government officials, and educators. Other DPP leaders said that this would be a bigger issue for winning votes than it had been in the past.[71]

At a press conference organized by Lin Yang-kang supporters, Chen Chen-sheng, former presidential press officer, accused President Lee of pressuring government employees to participate in campaign activities and questioned whether large amounts of money used in the campaign by the KMT were not taxpayer money. Chen called for a Control Yuan investigation and said he would reveal more in daily statements.[72] Meanwhile, the New Party sought to stop Lin and Chen Li-an supporters from criticizing each other and promised to support the team with the largest following.

The second week into the campaign period, the vice presidential candidates spoke at an Election Commission–sponsored forum. Premier Lien Chan spoke of political and economic stability, successful efforts to turn Taiwan into an Asian regional hub, and the great amount of political experience that he and President Lee brought to their jobs. Hau Pei-tsun attacked Lee and the "Taiwan independence camp" as going down the "road to death." He noted that as a Mainland Chinese on a ticket with a Taiwanese, the two would guarantee an end to provincial rivalries. Speaking third, Frank Hsieh spoke in Hakka and Ami (one of the Aboriginal languages) and also Taiwanese and Mandarin, calling for respect for Taiwan's minorities. He spoke of Taiwan as a multi-cultural society and promised mother-tongue education. He also attacked the KMT's cultural policies. Wang Ching-feng said that Chen Li-an's choice of a woman as his running mate proved his support for women's issues, while calling for a more passionate society. Three vice-presidential candidates (all but Lien Chan) called for presidential debates.[73]

Elsewhere, Lin Yang-kang's campaign office made issue of Lee Teng-hui's alleged membership in the Chinese Communist Party at one time—disseminating to the public copies of an article about this matter by journalist Li Ming written in *Ming Pao* (a Hong Kong newspaper). According to Lin, Lee Teng-hui had contact with Communists in Taiwan in 1946 and was recruited by an individual named Yeh Cheng-sung, who was later executed. The article further stated that Lee was still contacted by the police in Taiwan in the 1970s about his former associates. This story, being old news, was apparently brought up at this time to counteract the boost Lee had received from the Nobel Peace Prize nomination. The Lin-Hau camp also repeated a statement from a Swedish newspaper that said that it was possible to buy a Nobel Prize and assailed the KMT in connection with a Government Information Office expenditure of US$100,000 to place an article by Lien Chan in the U.S. journal *Foreign Affairs,* suggesting that this was taxpayer money being used for election advertising.[74]

Chairman of the DPP Shih Ming-teh, pursuing a favorite party theme, attacked the KMT for using people with gangster backgrounds in their campaign. He said Taiwan had survived "white terror" (refer-ring to the KMT's use of police power and censorship in the past) and would now survive "black power" (referring to organized crime). Shih made specific reference to the assault on the party's secretary general outside of DPP headquarters the previous day and said that Lee Teng-hui's administration had encouraged an increase of criminal influence in politics. The DPP, he declared, would organize a protest march soon.[75]

As the campaign continued Peng Ming-min accused President Lee of not mentioning the unification of China during his campaign, a position he had publicly supported many times. Lin Yang-kang demanded that President Lee take a leave of absence so that he would not be using public funds in campaigning. He also accused Lee of making inflammatory remarks during the campaign to provoke Beijing so that he could then declare martial law and postpone the elections. On the campaign stump Lee's daughter called Lin a "defeatist." Chen Li-an seemed to want to stay clear of accusations and continued to tour and make issue of environmental matters.[76]

Meanwhile the DPP joined Lin Yang-kang in attacking Lee Teng-hui for his past Communist ties. Peng Ming-min, in fact, went even further, saying that, according to documentary evidence, a "bandit cadre" named Lee Teng-hui was arrested in 1949 and provided a list of names of Communist activists to the police after which several people were arrested and executed. Peng obliquely blamed Lee for their deaths. Seemingly working in tandem with the DPP on this issue, the Lin-Hau camp then presented a campaign commercial that included a similar charge testified to by a policeman who had interrogated Lee. All of this prompted the Presidential Office to issue a denial and threaten legal action against people making false accusations. Lee's spokesperson said that the person mentioned in the documents in question could not have been Lee because of discrepancies in provincial origin and age.[77] In another case DPP supporters staged a protest outside the offices of the *Independence Evening News* because the newspaper had published a story saying that Peng Ming-min did not have the support of the party and appeared to have quit the campaign. DPP leaders explained that Peng was preparing for a television debate. Campaign executive director Pang Pai-shien declared, "The KMT and the Communists are joining hands in order to smear and divide the DPP."[78]

On March 18, just five days before election day, Tainan County Commissioner Chen Tang-shan threatened to sue Lee Teng-hui over the use of a campaign advertisement that portrayed him as supporting Lee because he had presented Lee with a pineapple and had made a few friendly comments during one of Lee's visits to Tainan. The perception that Commissioner Chen supported Lee also came from the fact that he had, in contrast, been absent during Peng Ming-min's visit. This provided the opportunity for Lee's campaign people to boast that many DPP politicians (Chen having ties to the DPP) supported Lee rather than Peng. Chen stated that the use of his comments constituted a violation of the Election Law and that he would take legal action.[79]

As the campaign entered its final days, the Lee-Lien team adopted a strategy of trying to convince voters (even though there were no polls to cite) that they would win and that everyone should "jump on the bandwagon." The Lin-Hau team tried to give the impression that they were gaining momentum by holding large rallies and by buying news-paper advertisements. They also continued with negative campaigning, making additional charges that Lee Teng-hui had been a Communist in the past and that he was covertly supporting independence. Chen Li-an remained more low-key in his campaign, apparently trying to pick up votes from urban, young, white-collar voters opposing Lee. Some said that Chen perceived that, because of his age, he was the only possible candidate among those running who might run again in 2000 and that he wanted to run a "gentleman's campaign." Peng Ming-min apparently thought he could get more votes by conceding victory to the Lee-Lien ticket in the hopes of persuading more DPP supporters not to vote for Lee (because he did not need their support) while claiming the second place position.[80]

There were several pitches by supporters of candidates to get competitors to drop out of the race, though in most cases these were not serious and had to be considered campaign ploys. Several noted personalities and officials supporting the DPP signed an open letter asking Lee Teng-hui to drop out of the campaign. Included were Huang Hsin-chieh, former head of the DPP; Li Chen-yuan, Academica Sinica scholar; Kao Chun-ming, Presbyterian Church leader; and Tsai Chung-poh, ROC Rotary Club director. The letter stated that Lee had provoked problems with Beijing, had allowed money politics to pollute Taiwan, and had not answered charges that he was formerly a Communist. Frank Hsieh hinted that Lee had made a deal with Beijing, based on the news that there were assassination attempts against other candidates but not Lee.[81] Chen and Lin each talked about the other resigning and the New Party, though trying to mediate between the two, said it would unequivocally support Lin because he had a better chance of winning.[82]

The Beijing Threat Factor

Before and during the campaign, the People's Republic of China threatened Taiwan in various news releases and official statements, conducted military maneuvers, and even fired missiles to targets in close proximity to two of Taiwan's port cities, all in an effort to intimidate the government and the population and to influence the voters who were going to the polls on March 23. The "Beijing factor" had an undeniable impact on the campaign and on the election results.

It was not the first time Beijing had tried to intimidate Taiwan militarily; however, the reaction in Taiwan this time was noticeably different than in the past. The People's Liberation Army (PLA) had conducted missile tests in the Taiwan Strait after President Lee's visit to the United States in June 1995 to express its displeasure with what it interpreted to be an expression of Taiwan independence (though Lee and most people in Taiwan saw Lee's visit as simply an effort to carry on what Lee labeled "pragmatic diplomacy" and prevent Taiwan from being isolated). The PLA subsequently sought to influence the December 1995 election through similar threats and military exercises and tests during the campaign. Generally, in both cases Beijing evoked the result it wanted, and it was no doubt encouraged by this success to try again in this even more important election.[83]

Another event that explains the Taiwan electorate's reaction was Beijing's advanced warning it would conduct military exercises during the period before the March 23 elections; thus, when the time approached Taiwan was in many ways prepared. Beijing also presented its reasons for conducting the tests, though its explanation was not very credible in Taiwan. In early March PRC leaders announced that if Taiwan were to drop its independence drive, tension in the Taiwan Strait would ease. The situation was "totally the result of Lee Teng-hui visiting the U.S. and his attempt to create two Chinas," said a Foreign Ministry spokesman.[84]

A third factor, again thinking of the effect on the voter, was the fact the U.S. Congress, and to a lesser extent the White House and the Department of State, condemned the exercises and tests. Congress responded immediately, offering Taiwan various assurances. Specifically, Congress blamed Beijing for the conflict and therefore discussed changes in the Taiwan Relations Act (Section 3a and 3b) that would suspend the 1982 August Communiqué's promises to decrease and ultimately end arms sales to Taiwan, which seemed to contradict provisions in the TRA.[85] Congress also debated changing the name of Taiwan's representative offices in the United States from Taiwan Economic and Cultural Representative Office (which does not suggest that it has an official diplomatic functions) to Taipei Representative Office, to officially welcome President Lee if he wished to visit the United States again, and to support Taiwan's admission to the World Trade Organization.[86] Congress' actions also no doubt helped incumbent Lee Teng-hui.

Fourth, Republican candidate for the presidency Robert Dole stated that he would support Taiwan's reentry into the United Nations. Concerning another Lee visit to the United States, he said ostentatiously, "OK with me." He also asserted that the United States had a commitment to Taiwan if the People's Republic of China attacked the island.[87] Parris Chang, a DPP member of the Legislative Yuan, invited several noted Americans to Taiwan, including former CIA director James Woolsey and Admiral Edney, to discuss the crisis. They averred that the United States would act to help Taipei if Taiwan were attacked and stated that Taiwan needed more anti-ballistic missiles immediately.[88]

Finally, international public opinion favored Taiwan, which has not always been the case when Beijing and Taipei have been at odds. Japanese Prime Minister Hashimoto called on Beijing to pursue a peaceful settlement of the issues.[89] Former Singapore Prime Minister Lee Kuan Yew suggested Beijing give Taiwan "international space" and declared that countries in the region did not understand why China could not be patient.[90] Hong Kong Governor Chris Patten said the tests would damage confidence in the region.[91]

In its riposte to the support given Taiwan, Beijing warned of "serious consequences" of foreign intervention and accused Taiwan of trying to enlist the help of foreigners to boost Taiwan and betray China.[92] Beijing, however, also, in what appeared to be a concessionary move, declared that it would cut its troop strength if the United States would stop selling arms to Taiwan.[93]

Taipei responded in a variety of different ways: Minister of Defense Chiang Chung-ling asserted that Taiwan was prepared for Beijing's aggression and could defend the island. He also said that ROC forces would be compelled to counter-attack if any missiles fell within the country's territorial waters, which extend 21.6 kilometers, or 12 nautical miles, from the coastline (which the test off Taiwan's northeast coast could do, as it was expected to take place 20 kilometers from shore).[94] Premier Lien Chan called the tests provocative and issued a statement calling on Beijing to cancel its plans. He said they would interfere with the coming elections and would "jeopardize regional peace and stability." He also asserted that President Lee was pursuing a policy of reunification and that he opposed Taiwan independence.[95] Other Taiwan authorities, no doubt speaking for the president, declared that they did not think the People's Liberation Army would invade the island. Taipei meanwhile put out feelers, saying that "one China" should be discussed and defined.[96] Government leaders appeared to be at once playing down the threat (in order to prevent public panic), offering concessions (so as to avoid being labeled in any way the cause of the crisis and to win international public opinion), and staying tough (to give the impression that President Lee was strong and confident).

This three-pronged strategy may suggest a confused policy but probably, instead, reflected a flexible, multifaceted response guided by the
fact that the conflict was clearly a campaign issue—perhaps the central
one.

On March 7, the day before the missile firings began, the Foreign
Ministry in Beijing said that the missile tests were intended to "safeguard China's sovereignty and territorial integrity" and were "a good
move in attacking the acts of pro-independence forces to create 'two
Chinas' or 'one China and one Taiwan.'"[97] The U.S. Department of
State in response called the tests "irresponsible" and sent messages so
stating to Beijing through its ambassador in the United States Li Daoyu
and Ambassador James Sasser in Beijing. Anthony Lake, national
security adviser to President Clinton, said that a military attack would
have "grave consequences." The Senate suggested consultations in
view of the threat and the U.S. commitment to Taiwan contained in the
Taiwan Relations Act. Senator Frank Murkowski, an expert on Asia,
suggested that the tests constituted a "virtual blockade" of Taiwan's
ports.

In Taiwan, on the Tuesday and Wednesday before the tests, the
stock market dropped 120 points (closing at 4,750). However, this was
only a small portion of its value and less dramatic than the decline that
occurred after the first missile tests in the summer of 1995. Taiwan's
minister of defense reported that defense spending would increase 3.8
percent to 21 percent of the budget in the next fiscal year, but since this
was a long-range projection it could hardly be considered provocative.[98]

Before the tests started all of the presidential candidates announced
their assessments of the situation and policies in response to the crisis.
President Lee stated that the tests were the product of a power struggle
within the leadership in Beijing and reflected the internal discord there.
He said: "They are struggling for power because they have no system
for picking a leader, and must use force to settle the dispute." He
further asserted that Beijing "fear[ed]" Taiwan's democratization and
felt threatened that people would see Taiwan's example and rise up
against the government. Lee sought to explain the crisis in terms of
what was happening in Beijing and the irrationality of Chinese leaders
there.

Peng Ming-min stated that the crisis happened because of the
"insufficient internationalization" of the Taiwan question, which he
said was an outcome of the KMT's one-China policy. Peng's tack was
to blame the government's past policies, in particular its one-China

policy, for the problem. But Peng was also provocative: He announced that Taiwan should "immediately cease" any cooperation with Beijing and that the government should consider its own war games off the coast of Shanghai or Guangdong Province.

Chen Li-an blamed Lee Teng-hui for the crisis and suggested that he drop out of the race, saying it would be "Taiwan's saving grace." He stated that Lee's "headstrong character" had brought Taiwan "nothing but danger." He further added, "If you vote for Lee Teng-hui, you are choosing war."

Lin Yang-kang called for Beijing to stop the tests but said that Lee's "covert independence campaign" was the cause of the crisis and that the president was using "the people, their families and their property as bargaining chips." He maintained that a stance of "no consideration of Taiwan independence" could preserve Taiwan's security.[99]

On the eve of the missile tests, both sides postured and sent warnings. The vice Chairman of the Chinese Communist Party's Central Military Commission, Liu Huaqing, declared that the PRC had no intention of invading Taiwan and furthermore would never use its military to compete on the world stage.[100] At the same time, however, Beijing rejected President Lee's peace overtures, saying that he was a "sweet-talking chameleon."[101] Chinese leaders also threatened the United States, saying that war would result if that nation intercepted its missiles.[102] Deng Xiaoping, however, spoke in less provocative terms, saying simply that he was "concerned about reunification."[103]

On the other side of the Taiwan Strait, Minister of Defense Chiang denied he said that Taiwan would retaliate if a missile landed inside Taiwan's territorial sea boundary.[104] However, on another occasion he said that the Republic of China would "fight" any encroachment on its territory.[105] President Lee, meanwhile, played down the threat.

The U.S. Department of State again warned Beijing of "serious consequences" if a missile went astray.[106] Yet it took no action to evacuate U.S. citizens from Taiwan.[107] The House of Representatives demanded that the White House provide defense guarantees to Taiwan. The White House said the tests were "not helpful."[108]

The tests began on March 8. The People's Liberation Army fired three M-9 surface-to-surface missiles (built in China but patterned after Russian-built SCUD missiles), two west of Kaohsiung and one east of Keelung—but they did not pass over Taiwan. That day and the following day, the war of words—most casting blame, some rather moderate —continued. China's Defense Minister Chi Haotien said Lee was trying to create two Chinas and quoted from one of the founders of the

Red Army who stated that Chinese would suffer "humiliation until Taiwan [was] liberated."[109] Jiang Zemin declared that the PRC "would not halt the struggle against an independent Taiwan until Taiwan gives up."

The Mainland Affairs Council in Taipei called Beijing's tests "dangerous behavior" but did not elaborate very much.[110] The government at the same time published intelligence reports indicating that Beijing did not intend to escalate the conflict.[111] All of the presidential candidates continued to criticize Lee for causing the crisis. Lin Yang-kang, however, admitted that in the short-term the crisis was helping Lee but said that this could change.[112] Meanwhile, the price of rice rose appreciably due to hoarding and the number of people seeking immigration visas increased as reflected in a rush on hospitals for physical examinations.[113]

Beijing escalated the conflict on March 9, announcing that it would conduct live ammunition tests 55 kilometers from the Pescadore Islands (an island group off Taiwan's west coast and territory of the Republic of China) and that ships should not enter the waters in that vicinity from March 12 to 20. Minister of Trade Wu Yi blamed President Lee and said his actions had provoked the PRC to conduct these tests.[114] The next day it was reported that the People's Liberation Army would conduct a large exercise near Taiwan from March 21 to 23 involving 150,000 troops, 300 planes, and 5 guided-missile destroyers and frigates as well as 4 submarines and a number of Sukhoi-27 fighters that Beijing had recently acquired from Russia.[115]

Taipei responded by announcing that it was opening a new missile base on the Pescadore Islands ahead of schedule. The base, it said, was equipped with Sky Bow II missiles. Also released was an opinion poll that indicated that support for unification had fallen from 20 percent to 16 percent, while support for independence had increased from 14 percent to 17 percent (while 46 percent favored the status quo).[116] The government also announced setting up a disaster center in case of war.[117]

In the face of heavy criticism from the PRC, President Lee countered that Beijing should be grateful to him for stabilizing cross-strait trade and for Taiwan investing so much money in China.[118] Nevertheless, competing candidates continued to blame Lee for the problem. Peng Ming-min charged that the government's five-decade-old one-China policy was to blame because it had given Beijing an excuse for what it was doing. He said if Taiwan became an independent country, China would lose its self-proclaimed sovereignty over Taiwan and could not claim the question of Taiwan's status to be an internal matter. In that case an attack on Taiwan would be viewed an invasion of one country by another and would be subject to international law. Lin Yang-kang and Chen Li-an took quite a different position, though one still critical of Lee. Both talked about a commonwealth between Beijing and Taipei similar to the European Union and advocated peaceful negotiations.[119]

Neither Beijing's escalated intimidation nor the harsh criticism of opposing candidates, however, seemed to hurt President Lee's popuarity; in fact, just the opposite. A local opinion poll put Lee far ahead of the other contenders with 40 percent of voter support compared to less than 15 percent for each of the others. Liang Shih-wu, director of the Public Opinion Research Center at the World College of Journalism and Communications, said Lee was expected to get 51.37 percent of the vote, compared to 19.49 percent for Lin, 17.26 percent for Chen, and 11.88 percent for Peng. Scholars said that the military exercises were scaring people but that the majority of citizens were angered, which helped Lee.[120]

At this juncture U.S. Secretary of Defense William Perry called Beijing's escalation "reckless" and "an act of coercion." He noted that the aircraft carrier USS *Independence* was 320 kilometers northeast of Taiwan and that the guided-missile cruiser *Bunker Hill* and the guided missile destroyer USS *O'Brien* were also in the area.[121] Two days later President Clinton ordered a second aircraft carrier, the USS *Nimitz* and five or six accompanying ships to the Taiwan Strait area while noting that the USS *Independence* would be positioned about 160 kilometers from the Taiwan Strait. Coinciding with this announcement Secretary of State Christopher called Beijing's actions "unnecessarily reckless."[122]

Taipei said that it welcomed the U.S. naval presence in the area to "safeguard peace." Premier Lien Chan then met with the Cabinet's emergency task force and intelligence organizations to discuss the situation.[123] The Ministry of Foreign Affairs announced that it would not give up its efforts to participate in the United Nations.[124]

Beijing seemed to alter its policy a bit on March 11: China's foreign minister, Qian Qichen, told reporters at a news conference that Taiwan's election was not democratic but, rather, "run by money and the mafia." He further said that it was part of an independence plot and that the winner of the election would remain "just a local government leader." Xinhua news agency rephrased Qian's words in even harsher language.[125] Meanwhile, a Hong Kong paper reported that Beijing's hostile policy toward Taiwan was ordered by Deng Xiaoping.[126]

Lee Teng-hui replied, saying that he could not help it if Beijing did not believe it when he said that he was not for independence. He also reiterated an earlier statement that Beijing was afraid of democracy in Taiwan because it would cause other nations to support Taiwan and evoke demands for democracy in China.[127] DPP Chairman Shih Ming-teh responded by organizing a boat trip along Taiwan's coast to reassure Taiwan's fishermen hurt by the tests and to demonstrate resolve against Beijing's threats.[128] The DPP also welcomed the arrival of U.S. aircraft carriers and delivered a message of special thanks to the office of the American Institute in Taiwan, located in Taipei.[129] Chen Li-an visited Quemoy where he spoke out in favor of the U.S. naval presence in the area.[130] He later qualified this position, saying that Taiwan should not depend on the United States and that the United States did not want to see a unified Taiwan and China.[131] Lin Yang-kang and his running mate, Hau Pei-tsun, spoke out against "foreign intervention" by the U.S. fleet. The New Party, on their behalf, purchased advertisements and issued campaign fliers suggesting that Taiwan might again be degraded by the presence of U.S. soldiers filling the bars and lowering the respect of the country. One piece of campaign literature asked: "In those days, where was the respect of our sisters and daughters? Maybe the streets will look like that again and where will the respect of the people be?"[132]

The next day it was reported that an unnamed government official had said that Taipei was sending a special envoy to China to explain that the election had nothing to do with independence. Li Yuan-tseh, the president of Academica Sinica and a Nobel Prize winner, was mentioned, although the Mainland Affairs Council said this was not true. DPP Secretary General Chiou I-jen said such a course would further endanger Taiwan. Meanwhile, another government official said there would be an "important announcement" about cross-strait relations shortly after the presidential election.[133] Subsequently, the government denied this report. A government official, however, did confirm that President Lee was considering a national conference to discuss relations with China.[134]

In response to China's fourth missile firing, which was accompanied by other exercises and the promise of live firings in a few days, seventy members of the U.S. Congress sponsored a bipartisan concurrent resolution that had the support of all congressional leaders, saying that the United States should defend Taiwan. Members of

Congress criticized the U.S. policy of "strategic ambiguity" as a cause of the crisis and said that a more clear policy needed to be enunciated.[135] Elsewhere, Vice Admiral Archie Clemins, commander of the Seventh Fleet, said that the fleet's presence in the area reflected Washington's "commitment to stability in the region."[136]

Several days before the election, Beijing lowered its threat level somewhat. Premier Li Peng suggested that war was not imminent and talked about economic development in Fukien Province, where Taiwan businesses were heavily invested.[137] U.S. officials also made some optimistic statements, even though it was reported that Beijing had threatened Los Angeles with nuclear bombing if the United States defended Taiwan in a future attack.[138]

Just before the voting, in a last chance effort to convey their campaign messages on television, the candidates reiterated their views about Beijing's intimidation. In fact, this issue was the main focus of all of the candidates' last comments. President Lee called the missile tests and threats "state terrorism" aimed at "dominating our historical presidential election." He urged the population "not to dance to Beijing's tune." He further stated the threats were the product of a power struggle in China. Both Chen and Lin blamed Lee for the problem. "Lee does not consider himself as Chinese, which is the main reason for Beijing's hardened attitude," said Chen. Lin restated a promise to visit China after becoming president and sign a peace treaty. Peng Ming-min hit Lin on the peace treaty issue, saying that he was against any plans "to sell Taiwan to China."[139]

Clearly, as the voters went to the polls, Beijing's threats were on their minds. In addition, they had heard many candidates' positions on the matter of the PRC's threats and its missile tests.

Election Results

In the presidential and vice presidential part of the election, incumbent President Lee Teng-hui and Lien Chan won 5,813,699 votes, or 54 percent of the votes cast. Peng Ming-min and his vice presidential running mate, Frank Hsieh, garnered 2,274,586 votes, for 21.13 percent of the total. Lin Yang-kang and Hau Pei-tsun received 1,603,790, or 14.90 percent. Chen Li-an and Wang Ching-feng won 1,074,044 votes, or 9.97 percent of those cast.[140]

Lee Teng-hui and Lien Chan could claim a big victory, with more than double the votes received by the second-place finishers and more than all of the other three teams combined. And they did. Before one-third of the votes were counted, KMT spokesman Hansen Chien declared a triumph. On the evening of the election, after all the votes had been tallied, President Lee proclaimed a victory "for Taiwan's 21 million people."[141]

Other candidates immediately conceded defeat, while the media called the Lee-Lien victory a resounding one. DPP presidential candidate Peng Ming-min, early in the ballot counting, stated that the Lee ticket had won. Subsequently, DPP Chairman Shih Ming-teh announced that he would resign. He declared, "With the result of the presidential election so bad, as chairman of the party I wish to apologize to all DPP members and friends." Lin Yang-kang announced that he "accepted the people's choice." The evening of the election, Chen Li-an thanked his supporters and expressed disappointment in losing the election.[142] A number of newspapers declared that the victory had given the Lee-Lien team a clear mandate.[143]

Indeed, the victory was a clear one for the KMT. The Lee-Lien ticket garnered 54 percent of the popular vote, compared to 52 percent received by KMT candidate James Soong in the 1994 gubernatorial race and 45.3 percent KMT candidates got on average in the 1995 Legislative Yuan election. Thus, this election victory could be viewed as a turnaround for the KMT, which had seen its voter support decline for a number of years, leading to speculation that it would eventually lose power.

Lee and Lien could also boast of winning twenty-four of the nation's twenty-five counties and cities. They failed to win only in Nantou County, Lin Yang-kang's home. Lee could also point to getting 90 percent of the vote in his hometown. In addition, the Lee team won more than 50 percent of the vote in all of Taiwan's counties except for Nantou and Taipei counties and Kinmen and Lienjiang counties on the Offshore Islands.[144] Finally, President Lee and his running mate did better than the pre-election polls had predicted.

Those who chose another interpretation than a momentous Lee-Lien victory noted that they barely won over half of the votes (70 to 80 percent constituting a good victory to some) or that they won a much smaller victory than the KMT routinely had won in the past. This, however, was not considered a very valid argument in view of the fact that Taiwan's democratization has meant closer elections. Analysts also pointed to disorganization and disarray and even splits in the campaigns of the opponents as major benefits to the Lee-Lien ticket, saying that they would have won a much smaller portion of the vote had this not been the case. Clearly all of the other teams had witnessed some problems. The DPP's candidate had been away from Taiwan for years and could boast of no important government service. The Lin ticket did not have a party; the New Party favored the ticket but technically stayed neutral. The Chen-Wang team had no party and suffered seriously from a lack of organization and money. Other observers noted that the Lee ticket benefited tremendously from a voter backlash against Beijing's intimidation.

In an effort to put a good face on their performance, the Peng-Hsieh team pointed out that many DPP supporters had voted for President Lee because they interpreted his tough statements toward Beijing as promoting an independent Taiwan. Regarding the issue of independence —the central tenet of the DPP's platform and an issue the party had supported from the time of its founding—one need only total the votes of the Lee and Peng teams, which would be over 75 percent, to see that the DPP had won on the most important and most salient issue of the campaign, said Peng. Lin and Hau supporters, in rationalizing the margin of their defeat, referred to earlier polls and declared that their candidates would have done much better had it not been for the backlash caused by Beijing, and furthermore that the Chen campaign hurt them. In sharp contrast to the DPP's interpretation of the election as mirroring support for independence, they noted the fact that the Lin and Chen teams together got more votes than the DPP, widely reputed to be the main or only serious opposition party. This, they said, was proof for a "third force" in Taiwan's political future.[145] Chen supporters mentioned that their candidate had lacked a large organization and money yet won nearly 10 percent of the vote—more than any independent candidate had ever before garnered in an election in Taiwan.[146]

Notwithstanding these "second opinions," the Lee-Lien ticket won a significant and meaningful victory in what was a hotly contested election that was considered fair by most observers. In other words, their victory was a genuine victory.

Why did the Lee team win? The most obvious reason is that both President Lee and Premier Lien had long records of outstanding government service. Lee was the incumbent president, having served in that office since Chiang Ching-kuo's death in January 1988. Lien had more years of experience in different positions in high office than anyone in government, at least anyone his age. Both Lee and Lien had furthermore garnered high public opinion ratings over a long period of time. Both were also regarded as having good academic backgrounds, both having attained Ph.D. degrees from prominent American universities. In short, in terms of qualifications, they were the best.

Second, the Lee ticket was advantaged by the strong party organization and talent behind them. The ticket was supported by a well-planned and organized campaign conducted by experienced and talented professionals. Similarly their well-run campaign did not lack for money at any time. The fact that they did well in the rural areas clearly demonstrated that their campaign was better organized and better financed then the others. The duo won more than 60 percent of the popular vote in eleven counties and fell below 50 percent only in the four counties mentioned earlier.

Third, the Lee ticket benefited from incumbency. Beyond the slight to moderate edge this position gives candidates in any democratic election, the Lee-Lien ticket gained because of the apprehension and fear that influenced voters in the weeks before election day. It is natural for any electorate to choose the known quantity when they are uncertain about the political situation and their country's future. Voter anxiety obviously resulted from Beijing's military threats. However, it also came from uncertainty about the stock market, housing prices, Taiwan's economy overall, and much more. For the voter who looked for a simple solution or the known quantity, the greater choices of candidates may have also helped the incumbents.

Fourth, Beijing's intimidation against Taiwan and its harsh, threatening, and nasty condemnations of President Lee caused a backlash. One KMT official declared, "We should give Jiang Zemin a medal. He is a super campaign aide."[147] It was difficult to say how much the backlash translated into votes; most put the figure at around 5 percent, but some figured as much as 10 percent.[148]

The foreign press almost unanimously interpreted the election results as a big victory for President Lee, while giving him a clear mandate. In addition, most foreign papers said the election was a rebuke and a setback for Beijing. The *New York Times,* in a front-page story, reported that the election results constituted a mandate and that Lee's victory "exceeded all expectations and was a forceful rebuke to mainland China." *Time* entitled its story on the election "Taiwan's Second Miracle" and spoke of a "political revolution." *Newsweek* said, "The balloting ratified a nation."[149] *The Economist* called Lee's victory a "sweeping mandate" and one that made Taiwan look more like "an independent country."[150] *Asahi Shimbun* said that Lee was the "first Chinese leader ever elected directly and justly."[151]

In the National Assembly race, the KMT won 5,180,714 votes, or 49.68 percent of the popular vote, giving it 180 seats (129 district seats, 43 at-large seats, and 11 seats representing Overseas Chinese). In the new National Assembly, the KMT would thus own 53.3 percent of the 334 seats. The DPP won 29.85 percent of the popular vote, taking ninety-nine seats (sixty-eight district seats, twenty-five at-large seats, and six seats representing Overseas Chinese). It would control 29.64 percent of the total seats. The NP got 13.67 percent of the vote, giving it forty-six seats (thirty-one district seats, twelve at-large seats, and six representing Overseas Chinese). It would have 13.7 percent of the seats. The Green Party got one seat, and independents won five seats (all district seats).[152]

The KMT lost significantly in terms of both the percent of the popular vote and the number of seats won, at least by comparison with the previous National Assembly election. In 1991 the ruling party had received 71 percent of the popular vote, for 254 seats. Its popular vote had declined by more than twenty points from the last election. This had to be considered a significant setback for the ruling party, and it was.

The defeat was not as big, however, as the numbers might suggest. The 1991 win was unusually large—caused by the fact that the DPP had put the independence issue in the platform and had saved many of its best candidates for the Legislative Yuan election the next year. The DPP was also split and did not run an efficient campaign. Instead, if one compares the KMT's performance in this election with other recent national elections, its performance in this election does not seem so bad. It was also only slightly below what had been predicted. Hsu Shui-teh, secretary-general of the KMT, said he was satisfied with the party's performance, noting that winning nearly 50 percent of the seats stood as proof for a "public acknowledgment" of constitutional reforms passed by the previous KMT-dominated National Assembly.[153]

Also ameliorating the KMT defeat was the fact that almost five years had elapsed since the previous election and this organ of government had been reduced in stature. There was clearly diminished interest on the part of the electorate about the National Assembly. It was difficult for candidates to raise money, and campaign rallies for the National Assembly were not well attended.[154] The DPP had spoken ill of the National Assembly for some time and had campaigned on a plank of abolishing the body altogether, and opinion polls indicated there was considerable public sentiment in favor of this proposal. The National Assembly's main function (electing the president and vice president) having been eliminated, it was questionable whether it should be allowed to survive. Finally, the presidential and vice presidential election eclipsed the National Assembly election in terms of public interest and press coverage.

In addition, the KMT put a number of its well-known and high-visibility appointed officials and civil servants in the race and most won (seven out of the eight running). Four were top vote-getters in their constituencies. Jason Hu, director-general of the Government Information Office, elected from Taichung City, won the largest number of votes of any candidate running. John Chang, head of the Overseas Chinese Affairs Commission, also won big. So did Chang Lung-sheng, head of the Environmental Protection Administration; Hsu Shiang-kueen, director-general of the Economics Ministry's Water Resources Department; John Ni, director-general of the Economics Ministry's Medium and Small Business Administration; Chien Tai-lang, director of the Ministry of Interior's Department of Population Administration; and Yang Jen-huang, chief secretary of the Mongolian and Tibetan Affairs Commission.[155]

Yet, because of its loss overall in the National Assembly, the KMT's capacity, without compromise or building a coalition with one or more of the other parties, to pass constitutional amendments (which require a three-fourths majority) waned. It may have other difficulties in conducting business, even electing a speaker and other officers. Confirming top presidential appointments may also become a problem.[156]

The DPP increased its seats in the National Assembly as a result of this election from 66 to 99—a 33-member increase. Clearly the DPP will play a more important role in the new National Assembly. Its leadership, however, did not claim a big victory—noting that, in terms of popular vote, it won close to 30 percent, which is considered the standard level of support for the main opposition party.

The NP, established in 1993, did not participate in the 1991 election so its figures in popular vote and seats cannot be compared with what it had before. New Party leaders, however, claimed a victory on the basis of its popular vote, which was higher than it got in the 1995 Legislative Yuan election when the NP turned in a very good performance. NP Secretary-General Jaw Shao-kong also mentioned that his party had defeated KMT candidates in ruling-party strongholds on the Offshore Islands and that the number of seats won exceeded pre-election predictions.[157]

Notwithstanding the diminished interest in National Assembly seats by potential contenders and questions over the continued existence of the body, the new National Assembly race attracted young and talented candidates. Over 65 percent of the winners were under fifty years of age (2.10 percent under thirty, 22.46 percent between thirty and thirty-nine, 41.02 percent between forty and forty-nine), and almost 90 percent (88.93) were under sixty. Over 75 percent (76.95) were college educated, including 17.37 percent with Ph.D. degrees. Fifty percent had business backgrounds.[158] And the race attracted voter interest. Voter turnout was 76 percent—a significant increase over the 1995 Legislative Yuan election (when voter turnout was 67.64 percent) and comparable to the 1994 gubernatorial, Provincial Assembly, metropolitan mayoral, and metropolitan city council races (when the turnout was 76.76 percent).[159]

The problem of vote-buying was also appreciably less in this election than in previous ones, which was a positive trend. Minister of Justice Ma Ying-jeou said it was the "cleanest in the history of Taiwan's democratic evolution." He compared the number of cases resulting from the previous National Assembly election, 250, to 110 this time. He also noted that only 21 cases of vote-buying had been reported in the presidential part of the election, involving only 33 people. He attributed the changed situation to his "war on vote-buying" and to the sense of honor of the people, who were on good behavior because of the historic nature of the election.[160]

Conclusions

This election was without a doubt Taiwan's most significant election ever. President Lee, Premier Lien, and other KMT officials ostentatiously labeled it the first direct, popular election of a top political leader in 5,000 years of Chinese history. This statement was not an exaggeration. It was a poignant observation and says something that will be remembered by people in Taiwan for a long time. In short, this election was epoch-making.

It will also be remembered elsewhere. In fact, this election will likely permanently change the nature of discourse throughout the world about Taiwan. It will cause Taiwan to be seen in a different light—as did the Tiananmen Massacre for the People's Republic of China —except it will forever give Taiwan a positive image in terms of its successful transition from an authoritarian system to a democratic one. It may well be that no serious writer will ever call Taiwan a dictatorship again. Thus it was an event that may be defined as a turning point or a watershed event in Taiwan's history.

Not only was this election a momentous one for general reasons, it has important specific implications. It will impact the political future of East Asia. It will set precedents in Taiwan and change its polity in some important ways.

First, this was an election that may well redefine what democracy means in Asia. Hong Kong's Democratic Party legislator Martin Lee commented that it "completely exploded the myth that democracy is somehow unsuitable for Chinese people."[161] It may, in fact, become a rallying cry for advocates of democracy in China. This could be either in the short-run or the long-run. Clearly officials in Beijing were watching this election as were many people in the People's Republic of China. The effect may be greater than anyone can predict because it came at such a critical time. China is at a crossroads in terms of its new leaders and what kind of political change, systemic or otherwise, they will adopt. China's second generation was installed in power after Deng's death and the third generation seems not far behind. Both will be looking for models for change. Taiwan's election may also influence the future of Hong Kong inasmuch as both China and the rest of the world now have to wonder why Hong Kong should not be given a chance to democratize.

Second, this election sent the message that Taiwan may or may not be part of China. There are reasons and trends to predict that it may be either. Economic trends are linking the two. An East Asian economic bloc is forming. China and Taiwan, obviously, are in the same bloc, and the two are trading—a lot. Taiwan is investing huge amounts of money in China. A "Greater China" bloc is also evolving. Politically, however, trends do not favor integration. Taiwan is far ahead (even further than most realized because of this election) of the People's Republic of China in terms of political modernization. This trend must be reversed before the Taiwan issue can be resolved in favor of one China. The implication is that if Beijing does not catch up to Taiwan in political development of the democratic kind (and it is unlikely Taiwan will regress), the Republic of China will remain on its own—as a sovereign and independent country. This reality is likely to affect China's future: whether it evolves toward a democratic and decentralized federation, retreats to tyranny and isolationism, or fragments.

Third, one must ask what influence Beijing had on the results of the election. In other words, did its intimidation and threats change the way the voters voted? The answer seems obvious: It did. But it did not influence the voters in the way China wanted. In other words, there was a backlash. This reaction was a marked contrast to Beijing's influence on the Legislative Yuan election three months earlier. It may be that Chinese leaders in Beijing calculated that they could repeat their earlier performance. If so, they were wrong. The first time they used intimidation to influence an election, Taiwan reacted with shock and fear. This time the reaction was anger. In short, the backlash effect was considerable and offset whatever apprehension Beijing might have created in hopes of turning voters against President Lee. This time was different also in the sense that the electorate had a clear choice of staying the course and voting for the incumbent and the status quo. President Lee clearly represented the status quo about the matter of independence or unification. The opinion polls confirmed this view. President Lee received as much as 10 percent more popular vote than the polls were predicting several weeks before the election.

Fourth, the election events, meaning Beijing's military threat, tested the U.S. commitment to Taipei. Washington came quickly to Taiwan's rescue and did it in a way that was not too antagonistic, yet sent a clear message. One would conclude that for Taiwan the "American card" was genuine. Beijing backed down. Thus it gave the people of Taiwan reassurance. Its citizens can be more confident Washington will act to preserve Taiwan's democratization in the future. But it was also a special time in the United States. The Republicans were in control of Congress and it was an election year for an incumbent president who did not enjoy a good reputation in the realm of foreign policy or a good image with the military. Washington may act differently next time. People in Taiwan also have to ponder how long the United States can guarantee their security in view of the decline of U.S. military power and the rise of China's. Perhaps it will last only a decade. That being the case, Taiwan may need to seek other allies. Alternatively, it needs to come to terms with the People's Republic of China. Perhaps it needs to do both.

Fifth, Taiwan's presidential election may change the thrust of the debate about democracy for the countries of East Asia. Many have assumed that Asian countries would evolve in the direction of what many have called Asian democracy, which was thought to be different from Western democracy in many ways. Taiwan represents the essence of Asian democracy in seeking to avoid the excesses of the liberal ideals of democracy in the West: going too far with individual rights (as opposed to the rights of the society), excessive taxes and welfare, the break-up of the family, apathy toward the aged, ultra-egalitarianism, and other facets of 1960s Western democracy and its legacy. Yet, Taiwan has moved quickly to adopt broadly participatory democracy with open and active campaigns and elections where public opinion plays a major role. Perhaps Taiwan's democracy, as reflected in its elections, especially this one, will help bridge the gap between Asian-style and Western-style democracy.

In domestic political terms, there are also implications for Taiwan. The election set some precedents while it changed Taiwan's political scene in some important ways. First, the consensus is that the KMT won the election. In the first direct presidential election ever, for President Lee and Premier Lien to win a resounding victory meant that the KMT scored a big victory. KMT officials were happy—with justification: The ruling-party seemed to have a better future after this election than before. It seems less likely that the KMT will lose its ruling party status in the foreseeable future than it appeared before the election. It is likewise good reasoning judging from the fact that other nations congratulated President Lee and interpreted his victory as a good thing and that this rubbed off on the party. Moreover, it was a victory for the KMT inasmuch as the Lee-Lien ticket did much better than the polls suggested they would. They won appreciably more than 50 percent of the vote, which some had speculated they needed in order to have a mandate. Finally, this interpretation follows from the fact that the presidential election dominated the news during the campaign and after the election, whereas the National Assembly race, where the KMT did not perform so well, got little attention.

Second, the KMT victory and the election itself say something about the matter of Taiwan's political party system and whether it is a multi-party, two-party, or one-party system. The presidential election results would suggest that Taiwan may have regressed to a one-party-dominant system as it was in the past; or, perhaps it is a multi-party system (counting independents). Since these two propositions seem to have some basis in fact yet do not by any means reflect long-term trends, the question of Taiwan's party system persists. The DPP's poor performance was in large part due the fact that many of its supporters voted for the Lee-Lien ticket; this seems to suggest that the largest opposition party has not lost strength and will continue to play the opposition role it has for nearly a decade. Its performance in the National Assembly election also suggests it is not ready to be given a lesser status. The poor performances of the Lin-Hau and the Chen-Wang tickets may suggest the "third wave" is going nowhere. Yet their losses must be seen against the fact that the two pairs of candidates on the right took voting strength from each other. Their contention that together the "right" got more votes than the DPP suggests there is a "third wave." So do the polls that put the Lin-Hau ticket significantly ahead of the Peng-Hsieh ticket only a few weeks before the election, only to drop because of the "Beijing factor." Lin and Hau were also hurt, it appears, by their opposition to the U.S. military presence in the area and by what seemed to be a failed attempt to stir up anti-foreign feelings to their advantage.

One might conclude, from the fact that the Lin-Hau and the Chen-Wang tickets did not perform up to expectations, that party affiliation is needed to win in any future presidential contest. However, it may be too soon to say this in view of the fact that they probably took too many votes from each other. Still, party identification seemed to be an important part of this election. Independent candidates may be discouraged from running in the future. Provisions in the election law making it difficult for a less-than-serious candidate to win will also make it difficult for independents.

The fact that Chen, a devout Buddhist with a female running mate, did not perform well suggests that Taiwan is a country where voters do not pay attention to religion or women's issues. This conclusion seems to conform to superficial evidence about Taiwan's political culture. There is very little religious discrimination in Taiwan--perhaps less than in any nation in the world. Thus voting based on religion has never been commonplace in the past. Nor have there ever been good prospects for forming a religious party, an issue broached during the campaign. Finally, Lee Teng-hui is identified as a Christian in a nation where Christians number less than 3 percent of the population, and unlike other presidents (Chiang Kai-shek, Yen Chia-kan, and Chiang Ching-kuo, who were also Christians), he has often talked about his beliefs and has frequently quoted the Bible. Still there was no anti-Christian vote.

Likewise for female voting. Wang did not make much of women's issues and certainly did not advocate feminism or women's liberation or identify herself often as a female. Women in Taiwan are concerned with issues when they vote, not gender. Also, they have been represented quite well in politics for some time. Certainly they do not view themselves as an oppressed group as in other countries, including the United States.

Third, the election appears to offer some hints about solutions to constitutional questions. The same goes for future campaigns. Clearly the KMT will have difficulty pushing through constitutional amendments without support from either the Left or the Right: the DPP or the NP. It does not now have the voting strength in the National Assembly to change the constitution. This task, thus, may be delayed. Or the KMT will have to seek votes or allies.

Fourth, political campaigning may be different in the future. Vote-buying was down in this election. It may not be such a good issue for the opposition in upcoming contests. Moreover, it was reduced in importance because of the KMT's Minister of Justice Ma Ying-jeou. In short, the party that was the biggest culprit must also be given credit for doing something about the problem. And yet, if Ma is relieved of his job and his successor is lax on the problem, it may reappear and become a serious issue once again. Negative campaigning was a hallmark of this election. It was more prevalent and more potent than at any time in the past. Much of it was directed against President Lee; yet he won. Lee's victory may send a signal making negative campaigning less popular in future elections, unless candidates feel that it at least draws attention to those who use it.

1. For an assessment of Taiwan's previous elections, see John F. Copper with George P. Chen, *Taiwan's Elections: Political Development and Democratization in the Republic of China* (Baltimore: University of Maryland School of Law, 1984); John F. Copper, *Taiwan's Recent Elections: Fulfilling the Democratic Promise* (Baltimore: University of Maryland School of Law, 1990); John F. Copper, *Taiwan's 1991 and 1992 Nonsupplemental Elections: Reaching a Higher State of Democracy* (Lanham, MD: University Press of America, 1994); John F. Copper, "Taiwan's 1994 Gubernatorial and Mayoral Elections," *Asian Affairs* (Summer 1994); John F. Copper, Taiwan's 1995 Legislative Yuan Election (Baltimore: University of Maryland School of Law, 1996).

2. The Temporary Provisions were amended on two other occasions, though in not such important ways.

3. Hung-mao Tien, *The Great Transition: Political and Social Change in the Republic of China* (Stanford: Hoover Institution Press, 1989), p. 113.

4. See Tien, *The Great Transition*, p. 156.

5. In the late 1960s KMT candidates at all levels won between 78 and 92 percent of the time. This began to change a bit in the 1970s and 1980s, but the DPP did not perform well in an election until 1989. See The Kuomintang: A

Brief Record of Achievements, cited in Ralph N. Clough, *Island China* (Cambridge, MA: Harvard University Press, 1978), p. 50.

6. See comments by Hong Yeh-chin in Harvey J. Feldman (ed.), *Constitutional Reform and the Future of the Republic of China* (Armonk, NY: M. E. Sharpe, 1991), p. 9.

7. Edwin A. Winckler, "Taiwan Transition?" in Cheng and Haggard (eds.), *Political Change in Taiwan*, p. 232.

8. See Ts'ai Ling and Ramon H. Myers, "Achieving Consensus Amidst Adversity: The Conference to Decide the Republic of China's Destiny," *American-Asian Review*, Fall 1991.

9. See Hungdah Chiu, "The National Affairs Conference and Constitutional Reform in the Republic of China on Taiwan," and James A. Robinson, "The ROC's 1990 National Affairs Conference," *Issues and Studies*, December 1990.

10. Sixty-five favored an electoral college, fifty-two favored a direct election system, and twenty wanted no change. See chart in Jaushieh Joseph Wu, *Taiwan's Democratization: Forces Behind the New Momentum* (Hong Kong: Oxford University Press, 1995), p. 65.

11. Ramon H. Myers, "Building the First Chinese Democracy: the Crisis and Leadership of President Lee Teng-hui," in Jason C. Hu (ed.), *Quiet Revolutions on Taiwan, Republic of China* (Taipei: Kwang Hwa Publishing Co., 1994), p. 56.

12. See Copper, *Taiwan's 1991 and 1992 Nonsupplemental Elections*, p. 30.

13. The KMT spoke of constitutional change, "streamlining" the office of the president and other reforms, but on many were not specific. See Copper, *Taiwan's 1991 and 1992 Nonsupplemental Elections*, pp. 23–30.

14. For example, see Constance Squires Meaney, "Liberalization, Democratization, and the Role of the KMT," in Tun-jen Cheng and Stephen Haggard (eds.), *Political Change in Taiwan* (Boulder, CO: Lynne Rienner Publishers, 1992), p. 104, and Edwin A. Winckler, "Taiwan Transition?" in the same publication, p. 232. In 1991, President Lee spoke of a "second phase" of constitutional reform after the election of the second National Assembly, which some have taken to mean he planned on pushing a direct presidential election system. See "Constitutional Reform, National Unification and the Future," Politique Internationale, July 1, 1991, reproduced in Lee Teng-hui, *Creating the Future: Towards a New Era for the Chinese People* (Taipei: Government Printing Office, 1993), p. 73.

15. Myers, "Building the First Chinese Democracy," p. 64.

16. Wu, *Taiwan's Democratization*, p. 131.

17. Yu-shan Wu, "Taiwan in 1993," *Asian Survey*, January 1994, p. 47.

18. For details, see John F. Copper, "The KMT's 14th Party Congress: Toward Unity or Disunity? in Cynthia Chenault (ed.), *Modernizing East Asia: Economic and Cultural Dimensions of Political Change* (New York: St. Johns University Press, 1989)

19. Virginia Sheng, "Independents Fault Sign-up Rules; One Presidential Hopeful Abandons Race in Protest," *Free China Journal,* January 12, 1996, p. 2.

20. "Presidential Election Rules 'Too Strict,'" *Asian Bulletin*, March 1995, p. 25.

21. "Surprisingly Few People Returning to Vote," *China Post*, February 28, 1996, p. 1.

22. For further details and background, see Tun-jen Cheng, Chi Huang, and Samuel S. G. Wu (eds.), *Inherited Rivalry: Conflict Across the Taiwan Strait* (Boulder, CO: Lynne Rienner Publishers, 1995).

23. For an analysis of Taiwan's view on this subject, see John F. Copper, "Taiwan and the New World Order," *Journal of East Asian Affairs*, Winter/ Spring 1995.

24. See Hungdah Chiu, *Koo-Wang Talks and the Prospect of Building Constructive Relations Across the Taiwan Strait* (Baltimore: University of Mary-land School of Law, 1993).

25. For details on this document and its meaning, see John F. Copper, *Words Across the Taiwan Strait: A Critique of Beijing's "White Paper" on China's Reunification* (Lanham, MD: University Press of America, 1995).

26. Hung-mao Tien, "Taiwan in 1995: Electoral Politics and Cross-Strait Relations, " *Asian Survey*, January 1996, p. 34.

27. For further details, see "ROC President Makes Six-Point Policy Speech on Relations with Mainland," *Asian Bulletin*, June 1995, p. 25.

28. Julian Baum, "A Case of Nerves," *Far Eastern Economic Review*, July 20, 1995, p. 26.

29. Tien, "Taiwan in 1995," p. 36.

30. Julian Baum, "Idling Threat," *Far Eastern Economic Review*, April 13, 1995, p. 29.

31. The author was in Taiwan at the time and heard this from a number of diplomats and officials.

32. "PRC to Hold Another Drill: Report," *China Post* (international edition), November 30, 1995, p. 1.

33. "China Finalizes Strategy for Taking Taiwan: HK Newspaper," *China News* (domestic edition), December 1, 1995, p. 1.

34. For details, see Copper, *Taiwan's 1995 Legislative Yuan Election,* pp. 34–35.

35. Tien, "Taiwan in 1995," p. 37.

36. Julian Baum, "He's No China Doll," *Far Eastern Economic Review*, August 31, 1995, pp. 17–20.

37. See "Raising the Stakes," *Asiaweek*, September 8, 1995, p. 28.

38. Julian Baum, "Party Crasher," Far *Eastern Economic Review*, August 31, 1995, p. 20.

39. Tien, "Taiwan in 1995," p. 38.

40. See "Raising the Stakes," p. 28, and Julian Baum, "Up and Running," *Far Eastern Economic Review*, September 7, 1995, pp. 14–15.

41. "President Lee Announces Intention to Stand for Re-Election in 1996," *Asian Bulletin*, October 1995, p. 37.

42. Ibid., pp. 37–38.

43. Baum, "Up and Running," p. 14.

44. Ibid. 15.

45. "Open Season on Hau, Lin at CSC," *China News* (domestic edition), November 23, 1995, p. 2.

46. "KMT Mavericks Reject Party's Criticism," *China News* (domestic edition), November 23, 1995, p. 2.

47. "KMT Members Protest," *China News* (domestic edition), November 28, 1995, p. 2.

48. "KMT 'Needs Experience' of Being in Opposition," *China News* (domestic edition), November 30, 1995, p. 2.

49. "Elected KMT Deputies Want Lin, Hau Punished," *China News* (domestic edition), November 30, 1995, p. 2.

50. See Copper, Taiwan's 1995 Legislative Yuan Election, pp. 25–34.

51. "Chen Visits Retired Servicemen," *China Post*, (international edition), February 24, 1996, p. 1.

52. Christopher Bodeen, "Lee Airs Views on Mainland China," *China Post* (international edition), February 24, 1996, p. 1.

53. Christopher Bodeen, "Peng Urges Independence in the Event of a PRC Attack," *China Post* (international edition), February 24, 1996, p. 4.

54. R. L. Chen, "Candidates Speak Out," *China Post*, (international edition), February 26, 1996, p. 1.

55. R. L. Chen, "Cross-Strait Policies Outlined," *China Post* (international edition), February 26, 1996, p. 1.

56. "KMT Wants Reformed Constitution," *China Post* (international edition), February 26, 1996, p. 4.

57. The present electoral system in use in Taiwan resembles the system in Japan and has been blamed for creating "money politics" there. The KMT, by proposing change, also puts the other parties in an awkward position since a single-member district system would probably help KMT candidates, forcing the other parties into debates and advocacy of more at-large seats.

58. "Hopefuls Kick Vote Drive into High Gear," *China Post* (international edition), February 26, 1996, p. 4.

59. "Lin Backers Threaten to Storm TV Station," *China Post* (international edition), February 26, 1996, p. 1.

60. "DPP Leaders Rally Behind Candidates," *China Post* (international edition), February 26, 1996, p. 1.

61. "Lin Backers Threaten to Storm TV Station," *China Post* (international edition), February 26, 1996, p. 4.

62. "We're Ready for Anything, Says Lee," *China Post* (international edition), February 27, 1996, p. 1.

63. "Peng Warns of Another 2-28 Incident," *China Post* (international edition) February 27, 1996, p. 1.

64. "Lee Says Not to Be Complacent," *China Post* (international edition), February 27, 1996, p. 1.

65. R. L. Chen, "Mainland China Still Preparing Exercises," *China Post* (international edition), February 28, 1996, p. 1.

66. "Candidates Get Needed Donations," *China Post* (international edition), February 28, 1996, p. 1.

67. Christopher Bodeen, "Park Renamed for 2-28," *China Post* (international edition), February 29, 1996, p. 1.

68. "Lee Nominated for Nobel Prize," *China Post* (international edition), March 1, 1996, p. 1.

69. Ibid.

70. Ibid.

71. Christopher Bodeen, "Peng Issues Public Welfare Proposals," *China Post* (international edition), March 1, 1996, p. 4.

72. Stephen Grauwels, "Presidential Press Officer Accuses Lee," *China Post,* March 1, 1996, p. 4.

73. Christopher Bodeen, "Vice President Candidates Air Views," *China Post,* March 4, 1996, p. 1.

74. Stephen Grauwels, "Lin Says Lee Joined The Communists," *China Post,* March 4, 1996, p. 3.

75. R. L. Chen, "DPP Chief Declares War on Gangland Influence," *China Post,* March 1, 1996, p. 1.

76. "President to Unveil New Policies Soon," *China* Post, March 5, 1996, p. 1.

77. "Rivals Accuse Lee of Communist Past," *China Post*, March 15, 1996, p. 4.

78. Stephen Grauwels, "Newspaper apologizes to DPP's Peng," *China Post*, March 16, 1996, p. 4. The Independence Daily News is a paper that had long supported the opposition, but it was bought by a KMT member of the Taipei City Council in 1995.

79. "Official Threatens to Sue President," *China Post*, March 18, 1996, p. 1.

80. See Christopher Bodeen, "Lee Goes for Common Touch, Observers Say," *China Post*, March 20, 1996, p. 4.

81. Stephen Grauwels, "DPP Friends Call on Lee to Quit Race," *China Post*, March 22, 1996, p. 1.

82. "Independents Battle for Undecided," *China Post*, March 22, 1996, p. 1.

83. For details on Beijing's 1995 threat, chapter 3 and Copper, *Taiwan's 1995 Legislative Yuan Election*, especially pp. 19, 20, 29.

84. Joe McDonald, "Drop Independence Drive and Tension Would Ease, Says PRC," *China Post* (domestic edition), March 2, 1996, p. 1.

85. For background details on this issue, see John F. Copper, *China Diplomacy: The Washington-Taipei-Beijing Triangle* (Boulder, CO: Westview Press, 1992), pp. 46–56.
86. "U.S. Moves to Change TRA," *China News* (domestic edition), March 1, 1996, p. 1.
87. "Dole Says He Would Support Taiwan's Reentry Into UN," *China Post* (domestic edition), March 5, 1996, p. 1.
88. *China News* (domestic edition), March 5, 1996, p. 1.
89. "Japan PM Calls on Beijing to Pursue Peaceful Settlement," *China Post* (domestic edition), March 3, 1996, p. 1.
90. "Lee Kuan Yew said Beijing Needs to Negotiate to Give Taiwan 'International Space,'" *China Post* (domestic edition), March 4, 1996, p. 1.
91. Hilton Shone, "Asia Cool to Test Report," *China Post* (domestic edition), March 6, 1996, p. 1.
92. "Don't Intervene in ROC Issue, PRC Tells World," *China News* (domestic edition), March 4, 1996, p. 1.
93. *China News* (domestic edition), March 7, 1996, p. 1.
94. "PRC Announces More Missile Exercises," *China Post* (domestic edition), March 6, 1996, p. 1. Also see editorial in *China Post* (domestic edition), March 4, 1996, p. 2, for additional details.
95. Stephanie Low, "Officials Launch Protest Against Military Plans," *China Post* (domestic edition), March 6, 1996, p. 1.
96 "'One China' Definition Should Be Discussed: SEF," *China Post* (domestic edition), March 5, 1996, p. 1.
97. "Beijing Admits Motives Behind Tests," *China Post* (domestic edition), March 8, 1996, p. 1.
98. "Defensive Arms Beefed Up on eve of PLA Drills," *China Post* (domestic edition), March 8, 1996, p. 1.
99. Christopher Bodeen, "Presidential Candidates Differ on Handling Crisis," *China Post* (domestic edition), March 4, 1996, p. 1.
100. "China Will Never Invade Any Country, Military Leader Promises," *China News* (domestic edition), March 7, 1996, p. 1.
101. "PRC Rejects Lee's Peace Overtures," *China News* (domestic edition), March 7, 1996, p. 1.
102. "Intercepting Missiles Would Mean War: Beijing," *China News* (domestic edition), March 8, 1996, p. 1.
103. "Deng Said Concerned About Reunification," *China Post* (domestic edition), March 7, 1996, p. 16.
104. "Minister Denies Reprisal Threat," *China Post* (domestic edition), March 7, 1996, p. 1.
105. "ROC Will 'Fight' Encroachment," *China News* (domestic edition), March 7, 1996, p. 1.
106. "U.S. Warns Beijing," *China News* (domestic edition), March 8, 1996, p. 1.

107. "AIT Not Evacuating U.S. Citizens," *China News* (domestic edition), March 7, 1996, p. 1.

108. Bill Wang, "Tests Not Helpful: White House," *China Post* (domestic edition), March 7, 1996, p. 1.

109. "China Continues War of Words with Lee," *China News* (domestic edition), March 9, 1996, p. 1.

110. "MAC Protests Beijing's 'Dangerous Behavior,'" *China News* (domestic edition), March 9, 1996, p. 1.

111. "No Sign PRC Is Raising Stakes: Report," *China Post* (domestic edition), March 9, 1996, p. 2.

112. Norman Wei, "Support for Lee Expected to Wither in Time," *China News* (domestic edition), March 9, 1996, p. 2.

113. "Number of Immigration Seekers Sees Increase" and "Rice Hoarders Hit with Higher Prices," *China News* (domestic edition), March 9, 1996, p. 3.

114. "China to Stage Live Fire Drills Starting Tuesday," *China News* (domestic edition), March 10, 1996, p. 1.

115. Jane MacCartney, "More PLA Exercises May Follow Voting," *China Post* (international edition), March 11, 1996, p. 1. This was a Reuters story based in part on information carried in Sunday's *Yomiuri Shimbun*.

116. "New Missile Base Opening Moved Up," *China News* (domestic edition), March 10, 1996, p. 1.

117. "Taipei Sets Up Disaster Center in Case of War," *China Post* (international edition), March 11, 1996, p. 4.

118. "Beijing Should Thank Me: President Lee," *China Post* (international edition), March 11, 1996, p. 1.

119. R. L. Chen, "Candidates Blast President Over Tensions," *China Post* (international edition), March 11, 1996, p. 4.

120. R. L. Chen, "Military Threats Seen as Failing to Diminish Lee," *China Post* (international edition), March 11, 1996, p. 4.

121. "U.S. Navy Monitoring Missile Exercises," *China News* (domestic edition), March 10, 1996, p. 1.

122. Dana Priest and Judith Havemann, "Second Carrier Group Headed Toward Strait," *China Post* (domestic edition), March 12, 1996, p. 1. This piece was reprinted from the *Washington Post*.

123. "Approaching U.S. force welcomed," *China Post* (domestic edition), March 12, 1996, p. 1.

124. Christopher Bodeen, "ROC Firm on U.N. Bid, Rejects Threats," *China Post* (domestic edition), March 12, 1996, p. 1.

125. "Presidential Election 'Not Democratic,'" *China News* (domestic edition), March 12, 1996, p. 1.

126. Ming Pao, March 11, 1996, cited in "Deng Ordered Toughening of Policy Toward Taiwan," *China News* (domestic edition), March 12, 1996, p. 1.

127. "Lee Says It Is Beijing's Fault For Not Believing Unification Stance," *China News* (domestic edition), March 12, 1996, p. 1.
128. Yi-chin Ho, "DPP Officials to Set Sail in Protest of China Drills," *China News* (domestic edition), March 12, 1996, p. 2.
129. "DPP Members Laud Carrier's Arrival," *China Post* (domestic edition), March 15, 1996, p. 19.
130. Peter Harmsen, "Independent Chen Visits Kinmen Island," *China Post* (domestic edition), March 14, 1996, p. 16.
131. Joanna Ku, "'Don't Rely on US Help,' says Chen," *China News* (domestic edition), March 15, 1996, p. 2.
132. "Some in Taiwan Echo Beijing Concerning US Role in Crisis," *China News* (domestic edition), March 19, 1996, p. 1.
133 "Special Envoy May Be Sent to Talk to Beijing: Report," *China News* (domestic edition), March 14, 1996, p. 1.
134. "Lee Mulls Meet to Ease Tension," *China News* (domestic edition), March 16, 1996, p. 2.
135. "Seventy US Congressmen Sponsor Call to Defend Taiwan," *China News* (domestic edition), March 14, 1996, p. 1.
136. "Carrier 'Can Handle Contingencies,'" *China News* (domestic edition), March 14, 1996, p. 1.
137. "PRC Premier Signals War Unlikely," *China Post* (domestic edition), March 16, 1996, p. 1.
138. Charles Aldinger, "Mainland Won't Attack: U.S. Official," *China Post* (domestic edition), March 16, 1996, p. l, and Jim Wolf, "PRC Gave Nuclear Warning to U.S.: Lord," *China Post* (domestic edition), March 19, 1996, p. 1.
139. Joanna Ku, "Candidates Give Last TV Speeches," *China News* (domestic edition), March 18, 1996, p. 2.
140. These are official results from the Central Election Commission. The total number of votes cast was 10,766,119. There were 14,313,288 eligible voters. See data chart in China Post, March 24, 1996, p. 1.
141 "Lee Wins Mandate," *China News*, March 24, 1996, p. 1.
142. Stephen Grauwels, "Shih Ming-teh Resigns as Chairman of DPP," *China Post*, March 24, 1996, p. 1, Christopher Bodeen, "Lin Bows to Lee, Reviews Campaign," Stephen Grauwels, "Weary Peng Offers Quiet Congratulations," and Christopher Bodeen, "Chen to Pursue Campaign Ideals," *China Post*, March 24, 1996, p. 2.
143. See, for example, "Lee Wins Mandate," *China News*, March 24, 1996, p. 1.
144. See data chart in *United Daily News* (in Chinese), March 24, 1996, p. 2.
145. R. L. Chen, "Lee Wins," *China Post*, March 24, 1996, p. 1.
146. Mark Wu, "Support for Independents Signals New Political Era," *China News,* March 24, 1996, p. 3.
147. William Kazer, "Lee's Win Seen as Rebuff to PRC," *China Post*, March 24, 1996, p. 5.

148. The author interviewed a number of officials and experts after the election. Most put the "PRC benefit" for Lee at 5 percent or a bit more. Some earlier polls gave Lee only 45 percent of the popular vote, nearly 10 percent below what he got, leading some to suggest a higher figure.

149. Joe Kline, "The Spiritual Power of Democracy," *Newsweek*, April 1, 1996, p. 34.

150. "The Day Taiwan Stood Up, "*Economist,* March 23-29, 1996, p. 37.

151. Cited in *World Press Review*, May 1996, p. 20.

152. See data chart *in United Daily News*, March 24, 1996, p. 2.

153. Susan Yu, "KMT Wins Slim Assembly Edge; DPP, New Party Build Up Strength," *Free China Journal*, March 28, 1996, p. 2.

154. James A. Robinson, "Little Noticed Assembly Vote May Hold Key to New Reforms," *Free China Journal*, March 28, 1996, p. 7.

155. Yu, "KMT Wins Slim Assembly Edge: DPP, New Party Build Up Strength," p. 2.

156. In fact, there was talk of this at the time of the election. This writer heard discussions about whether the position of speaker, which was widely rumored to go to Foreign Minister Frederick Chien, might be blocked by opposition delegates.

157. Ibid.

158. Ibid. Also see data chart in *United Daily News*, March 24, 1996, p. 10.

159. "76 Percent of Voters Decide Next President," *China News*, March 24, 1996, p. 3.

160. Christopher Bodeen, "Vote-buying Cases Down, Says Ma," *China Post*, March 22, 1996, p. 1.

161. Cited in Richard R. Vuylsteke, "A Victory for Democracy," *Free China Review*, May 1995, p. 4.

Chapter Four
The KMT's 15th Party Congress:
The Ruling Party at a Crossroads

Introduction

For four days from August 25 to 29, 1997, the ruling Nationalist Party or Kuomintang (KMT) in Taiwan (officially known as the Republic of China) held its 15th Congress. The meeting's venue was the International Convention Center adjacent to the Hyatt Hotel in Taipei; attendees were party delegates, other party members, dignitaries, visitors and observers. The mood of the meeting was somber. There was a distinct feeling among party leaders and delegates to the congress alike was that the 103-year-old party faced serious problems and challenges.

Four years had passed since the KMT's 14th Congress and nine years since the 13th, both of which witnessed sweeping changes in the make-up of the party, party rules and procedures, and the direction of reform in the party.[1] Both meetings also were replete with controversy and came at critical junctures in terms of ROC's politics and the role of the ruling party in that context. This meeting was similar in many respects to those two previous congresses. However, in some ways it was very different: There was no leadership struggle at the top; nor was there a problem of open factionalism. Even more than the previous two congresses, however, the mood at this meeting was one of apprehension, reflecting the widely-held perception, even apprehension, that the KMT's future was in doubt and that the ruling party was truly at a crossroads as it had never been before.

The Congress convened on the heels of three major elections, controversy over amending the Constitution, and new alignments or realignments of Taiwan's political parties. The meeting also took place in the midst of an inter-party dispute that centered on the downsizing of the provincial government and pitted the provincial governor James Soong against President Lee Teng-hui. A pending reshuffling of cabinet posts and the resignation of the premier and a new appointment to that office were also on the minds of KMT leaders as well as delegates to the Congress in August. So were the issues of crime and political corruption, both of which weighed heavily on the ruling party which, to the public, bore the responsibility. These problems were seen as sorely hurting the KMT's public image and its hopes for performing well in fall local elections.

The congress accomplished the ratification of new policies and in some ways energized the party at a time when it very much needed it. It also saw some wounds healed, though certainly not all of them, while it created some new ones. In an effort to avoid controversial personnel changes, the party installed a "new" (though not changed drastically) second-echelon leadership. President Lee was re-elected chairman of the KMT with a larger vote count by a good margin than at the previous congress. Governor James Soong, when the vote was taken for Central Committee membership, won the largest number of delegates votes, which did not please President Lee while creating a field day for the media to comment on their feud.

In the pages below the author will assess relevant precursory events to the Congress or the context in which the KMT's 15th Party Congress was held. Clearly it was convened at an eventful time for Taiwan politically. Also analyzed are the immediate problems the KMT faced at the time as well as changes in personnel, party policies, and reform. Finally, comments will be made about the significance of the party gathering on the future of the KMT.

The Political Situation Prior to the Congress

To comprehend what transpired at the KMT's 15th Party Congress and why, as well as its final results, it is necessary to examine events at least three years prior to the congress, especially the mid-1990s elections. In addition, it is instructive to look at political trends in Taiwan together with specific problems that plagued the KMT during the months before the Congress. The issues that the ruling party faced at this time were generally not new and even the new ones had a history, but they were in many ways more acute.

In 1994, the Republic of China held elections for the provincial governor (for the first time in history), the two metropolitan city mayors (the offices having been made appointed positions in 1964 and 1977 respectively) and the provincial assembly and the metropolitan city councils.[2] Former KMT Secretary-General, and Lee confidant whom President Lee had recently appointed provincial governor, James

Soong, won the governors race for the Nationalist Party handily with 52 percent of the popular vote. The KMT, in addition, did unexpectedly well in the Kaohsiung mayoral race with party stalwart Wu Den-yih. It lost, however, in the Taipei mayoral race to the opposition Democratic Progressive Party's (DPP) Chen Shui-bian. The KMT also performed poorly in the Taipei city council race.

Soong was inspiring candidate with a charismatic personality and enjoyed a reputation for being incorruptible and a man of the people. In addition, he had the support of President Lee Teng-hui. Soon thus won notwithstanding the opposition's attempt to use the "ethnic (technically provincial origin) card" against him. Lee, observers said, "owed" Soong a debt of gratitude for his strong, some say daring, support of Lee following the death of President Chiang Ching-kuo in 1988 when Lee, who was then vice-president, became president but was challenged when he sought to assume the chairmanship of the party. In any event, Lee's endorsement of Soong and his campaigning for him helped Soong win by a significant margin, though he probably would have been victorious without Lee campaigning for him. The election, which was the most "national" of any election ever held in the ROC (in the sense that the political parties had to campaign nationwide and in some other respects as well) was also well organized by KMT professional campaign workers and not so well handled by the opposition parties.

The election victory catapulted Soong upward in terms of him becoming a future candidate for premier and even president in the year 2000. His subsequent credible, if not stellar, performance in office added to that perception, as did the fact that he rallied a large coterie of employees of the provincial government behind him.

The election and Chen Shui-bian's subsequent performance in office did the same for his career and evoked speculation that he may be the next president in the event the KMT falters and the DPP shows strength in coming elections. Chen was seen as a dynamic, clever and promising politician. Also Wu Den-yih saw his career potential improve.

On the other hand, both the campaign and the election were fraught with widespread cheating, vote-buying being the most common of the problems in this realm. Also, for the first time, a third party—the New Party (NP) competed in a major election, though only meaningfully in the Taipei mayoral race and the Taipei city council races. Nevertheless the NP tried and was to a considerable degree successful in portraying itself as a clean party and the others, but especially the KMT, as a corrupt party that bought elections. In terms of public perception, political corruption had already become a very serious problem and was a matter that patently needed government and ruling party attention because it was perceived as getting much worse. Meanwhile, Taiwan's political system had taken another big step forward in terms of democratization, making the corruption problem an even more visible one.

In 1995, the KMT suffered a serious setback in the December Legislative Yuan election. In fact, the ruling party nearly lost its majority in the national lawmaking body of government. As a result of its poor performance, its plurality of seats in the Legislative Yuan, for the first time ever, became razor thin. Thinking of this possibility, coalition governance was discussed by observers and the media going into the election. It indeed became a reality later as the Nationalist Party did not come away from the election with enough seats to pass some bills —party discipline being weak and KMT attendance sometimes being lax. Pundits meanwhile attributed the KMT's "defeat" to its steady decline in the context of democratization (necessitated by a need for party competition) and to the ruling party's deteriorating image that was largely a product of the public's disgust with corruption.

Others attributed the KMT's setback to missile tests conducted by the People's Republic of China's People's Liberation Army (PLA) during the run-up to the voting. It had an immediate and transparent impact on the stock market, land prices, applications for visas to other countries, and more. The populace was obviously intimidated and fearful. Some blamed President Lee. Lee had made a trip to the United States in June to his alma mater, Cornell University, and though he made a hit in the U.S. and was applauded by the U.S. and Western media and the trip seemed to help Taipei overcome and even crack Beijing's efforts to isolate the ROC diplomatically, many viewed the sojourn as unnecessarily provocative while reflecting Lee's pro-independence bent.

The KMT was also hurt, in terms of voters' support, by serious divisions in the party resulting from several party heavyweights expressing their opposition to President Lee and two (three counting one vice presidential candidate) announcing their candidacies for the presidential election the coming March. Chen Li-an, who had been Minister of Economic Affairs in the late 1980s, Minister of National Defense in the early 1990s and President of the Control Yuan, was the first to challenge Lee. He dropped his membership in the KMT to do this and registered as an independent just as Lee was given the KMT's nomination. Lin Yang-kang, who was known as the country's top Taiwanese campaigner and a politician that was considered in line for the presidency, also opposed Lee. So did Hau Pei-tsun, who was one of the nation's foremost military heroes, a past Minister of Defense, and Premier up to early 1993, and who had been feuding publicly with President Lee while in the premiership. Lin and Hau joined forces to run against Lee and did so as independents, though they did not resign their membership in the KMT. In fact, their actions stirred up a heated debate in the party provoked by members who wanted to have them expelled.

The New Party did especially well at the polls in the December 1995 Legislative Yuan election, increasing its representation in the lawmaking branch of government by threefold. The DPP increased its seats, though many of its leaders, especially some that promoted Taiwan's independence, lost. The KMT during the campaigning, promised to do something about vote buying, which had become an even bigger concern to the electorate. Minister of Justice Ma Ying-jeou had a number of candidates arrested, most being from the KMT, which earned him the wrath of many in his party for his actions. Meanwhile, cynics said that he was not being allowed to do his job and predicted he would not be kept in that office. Crime had also become a serious issue of widespread public concern due to an overall increase in the crime rate and a rash of sensational crimes, including kidnappings and murders (even though crime was still not a serious problem in Taiwan measured by global and especially by U.S. standards).

In March 1996, just three months after this election, the Republic of China held its first ever direct presidential election contest. President Lee and his running mate Premier Lien Chan ran against two sets of independent candidates (mentioned above) in addition to the DPP's Peng Ming-min (known as the father of Taiwan independence) and Frank Hsieh, a younger DPP activist. The PLA again staged military exercises and conducted missile tests to influence the election. The missile tests, actually a series of tests, involved the use of live warheads that hit close to Taiwan's two major ports and were, as a consequence, even more provocative than the ones done in 1995. Sea and air lane had to be closed. In direct response to the PRC's actions, the United States dispatched two aircraft carriers, each carrying nuclear weapons and accompanied by a flotilla of ships, to the area. This time, however, the PLA's intimidation backfired and its actions succored President Lee and Premier Lien since the tests evoked anger among Taiwan's voters rather than shock and fear as in 1995. Further helping the Lee ticket were Lee's experience, a well-organized KMT campaign, division and disarray among the other candidates' camps, and a number of other factors. Thus Lee Teng-hui and Lien Chan won an impressive victory. The two garnered 54 percent of the popular vote. Many DPP voters cast ballots for Lee, seeing their own candidate as less than experienced while espousing unrealistic positions on a number of issues and seeing Lee as taking a tough stance against Beijing's threats and to some a supporter of Taiwan independence (or at least the status quo, Lee's views being to many fuzzy on this matter). The New Party, which supported Lin and Hau, was seen by the electorate as pro-PRC at a time when ill-feelings toward Beijing ran high. In addition, their promotion of clean politics and an anti-isolationist foreign policy influenced few voters in the context of an external threat.

The election was heralded throughout the world as a gigantic step forward in Taiwan's process of democratizing, the Western media proclaiming it the first such election in 5,000 years of Chinese history. Clearly President Lee had a new and, apparently, very strong mandate.

Simultaneous with the presidential election was a National Assembly election contest. Questions about the future of that "parliamentary" body, since its most important function had heretofore been to elect the president and vice-president, arose during the campaign, the election and afterwards. The opposition DPP, which in 1991 had put the issue of independence in its platform and this among other factors caused it to lose big in that National Assembly election, pursued a much more intelligent campaign. And, this time the DPP performed very well. In fact, its "victory" (read big gain in seats, but not a majority) sent the message that President Lee was doing well but the KMT wasn't and in the future the ruling party would see its fortunes rise or fall depending on Lee. While this was far from the whole story, it was the most widely heard explanation for the one-dimensional KMT victory.

During the campaign the issue arose of President Lee "winning," and thereby having a mandate, only if he bested James Soong's popular vote of 52 percent. Selecting Lien Chan, a Taiwanese, as his running mate, while Lien remained premier, meanwhile signaled that the top political leadership in Taiwan was going to be (except for Soong) totally Taiwanese. Before there had been a balance (with Lee's previous vice-president having been Mainland Chinese and all premiers before Lien having been Mainland Chinese). It is also worthy of note that the challenge to Lee in this election came from Mainland Chinese, many who supported Chen Li-an (who is a Mainlander) or Lin Yang-kang (because of running mate Hau, an outspoken anti-Lee Mainland Chinese) and not so much from the DPP. Some said this caused President Lee to distrust Mainland Chinese (or to distrust and dislike them more, according to those who already saw him as pushing Mainlanders out of the KMT, witnessed by what happened at the 14th Party Congress when a number abandoned the party to form the New Party) and seek to make the government totally Taiwanese. KMT cooperation with the DPP rather than the NP in the Legislative Yuan at this time was also a factor as was a friendly relationship between President Lee and Taipei Mayor Chen.

In December, the Presidential Office hosted a National Development Conference to debate a number of monumental, some of them systemic, political problems and recommend solutions.[3] Probably President Lee hoped to repeat what a similar National Affairs Conference had done in 1990 (which among other things had recommended the retirement of the "elder parliamentarians" that were elected when the ROC government held elections on the mainland or were subsequently appointed to office, and had terminated the Temporary Provisions to the Constitution, which negated a number of civil and political liberty provisions in that document after which these reforms were adopted).[4] However, instead of proposing reforms that could be easily implemented and which would make the government popular, the recommendations of the National Development Conference had the opposite effect. The most important recommendation coming from the Conference was to reduce in size or eliminate the provincial government. This immediately provoked James Soong to tender his resignation (though it was not accepted). A storm of protest followed, generated by those who saw this as tantamount to declaring Taiwan independent, joined by provincial government employees and related businesses (which were numerous) and supporters of Soong. The National Assembly subsequently became bogged down in writing constitutional amendments to operationalize the National Development Conference's recommendations. This further confused the public about the reforms of the polity and was presented in ways the public did not care about or knew little.

By early spring, it was quite apparent the government and the ruling KMT were suffering from a conspicuous decline in public support. The controversy over the constitutional amendments, in part, caused this. The other main issues were crime and corruption. Even some high officials and some noted citizens had been the victims of extortion, violence and kidnappings. The government, including President Lee and Minister of Justice Liao Cheng-hao (Ma Ying-jeou having been transferred to the position of minister without portfolio), railed against crime and promised action. Yet, a KMT legislator, Luo Fu-tzu, who is widely regarded to have gang ties, sat as the chairman of the Legislative Yuan's judiciary committee. With only a two seat majority in the lawmaking body, KMT leaders were reluctant to do anything.[5] A 21st Century Foundation poll conducted at this time reflected that 61 percent of respondents were dissatisfied with the lawmaking body of government.[6] Most of the blame was put on the KMT.

The kidnapping of famous television star Pai Ping-ping's teenage daughter in April followed by a ransom demand for $5 million and then her torture and brutal murder, riveted public attention on the worsening crime situation in Taiwan and ties between criminals, including gangs and organized crime, and politicians. Citizens organized a protest demonstration which some observers said drew more than 50,000 people and was the biggest in Taiwan's history.[7] The protestors demanded government action and called for President Lee to "admit mistakes" and replace the cabinet, and for Vice-President and Premier Lien Chan to resign. Talk radio callers even suggested the country return to martial law. President Lee subsequently issued a public apology.[8]

On May 8, former Justice Minister Ma Ying-jeou resigned from his position of Minister Without Portfolio, saying he was "ashamed" over the recent crimes.[9] Ma had been known for his unflinching honesty and his undaunted efforts to crack down on vote-buying in several election campaigns. Some commentators called him the KMT's "last hope for reform." Vice-President and Premier Lien Chan subsequently appeared on a television talk show for the first time ever to try to convince the public that something was being done about the surge in crime.[10] A few days later, President Lee failed to present his state-of-the nation address to the National Assembly because of protestors from the New Party blocking his entry into the hall.[11]

The return of Hong Kong to the People's Republic of China by Britain on July 1 added further to Taiwan's woes. The PRC's newly acquired sovereignty over Hong Kong painfully reminded citizens in Taiwan of Beijing's claim to territory governed by the Republic of China and that Beijing had proclaimed only recently that Taiwan was next to be absorbed by the fatherland and even set a deadline. This in turn brought back memories of the PLA conducting missile tests in the Taiwan Strait in 1995 and 1996. Hong Kong becoming part of China also created serious problems for Taiwan relating to trade with and investment in China—both of which have grown to become very large in recent years, most of it passing through Hong Kong.

President Lee promptly and forcefully declared that Taiwan possessed sovereignty, that it was not like Hong Kong (which had been a colony) and Beijing's "one country, two systems" formula could not apply to Taiwan. The government forthwith refused to cancel military exercises in the Taiwan Strait just prior to Hong Kong's return to underscore its opposition to Beijing's demands. Meanwhile a public opinion survey in Taiwan recorded the largest citizen response ever in favor of independence; in fact, for the first time ever supporters of independence outnumbered advocates of a future linkup with China.[12]

Prelude to the Congress

Although the Nationalist Party or Kuomintang has democratized in recent years, clearly no longer operating as a single-party in an authoritarian state, it is still retained in some ways its Leninist-style organization. The Party Congress is comprised of delegates numbering approximately 2,300, chosen by election in advance (in July in this case) by the Party's full membership. The delegates to the Party Congress then elect, at the opening of the Congress, the Party Chairman (who then picks vice-chairmen) and the Central Committee (each delegate casting one vote for Chairman and 115 for the Central Committee). The Central Committee (a body which meets yearly to review policy) is made up of 200-plus members (230 in this case), or one in ten of the delegates. Since the Chairman is chosen first, he or she is able to submit a list of names that are his or her favorites or "recommendations" for seats on the Central Committee. Each nominee must, whether on the Chairman's list or not, be nominated and seconded by a minimum of eight delegates. Party Congress delegates vote for favorites among a group of over 600 candidates (640 to be precise at this Congress). After the Central Committee membership is decided, the Chairman then provides a list of appointed candidates (sixteen) for the powerful thirty-three member Central Standing Committee. The remaining seventeen are elected by the Central Committee.

The procedure for choosing the Chairman, the Central Committee and the Central Standing Committee were made more democratic at previous party congresses by the introduction of the secret ballot (voting previously was by delegates standing to be counted). Prior to this Congress, KMT leaders enlisted Acer Sertek, Inc. (Taiwan's premier computer company) to provide advanced technology to do the vote taking and counting by computer. Each delegate was given a PIN number to ensure confidentiality and results of the voting were made public within ten minutes of the last person casting his or her vote.[13]

The advancing of democratic procedures in the realms of vote casting and tallying was worthy of praise. Yet the fact that the Congress had to discuss and debate party policy less than a month after being elected—clearly not enough time to reflect and discuss issues intelligently and thoroughly—showed that reform was still needed. Making party policy and formulating the party's platform was primarily, in fact almost exclusively, left up to the top leadership, with the Party Congress serving as essentially a rubber stamp organization whose function it was to approve the party platform. During the debate on policy issues delegates were also distracted by colleagues meeting behind the scenes and forming factions to enhance their votes and doing horse trading for votes to the coveted Central Committee slots.[14] This does not prove that the KMT utilizes undemocratic procedures in electing its top leaders any more than other political parties throughout the world or even the other parties in Taiwan. In fact, simply looking at selection procedures, the KMT would probably be judged a fairly democratic party, even among parties in democratic countries.[15] Yet it was not viewed as very good, by either delegates or the media, in the context of the nation democratizing; nor did it help the KMT's image.

Also dampening the spirit of debate, but facilitating sorely needed party discipline, was the fact that a number of party members had been expelled, stripped of some their party privileges or disciplined, in the several months leading up to the Congress. As a matter of fact, only days before the 15th Party Congress opened President Lee was reported to have recommended harsh penalties for KMT "dissenters" in the National Assembly who opposed the KMT's constitutional reform proposals (the most important one being cutting the size drastically or eliminating the provincial government), including suspending party memberships of some for a period of time. (Earlier, one of the most outspoken critics of the reform in the National Assembly, Lu Hsueh-chang had been stripped of his party privileges.) It was also reported that Lee would reward deputies who had helped with the reform by pushing them for election to the Party's Central Committee.[16]

A more vexing problem facing the Party's leadership and party unity leading up to the Congress, however, was the rift between President Lee Teng-hui and Governor James Soong. As noted above, following the National Development Conference held in December 1996, at which time it was decided to drastically reduce in size or even get rid of the provincial government, Governor Soong tendered his resignation.

Premier Lien did not accept the resignation and Soong remained at his job and efforts were subsequently made to reach a compromise. But this proved elusive and the differences between Lee and Soong were vented publicly before the Congress. Both had strong support for their positions. Lee's position was reasonable inasmuch as the government needed to be streamlined and the cost of a dual or overlapping system was quite large.[17] Also, the opposition Democratic Progressive Party favored this change and its support was a *sine qua non* to make other constitutional changes (since the KMT did not have a two-thirds majority in the National Assembly). Finally, both constitutional and extra-constitutional changes were sorely needed at this juncture to make the system work after the rapid progress made in Taiwan in the realm of political development and democratization. Soong's position was that the governorship had just been made an elective office in a move to further the democratization process and that dealing with overlap in government should involve compromise. Further Soong argued that money could not necessarily be saved as provincial government employees had the right to transfer to other government positions and that outright elimination of the provincial government would reflect a dangerous two-China policy.[18]

In early July, little more than a month before the opening of the Congress, KMT leaders, particularly Secretary-General Wu Poh-hsiung and Yan Ying-chi, executive director of the party's Policy Coordination Committee, began pressuring KMT National Assembly deputies to vote for the "reform" constitutional amendment being debated at the time (including provisions to end election of the provincial governor).[19] Clearly, the party leadership, including President Lee Teng-hui, wanted the amendments passed before Party Congress. This led pundits to speculate at this time that the constitutional reforms were, in fact, a scheme against Soong (to deprive Soong of an official position of importance two years before the next presidential election, while adopting an absolute majority system of electing the president that would favor a candidate with party support rather than a popular candidate) to pave the way for a Lien Chan presidency in 2000.[20] Meanwhile, a special KMT organization called *Han Hsing* was established to push the reforms and support Lien, challenge Soong, and deal with another organization called *Tien Tan*, that was chaired by Deputy Governor Wu Jung-ming and promoted Soong.[21]

When the amendments passed in mid-July, Governor Soong challenged the central government to approve his earlier letter of resignation and summoned a press conference where he went public with his complaints about abolishing the provincial government.[22] Soong's move fanned the flames of controversy and evoked a crisis for the government and the KMT, since it was uncertain whether, if the Cabinet approved the resignation, it would be taking a legal action. Also it was unclear whether an election would have to be called immediately and KMT did not have a good candidate it could recruit quickly. Rumors about the government accepting his resignation spread, some said were started to test both Soong's and the public's reaction.[23] The upshot was that the KMT leadership chose not to dismiss a very popular KMT governor since that was certain to hurt KMT unity, increase ethnic tensions and hurt the ruling party's chances in elections for city mayors and magistrates in November. Shortly thereafter, it was reported that Lien Chan invited Soong to be his running mate in the presidential elections in 2000 and Soong bluntly rejected the offer, presumably because he had ambitions to be a presidential candidate himself.[24]

President Lee Teng-hui, as a result of the conflict, became more hostile toward Soong. In early August Lee said that Soong's actions constituted "an act of insurgency." He also intimated that he was aware of Governor Soong's efforts to block passage of the constitutional amendments and his use of his staff and supporters to campaign against the reforms. Lee, in addition, expressed dissatisfaction with Secretary-General Wu Poh-hsiung for defending Soong. But Lee reportedly said he did not want to accept Soong's resignation for fear of turning him into a "tragic hero."[25] President Lee refused to meet with Soong and his office declared there was no reconciliation in sight.[26] The fight reportedly prompted many KMT members to avoid Soong and even eschew discussions about him or mention his name.[27]

Meanwhile, Lee's popularity, along with Lien Chan's, continued to plummet as public confidence in the party waned. Amplifying Lee's and Lien's plight a large number of demonstrators rallied to complain of the breakdown of social order, with protestors in one parade carrying political caricatures of President Lee as Kei-pai lang-chun (a figure in Taiwanese opera with a face half white and half black—meaning two faced), while one of Taiwan's major newspapers (known for its anti-Lee stance) said Lee was "unable to distinguish right from wrong."[28] Lee's support in the party was also undermined by reports of close ties between him and Taipei mayor Chen Shui-bian, who was being touted as a strong possibility for winning the presidency in 2000 and alternatively by claims that Chen had manipulated Lee. Because of this and cooperation between KMT and DPP leaders on passing the amendments to the constitution, there was even serious talk of the KMT and the DPP merging, to the chagrin of many KMT stalwarts.[29]

A fortnight before the Congress opened, KMT officials announced that Soong would be nominated for a position on the Central Committee, but that the party would not muster support for him.[30] On August 23, the day before the Congress opened, Governor Soong arrived in San Francisco for a week-long visit. He said that he had taken the trip to avoid "unnecessary annoyances" and admitted that the trip was timed to coincide with the 15th KMT Party Congress. Soong also stated that he would not take part in any more KMT meetings or activities.[31]

Meanwhile, some other less-noticed controversies were seething. Leaders and members of the Legislative Yuan expressed their displeasure regarding its low representation in the KMT Central Committee and lobbied to increase it.[32] Women sought to increase their numbers by getting the party to agree on quotas. The military also seemed to be trying to exert some influence over the Congress.[33]

Just prior to the opening of the Congress, President Lee met with delegates and advised them that the "changing face of party politics" means that the KMT can no longer play a dominant role and must work hard to win public support. He also spoke of building up national defenses, improving social order, implementing an Asia-Pacific operations hub project, and implementing spiritual reform. He specifically addressed the matter of streamlining the provincial government saying that the central and provincial government overlapped by up to 95 percent.[34] Responses to his comments were mixed.

Political analysts and the media, both in Taiwan and abroad, saw the main issues to be resolved at the Congress and which, incidentally, were thought to reflect how the ruling party was faring were: (1) electing the party chairman, four vice chairmen and the Central Committee and the Central Standing Committee, (2) consolidating the party's leadership and preparing current leaders as the next generation of successors, (3) boosting party unity and preparing for local elections in November, (4) formulating a policy to deal with the People's Republic of China following the return of Hong Kong, (5) adopting measures to cope with social stability, especially the crime issue, and corruption.[35]

While there was no doubt that President Lee Teng-hui would be reelected chairman of the ruling party, there was some question about the percentage of vote he would receive. Polls indicated that he had support from over 90 percent of delegates and this figure was being cited as a goal and also juxtaposed beside his reelection with 82.5 percent of the vote at the last party congress. In other words, Lee was anticipating a big victory. The breadth of Lee's support among delegates to the Congress was considered important since many of Lee's policies were controversial within party ranks and his leadership of the party and the nation had been criticized widely in the media in the months leading up to the Congress due to the rash of crime and the lingering issues of corruption and constitutional reform. Lee was also thought to need a strong mandate to be able to decide who his successor would be and to continue to lead the party after his term as president ends in 2000 (assuming he will not run again, which he has said is the case, and inasmuch as his term as party chairman lasts one year after that). All of this may be summarized by querying whether, and when, Lee might become a lame duck.

The election of vice-chairmen was considered less than indicative of future trends or a new or changed party leadership since these positions are largely titular or ceremonial. On the other hand, there was some speculation that James Soong might be, or should be, given one of these positions. The Central Committee and its Central Standing Committee in addition to the Central Advisory Committee would, according to observers, reflect the make-up of the KMT's future leadership and would indicate who was rising and falling in terms of influence on party affairs. But there was little anticipation of broad change or even significant trend-setting.

In the realm of party leadership, inasmuch as the KMT is the ruling party and hopes to remain in power, party leaders were also thought to be future government leaders as well. President Lee, most observers perceived, supported Premier and Vice-President Lien Chan to be his successor. Lee also supported Vincent Siew to be elevated in rank and stature. Several months earlier Lien Chan had offered to resign from the premiership, due to the fact that the Legislative Yuan had challenged his holding that position while being concurrently Vice President, but more immediately due to a 50,000-person protest over a dramatic increase in crime. In July, Lien announced that he would step down from the premiership the following month. In August, less than a week before the opening of the Congress, President Lee named Vincent Siew the new premier. Siew was to be the nation's first Taiwan-born (Lien Chan was the first Taiwanese premier though he was not actually born in Taiwan) and the first to have been elected to the Legislative Yuan (over which he presides). He was also regarded as a smart politician, was well-liked by the public and was known as an expert on economic issues. Siew had also gained stature for winning a Legislative Yuan seat in 1995 against a tough DPP incumbent and for running President Lee's successful election campaign in 1996. If Siew, according to observers, did not receive a large number of votes to sit on the Central Committee, it would be a loss of face for Lee and a repudiation of his leadership. A large vote for Governor Soong, some opined, would have the same effect.[36]

The KMT also needed to demonstrate at the Party Congress that the party was unified and that it was prepared for the local elections in November. Clearly the party was much less split than at the two previous congresses in terms of challenges to the top leadership and party factions that were in contention. On the other hand, opinion polls indicated, and newspaper commentators concurred, that the KMT would not do well in the local (but important) elections in November. This evoked concern that the party was not in a healthy condition and that party members did not enthusiastically support the party platform and that many were seeking benefits for themselves and were not concerned very much about the future of the party. Speaking to the party's provincial committee in early August, Lee had made an appeal for party unity and devotion to the KMT, saying that all party members must set aside their own personal interests and honestly unite in unanimous support of the party's nominated candidates."[37]

The party's stance, which serves as the foundation for Taipei's foreign policy, on relations with Beijing became a sensitive issue in the wake of the return of Hong Kong to the People's Republic of China on July 1. President Lee was being assailed by the New Party for wrecking cross-strait relations and by the Democratic Progressive Party for not taking a tougher stance and one favoring independence. He was being criticized within the KMT for secretly supporting an independent Taiwan. Trade and investment across the Taiwan Strait was also a hot issue. Clearly the KMT needed to clarify its policies in a way that would send some positive signals to Beijing, the U.S. and the international community that would help the party's image.

President Lee and the KMT leadership were also the target of public anger and disgust over the rise of crime on the island. Both the president and other party leaders understood the party's future depended upon restoring social stability and confidence in the government and talked about these problems often. Poignantly underscoring the problem of crime just a fortnight before the opening of the Congress, a gun battle occurred in Taipei between police and kidnappers of the daughter of a famous singer during which one kidnapper was killed but two others escaped. Taiwan's top police official, the director of the National Police Administration, Yao Kao-chiao, resigned after this incident which happened at the same time members of the same gang abducted and tortured a local businessman.[38]

New Leadership and Personnel

Following a day of opening ceremonies, pomp, and speeches, on August 26 votes were cast for chairman of the party. President Lee Teng-hui, incumbent chairman of the KMT, ran unopposed —although a small group of party delegates tried briefly to organize opposition to Lee.[39] Of the 2,267 delegates to the Congress formally seated, 2,209 voted. Lee received 2,064 votes, or 93.4 percent of the votes cast. Delegates representing Taipei city and Overseas Delegates cast 100 percent of their votes for Lee. Provincial delegates voted overwhelmingly for Lee—giving rise to assertions that the central and provincial party organizations were working in tandem (meaning the issue of abolishing the provincial government was no longer dividing the party).[40] Inasmuch as Lee received a larger portion of the vote than at the 14th Party Congress held in 1993—82.5 percent—this was seen as a victory. Lee forthwith (the secret vote tallying being done by computer was finished in about two hours) received an official certificate from Li Yuan-zu, chairman of the Congress presidium, formally naming him party chairman; he immediately thanked the delegates for their support and declared that "with the help and synergy of other party members, the party could realize its goal of writing (its) achievements into history."[41] Lee also called on party members to "consolidate their efforts to develop Taiwan and to reform the party." He vowed to restructure the party and promote democracy in the nation.[42]

The high percentage of votes cast for Lee can be explained in large measure by the fact that he was unopposed in his run for reelection to the party chairmanship. In addition, holding the office of president and having been elected to that position in the nation's first direct election of an executive leader less than eighteen months earlier, Lee was the natural person for the job. Clearly, electing someone other than Lee would have created an untenable situation: the ruling party being led by a party leader that might oppose Lee's presidential policies or decisions. Worse still, the party head, who is not elected by the voters at large, would be able to contradict decisions made by someone who was popularly elected.[43] Hence, Lee was not opposed and his victory was widely anticipated.

The smooth election of President Lee to be party chairman for another four years suggested to some observers that the KMT was more unified than many previously thought and that the controversy over reforms that "froze" the provincial government was not as serious as perceived over the last several months, or had passed. Some viewed the vote, moreover, as giving Lee a mandate to push further political reform in the form of additional constitutional amendments and changes in the party's structure, rules and personnel, if he wanted. It also suggested that Lee's authority in the party would last beyond his term as president and hinted that he would be able to influence, if not decide, who the party's candidates for high office would be for the next four years. It would unquestionably strengthen Lee's authority within the party for at least a while, according to most observers.[44] It also had a positive effect on the meeting, since some perceived an absence of opposition to Lee meant that the party leadership was stronger and more unified. The business community demonstrated its approval of the vote as reflected in the fact that the stock market rose 105.37 points to 10,116.84 points—a seven-year high.[45]

Following his election to another term as party chairman, Lee appointed four party vice-chairmen: Vice President Lien Chan, former Vice-President Lee Yuan-zu, former Premier Yu Kuo-hua and former Examination Yuan President Chiu Chuang-huan. These appointments were approved immediately and without opposition—confirmed by 1,690 delegates simply raising their hands in approval.[46]

The listing of Lien Chan before the others, especially three older (in particular Li Yuan-zu, who was listed second at the last Congress) and in many ways more senior KMT leaders, was seen as both unusual and significant.[47] It was interpreted to be a signal by Lee that Lien was to be regarded the number two party leader. Lee likely also wanted it to be known, or underscore this to party delegates, that Lien was his choice for the party's nomination to be its presidential candidate in 2000—as opposed to Soong or some other top KMT official.[48] Lee may likewise have wanted to ensure that the KMT's leadership remain Taiwanese —Lien being the only Taiwanese among the vice-chairmen.[49] Being the "first vice chairman" would also, no doubt, help Lien succeed Lee as chairman of the party in 2001 when Lee's term expires. The previous day Lee rejected a proposal to appoint Governor Soong a fifth vice-chairman.[50] In fact, according to the press, he angrily refused to listen to this proposal.[51]

The Congress also voted to add 115 seats to the Party's Central Advisory Council (a group of mainly "elder statesmen" in the party, many of whom have retired from other duties). The Advisory Council going into the 15th Party Congress had 276 members. Among the previous members, two gave up their seats to run for Central Committee seats. The remaining 274 were reelected, which, with the addition of 115, made the body 389 in size—much too large to carry on good debate.[52] That, in fact, may have been the intent of the decision to enlarge the body; alternatively it was simply a place to put older, loyal party leaders while ensuring their continued support of the party's leadership and its policies.

The competitive election at the Congress was held the next day—for seats on the Central Committee. Three hundred and eighty-three candidates ran for 230 positions: 230 nominated by the Party leadership and 153 sponsored by fellow delegates. (Each delegate was allowed to vote for 115.) Of those nominated by the party, 165, or 71.1 percent, won seats. Among "independents" 65, or 42.5 percent, won.[53] (The make-up of the new Central Committee is discussed below.) In addition to winning, for many, the amount of votes garnered was important; it also mirrored party factionalism, disunity, and more.

Most surprising, and also revealing in terms of dissent within the party disunity or dissatisfaction with President Lee's leadership, especially the decision to abolish the provincial government, was the fact that Governor James Soong (who was placed tenth among nominees by the party hierarchy, i.e. President Lee) was the biggest vote-getter, with 1,696 votes. Soong's vote surpassed even that of Premier Siew, who had just been appointed premier and who was Lee's number one pick (the vice-chairmen not being considered in this list), by five votes. This was seen as a rebuke of President Lee and seemed to offset or dilute the significance of his large victory in terms of the strong support he got for reelection to the chairmanship of the party.

One writer called the large vote for Soong a "wake-up call" for Chairman Lee and other top party leaders and even the party in general, saying that it would give Lee "some pressure" and might even affect the direction in which he is leading the party.[54] Others opined that the strong vote for Soong reflected opposition to Lien Chan, who was seen as the strongest candidate to win the party's nomination as its presidential candidate in 2000. Still others said it had to do with the fate of the provincial government, which, despite overlap with the national government, had a good reputation for delivering services to the people, and because abolishing the provincial government seemed to be a move toward Taiwan independence.[55] Finally, 200-plus Overseas Chinese delegates were reported to have all cast votes for Soong as a protest against "party planning" and as a call for an end to party bickering.[56] Transcending this explanation, Soong was very popular with the party rank-and-file. A poll published by one of Taiwan's leading newspapers the day before the Congress reflected Soong was party members' first choice for "first" vice-chairman as well as the KMT's preferred presidential candidate in 2000.[57]

Premier Siew was second in the vote count, KMT Secretary-General Wu Poh-hsiung was third, Kaohsiung Mayor Wu Den-yih was fourth, former Minister of Interior Lin Song-cheng was fifth, Minister of Justice Lin Fong-cheng was sixth, Taiwan Provincial Lt. Governor Wu Rong-ming was seventh, Foreign Minister John Chang was eighth, Council for Economic Planning and Development Chairman Chiang Pin-kung was ninth and Legislator Huang Chao-shun (also director-general of KMT's Department of Women's Affairs) was tenth. Premier Siew was first on President Lee's list, followed by KMT Secretary-General Wu, National Assembly Speaker Frederick Chien, Examination Yuan President Hsu Shui-teh and Legislative Yuan Speaker Liu Sung-fan.[58] The top ten vote-getters, like Soong's strong showing, reflected disenchantment among delegates with the party's recommendations. Mayor Wu and former Minister of Interior Lin, who were number four and five respectively in the number of votes they received, were ranked only 21 and 42 on President Lee's list. Additionally, of the top ten, besides Soong, Premier Siew, Secretary General Wu and Foreign Minister John Chang, the remainder of the top ten vote-getters were not on the party recommended list of top candidates.[59]

Further supporting the view that there was opposition to Lee, or at least his recommendations, provincial government employees won much bigger than the party planners and Chairman Lee had hoped or expected. Representing the provincial government (besides Governor Soong and Lt. Governor Wu) were 17 other provincial government officials and 8 provincial assemblymen. All were elected with strong delegate support.[60] This was unexpected and ostensibly reflected concern by delegates about the fate of the provincial government and/or support for James Soong. Alternatively, they sought to send a signal to President Lee and party leaders that they did not want to follow the party leadership's dictates. Another factor was Soong's supporters and the advocates of not abolishing the provincial government were quite unified and well organized and lobbied for votes very successfully.

Members of the central government administration claimed 36 seats, which analysts considered a large number. Local government and party officials also did well. Legislative Yuan deputies did not—winning only 29 seats (compared to 32 gained at the 14th Party Congress). In fact, ten legislators failed in their efforts to win seats. National Assembly members likewise found their representation disappointing —winning but 32 seats (compared to 34 at the 14th Congress); 25 failed in their bids for a seat. Some parliamentary leaders, moreover, failed to win a seat. National Assembly caucus secretary-general Chen Tzu-chin did not win enough votes to become a member of the new Central Committee. Others did not attain a high ranking. KMT legislative whip, Yao Eng-chi, ranked only 119th in vote getting. Some observers thought this was odd in view of Taiwan's democratization in recent years and the increasing importance of the two parliamentary bodies in this context as well as the critical role the National Assembly had played (and presumably would continue to play in ensuing months) in amending the Constitution as Party Chairman Lee and other top KMT officials wanted.[61]

This, in fact, prompted analysts to see a rift in the party that might influence future bills and constitutional reform and/or a permanent decline in the influence of lawmakers in the party.[62] The top hierarchies of both the Legislative Yuan and the National Assembly were clearly unhappy with the results. KMT Legislative Yuan leaders had earlier expressed dissatisfaction with President Lee nominating only 26 of its members, in view of the fact six more than this number currently held seats on the Central Committee. The National Assembly fared better getting 37 nominations on Lee's list, but its leadership had hoped for a lot more than this.[63] Following the release of Lee's list, members of both bodies began lobbying behind the scenes to win seats, but as it turned out this had little impact. There are several factors that explain why members of the parliamentary bodies of government did not do better, among them the fight between the two bodies over the National Assembly's decision in revising the Constitution not to give the Legislative Yuan the authority to disapprove of the President's choice of premier, as well as tension between both bodies and between the two national parliamentary bodies and those advocating keeping the provincial government.

Some said women fared poorly. Given the demands women had made for more seats and their expectations, this was true. Women also made smaller gains than at the 14th Congress.[64] On the other hand women improved their numbers from the previous party congress (19 to 30) and attained more seats than the party planners recommended. Lee's list contained only 25 women. Legislator Huang Chao-shun, the top woman in the polling, got tenth place. She had been 66th on Lee's list. Another 29 women won seats, including Minister of Interior Yeh Chin-feng (twenty-third in votes) and Minister Without Portfolio Shirley Kuo (seventy-fourth in votes).

The military was reportedly not represented at all at the Congress. According to an earlier statement by top military leaders, soldiers would remain non-partisan and neutral. However, during the meeting it was rumored that 52 delegates at the conference, in fact, stood for, or spoke for, the military. This was subsequently denied by General Kung Fan-ding who declared that party organizations and activities are no longer allowed in the military, though he said individuals could participate in political parties and in this case they should not be defined as military.[65] In any event, observers and the media noticed when one notable military person, retired general Yang Tung-yun, head of the veterans' agency, was elected (the 14th Congress seeing no military person elected) to the Central Committee.[66]

Of the 230 names recommended by President Lee, 65 were defeated by delegates running on their own. This reflected the ability of a number of contenders to lobby or caucus for votes. It may also have been the product of a number of delegates voting for names not on the party list as a protest against Lee and/or the party's leadership. Clearly it was not anticipated that such a large number of delegates not on Lee's list would win. Secretary-General Wu tried to put a good face on this, saying that this was "only natural" when there was a free election, dismissing the importance of differences in the list of winners from the list of delegates recommended by the party.[67] Wu also argued that it was not too different from previous congresses.[68]

The new Central Committee was noticeably younger and more Taiwanese. Business interests were well represented: C.F. Koo (of the Koo group) was number 11 in votes; Wang You-tseng, chairman of Rebar, was number 40; President Enterprises chairman Kao Chin-yen was ranked 41; and Jeffery Koo of China Trust was 124. Ma Ying-jeou, even though having resigned from his government position, ranked 51 in terms of the number of votes he received.[69]

Following the Central Committee voting, the Taiwan Stock Exchange dropped 223.18 points. Investors apparently perceived that there was a power struggle going on in the ruling party and viewed the good performance of delegates representing the provincial government as reflecting strong dissent in the KMT over the issue of getting rid of the provincial government and the gravity of the conflict between President Lee and Governor Soong.[70]

Voting for the powerful Central Standing Committee presented fewer problems and much less dissatisfaction among KMT delegates to the Congress. The CSC, which was seated on August 28, was comprised of 16 members appointed by President Lee plus 17 elected by the Central Committee, an enlargement of two from the previous Central Standing Committee. Of the 17 elected, all were members suggested by party chairman Lee Teng-hui. President Lee putting Governor Soong on the list of 16 appointed members may have soothed feelings that were stirred the previous day with the election of the Central Committee. Also Secretary-General Wu Poh-hsiung met with 200 members of the Central Committee for lunch and pressured them to vote for Lee's favorites.[71] (For a list of both appointed and elected members of the Central Standing Committee, see Appendix I.)

The new Central Standing Committee is comprised of a larger number of Taiwanese: two-thirds of members (compared to 18 of 21 after the 14th Congress). Mainland Chinese only hold 10 of 33 seats. The overwhelming majority can be categorized as officials in some way: government, party or retired. Only two represent business, in contrast to the strong representation of business notables to the Central Committee. Three are women, compared to one after the 14th Congress. Aborigines were represented in this elite group for the first time.

New Policies and Programs

As noted above, delegates to the 15th Party Congress spent more time lobbying for positions on the Central Committee and doing other things than they did formulating new policies and programs. Also, many of the policies introduced for consideration by the delegates were presented in almost finished form by the top leadership with little debate or discussion needed or wanted. Nevertheless, a number of proposals and ideas, including some amendments to the Party constitution and plans for future KMT activities and policies, were put forward. Clearly the meeting was not devoid of new ideas, discussions and proposals.

The first day of the Congress delegates heard an address by KMT Chairman Lee Teng-hui, a party report from Secretary-General Wu

Poh-hsiung and an administrative report. Policy proposals and suggested amendments followed the two reports. President Lee's address and the two substantive reports reflected the party's leadership's views on new policies or directly promote them, or both.

President Lee's opening speech, as is usual for the chairman to give at a party congress, contained a summary of the KMT's history and an enumeration of the KMT's accomplishments. In short, the address was an opportunity to hype the party and in that context cite problems and broach solutions and new policies. Among recent achievements cited by Lee were: an "unprecedented election" in 1996 that constituted a major and final step in democratizing the country while garnering international acclaim; constitutional amendments passed for the purpose of "readjusting of the central government system and streamlining the government organizational structure;" stable economic growth; progress in promoting high-tech industries; and a national health insurance system. Lee listed problems relating to national security, citing the following as the most important: Beijing's military threats in 1996; social unrest that has been evoked by major criminal cases; and diplomatic relations, which, he said, though constituting a serious problem because of Beijing's efforts to isolate the Republic of China, were nevertheless welcomed by various governments and people. By putting crime and diplomatic relations in the category of national security, Lee may have calculated that he could deal with them more effectively; alternatively he sought to take advantage of his good image and strong public support in one area (dealing with Beijing's threats) to improve his and the party's poorer reputation on the other two, especially the crime problem. Lee, however, did not offer any specific policy recommendations; this was left to Secretary-General Wu and Vice-Chairman Lien. Chairman Lee then called for new policies and further efforts in the areas of ideological understanding, organizational quality and policy achievement. Specifically, yet still not in the form of a tangible policy recommendation, he summoned a more international outlook, abandoning "remnant bureaucratic and formalist work style," and communicating and consulting with other political parties. (For the text of his speech, see Appendix II.)

The speech, while short on policy specifics, was not unlike past party chairmen's speeches at party congresses. One, in fact, could say that President Lee, as is usual in such addresses at party congresses, sought to deal only with general ideas and leave concrete policy proposals to subsequent speakers.

Secretary-General Wu's speech address was, compared to Lee's, pessimistic. Clearly it was full of warnings. Wu declared, for example, that the KMT's power base is eroding and the next few years would be critical in determining whether the party would remain in power. He noted that while Chairman Lee managed to win a landslide election in 1996 in the first direct presidential election, the KMT attained just over 40 percent of the vote in the earlier Legislative Yuan election and in a simultaneous (with the presidential and vice-presidential election) National Assembly election. He called this evidence of the fact that the KMT's dominance in the nation's political arena is eroding. He spoke in harsh language about the fact many members did not understand the party's woes or its ultimate goals. He further iterated that party members have become apathetic and suspicious of the party's causes and goals. He specifically cited resistance to the KMT's restructuring and reform plans, illegal actions by a few members that have seriously undermined the party's image and have created an impression with the public that the KMT cannot wipe out money and gang-linked politics. He called for "soul searching." Wu reaffirmed the KMT's anti-communist, anti-independence policies. He said the party would cooperate with other parties but would not integrate with them. He declared that the KMT would work with the government to promote spiritual reform and eliminate political graft and organized crime. Finally, he asserted that the year-end local elections are "critical" to the party's future and promised that the party would nominate party standard-bearers with a clean image and professional capabilities.[72]

Vice-Chairman Lien Chan also addressed the delegates the opening day of the Congress. He focused on the issue of social order—an issue that has caused the KMT's reputation to suffer in the several months leading up to the Congress as well as Lien's own prestige and his image as a national leader (having been premier or head of the cabinet during the time crime and other social problems became much more acute) as mirrored in various opinion polls. He defended the cabinet's work and lauded its accomplishments. Lien, in fact, asserted that the government's bad reputation on the issue of crime was not deserved, citing a decline (from 1993 to 1996, criminal cases down 13.9 percent, firearms violations down 27.9 percent and intimidation and kidnap-pings down 24.2 percent).[73] He noted that the cabinet had enacted the Organized Crime Control Statute and the Anti-Money Laundering Act. He also pointed out that the government had revised anti-drug laws and had continued strong efforts to clean up organized crime. He declared that the government sought to build a solid social foundation for the

21st century, with greater safeguards for women, children, minorities, the elderly, and the physically and mentally disadvantaged.[74]

The administrative report presented at this time was rather routine and did not provoke much controversy or extensive comments. Subsequently delegates broke up into discussion groups to talk about various proposals and amendments. Three hundred and thirty-nine "cases" were submitted for discussion together with 262 political proposals and 77 party-suggested amendments. Business at this time was generally conducted in routine fashion. Many proposals were approved as a matter of course. Others were left for the Central Committee or the Central Standing Committee to finish.

Generally, in terms of the business conducted and the issues debated at the KMT's 15th Party Congress, the two most heated proposals made at the Congress were: (1) a bid for the appointment of Governor James Soong to be a fifth vice-chairman, and (2) a demand that women make up 25 percent of party members and for a woman also to be appointed vice chairman. Sixty-seven delegates put forward a motion to have James Soong made a vice chairman. Liu Tung-lung, one of the delegates who wrote the motion, said it would facilitate party unity. However, KMT Secretary-General Wu refused to comment on the proposal and Chairman Lee quickly parried the idea, saying it was his decision whom to appoint as party vice-chairmen.[75] Thus the issue in its immediate form died. But the controversy surrounding the dispute between Lee and Soong did not. Efforts were made by various party leaders to dampen the controversy at the Congress, especially given the media's focus on it, but the matter was not resolved and was left to others to deal with after the congress.

Delegate Lee Keng Kuei-fong, a professor at National Chengchi University, proposed that women account for at least 25 percent of party positions and that a woman be made vice chairman. She and her supporters pointed out that the opposition Democratic Progressive Party's charter mandated this and argued that the KMT should have just as many women in the party and as many in important and top positions. Her view was supported by former Minister of Interior Yeh Chin-feng, the first female to ever hold that position.[76] The party leadership thus proposed that the Congress adopt a rule requiring 10 percent women candidates be nominated for public office in the future, but went no further than this. The party hierarchy's position was that women did not need a quota rule inasmuch as they have done very well in attaining top positions in the party and the government and, furthermore, the party has done well in promoting female candidates and winning their support in elections, and, finally, passing a mandated quota would be demeaning. Some also pointed out there were three women members of the Central Standing Committee, compared to only one after the 14th Congress.[77]

A less attention-getting proposal submitted that created some controversy was to make county-level party heads elected rather than appointed by the top leadership.[78] This was dealt with quickly and with little heated debate, however, as few delegates were enlivened by the issue. Meanwhile, little was said about party primaries and there was no caucusing of delegates or protests or even heated speeches to oppose the party hierarchy's decision to abandon primaries. Nor was there much debate on the vitally important constitutional amendments, save the scrapping of the provincial government. Some thought these issues would generate some heated debate at the congress.[79]

Two other matters that did not receive much time or create controversy were minority rights and the economy. Aboriginal rights had been debated in top circles of the party and proposals were discussed by party members and in the media before the congress. There was but one decision made in this realm: A female aboriginal legislator, Chang Jen-syang, was put on President Lee's list of his appointments and won a seat on the Central Standing Committee—a first for the KMT. However, local newspapers did not respond in a positive way to the appointment because of her "mediocre record" in the Legislative Yuan and her lack of "noteworthy achievements."[80] Little other mention was made of minority rights and party leaders noticeably did not make much of this "historic" appointment.

The economy got short shrift compared to past congresses. This may be explained by the fact that opinion polls had recently shown that the public was not as interested in economic growth as it had been in the past and that most felt that economic development was proceeding at about the right pace. In fact, party leaders were trying to look for other issues to help put candidates in office in the coming elections and for this reason did not want to talk a lot about economic development at the congress.

Relations with the People's Republic of China, on the other hand, could not be ignored or played down. On August 26, midway through the 15th Congress, the party's Central Committee received a telegram from the Chinese Communist Party congratulating the KMT on the occasion of the congress while calling for talks "to end the state of cross-strait hostilities."[81] At the same time, however, Beijing rebuffed a proposal for better relations, saying: "Only when Taiwan authorities stop activities to split the motherland...can relations improve...."[82] A Ministry of Foreign Affairs spokesman also declared that President Lee's reelection to the position of KMT chairman "did not change Taiwan's status as part of China" and urged Taiwan to accept the "one country, two systems" formula for unifying the country.[83]

President Lee subsequently addressed the issue together with the party's policy toward Taiwan independence. While not announcing any new policies, Lee spoke in quite emphatic terms. He declared: "We will not, and there is no need, to seek so-called 'independence' since the Republic of China has been a sovereign nation for the past 86 years." He further stated that it is "our...goal to seek the reunification of all of China under freedom, democracy and prosperity on the principles of reason, peace and reciprocity." His words seemed to mirror the party's policy of "unification, but not now" or simply maintaining the status quo—which is what opinion surveys indicated is the desire of the population. Lee also had some harsh words, about the "hegemonic mentality of the Chinese communists" while asserting that Taiwan would never accept the "one-country, two systems" formula used by the People's Republic of China in incorporating Hong Kong. He likewise vowed to continue Taiwan's pragmatic diplomacy which has been loudly assailed by leaders in Beijing and which has been the subject of controversy at home as either good and should be pursued with greater strength and resolve, or too provocative. Lee stated that Taiwan will "adopt more flexible strategies to build stronger ties...and actively (try to) join activities of the United Nations and other world bodies...."[84] Later President Lee called on Beijing to "denounce the 'old-style hegemonistic mentality and join forces with Taipei to create peace and prosperity for the two sides of the Taiwan Strait."[85]

Toward the end of the Congress, delegates passed a resolution endorsing Lien Chan's administrative report while calling on the government to develop an efficient anti-crime system. The motion praised Lien for his leadership and the administration's successful work in completing constitutional reform, promoting pragmatic diplomacy and engineering stable economic growth. The report likewise lauded the KMT-led government's accomplishments in education, science and technology, and the nation's modernization. It called on the party to continue to push National construction projects and develop Taiwan into a Asia-Pacific regional business hub, heed the public's cry for better social order, and provide government services while eliminating waste from social welfare programs, especially the national health insurance program. Lastly the report recommended a step-by-step approach to dealing with China and in the development of cross-strait ties.[86]

In a KMT official declaration issued toward the end of the congress, the party leadership promised that the party would build clean and efficient government and develop Taiwan into a competitive technology stronghold and called on the people to foreswear ideological and regional differences and actively build a democratic society. In this declaration, party leaders expressed the view that the KMT had democratized the country as the Republic of China's founding father, Sun Yat-sen, wanted and that the congress had forged party unity.[87] Subsequently, at the closing ceremony of the 15th Congress, Chairman Lee repeated some of these tenets, urged the party to accept its historical responsibilities, and asserted that the KMT must keep in mind that "sovereignty resides with the people."[88]

Conclusions

For the KMT, the main objectives in holding this party congress, as with congresses in the past, were fostering party unity, installing new personnel, and deciding new policies. If these are taken as the criteria to decide whether this congress was a success or a failure, certainly one would have to say the results were mixed. This same thing, mixed results, may also be said about the efforts made in democratizing the party and getting ready for the next election campaign; in fact, the record here would be even less laudable. On the other hand, the KMT leadership did a credible job in avoiding or finessing issues that might have damaged party unity and morale, which going into this congress were of concern.

The KMT was obviously more unified than it was before, during, and after the 13th Congress and the 14th Congress in terms of the party's top leadership. At the 13th Congress, Lee Teng-hui's leadership of the party was challenged. He was not accepted by many of the old guard. At the 14th, a number of top party officials belonging to a group known as the non-mainstream faction of the party left the KMT to form the New Party. There was no such serious problem at this congress. Similarly, president and party chairman Lee Teng-hui was not challenged openly nor his leadership of the party seriously questioned. Being the incumbent and having already dealt with factionalism in the party (Lee's strongest opponents having already left the KMT), at least of the kind that might lead to the formation of a break-away party, Lee

had a distinct advantage. Also, Lee's winning an unprecedented election to become the first directly elected chief executive in the nation's
history was not far distant in the past and was certainly fresh in the
minds of most delegates. Finally, Lee's leadership of the party could
not be opposed strongly without doing serious damage to the party. All
of these things added up to a huge victory in terms of Lee being handily
reelected party chairman. This in turn meant that he could pick the
vice-chairman without serious challenge as well as the Advisory
Council.

When it came to electing the Central Committee and the Central
Standing Committee, things were different. Chairman Lee was challenged mildly at least, and in a sense rebuffed, or at least his leadership
goals were brought into question, in that James Soong garnered the
biggest number of delegate votes. Soong got this kind of support
because many party delegates were disappointed with Lee's leadership,
especially on the issue of downsizing or discarding the provincial
government. They were very aware of his feud with Soong and
supporting him was an easy and convenient, and safe, way to send a
message. Soong was also a popular figure and had the provincial
government behind him. Yet one cannot account for Soong's high vote
count simply by the fact that his close supporters rallied support for
him. Many delegates were troubled also by the fact that the KMT had
been plastered with the image of a corrupt party that was incapable or
unwilling, mostly the latter, of dealing with the crime issue—which
was connected in the minds of many to the corruption problem. Soong
was seen as a top leader that was not corrupt. Another issue was that
Lee had ostensibly chosen his successor: Lien Chan. Lien was not as
popular among the populace or the party's rank-and-file as Soong.
Many delegates, in addition, felt that Lee should consult them about
this, or even allow them to vote on the matter of his successor. Many
delegates connected this issue with the future of the party, about which
doubt was being cast at this time.

The vote tally for Lee's recommended list of candidates for the
Central Committee seconds this view. To some extent this can be
attributed to the fact that caucus groups had formed and vote trading
was endemic. In this context Lee's list did not mean as much as it
would have otherwise. Still, there seems to have been a general feeling
of resistance to Lee's leadership, or at least his dictating who should be
in this elite party core group. The figures are quite telling here. This,
however, does not apply to choosing the Central Standing Committee
as Chairman Lee has the prerogative (according to the party consti-

tution and there was little impetus to change this) of selecting most of this very elite body and could control the rest by arm-twisting and compromise. Also, Lee did not seek a Central Standing Committee too different than the last one or that delegates expected.

In terms of party morale, the 15th Congress accomplished little to change the rather low mood among both party delegates and party members. Party infighting over the matter of abolishing the provincial government had dampened the party's spirit. So did disagreements about other constitutional changes compounded by the fact the public did not comprehend very well what the KMT wanted to do. Clearly the system was in need of reform; but the reforms were neither understood nor supported by the public to the degree they should have been, given the fact that they were undertaken in response to the urgent need to fix a political system that had been democratized very extensively over the past fifteen to twenty years. One might say, as a consequence, that the party leadership's decisions were mostly correct, but it did not communicate very well. The hostility between the National Assembly and the Legislative Yuan, in terms of their powers relative to the other and both vis-a-vis to the Executive Yuan, spilled over into the party. Cooperation with the DPP in passing the amendments and in other ways was also troubling to many party members. So was the issue of independence. Lee was accused of being authoritarian on the reform of the government; yet, few opined that he wanted another term in office, which would, to his critics, explain his motivation for seeking to put more power in the presidency and the executive branch of government. President Lee had been walking on both sides of the independence issue. Some would say that his position on independence was both moderate and correct and according to opinion polls was popular. Still it was divisive and seemed to reflect a lack of policy rather than one that was supported by the majority of either party members or the population. Perhaps the best explanation for much of this is that Taiwan's politics have become very complex in recent years.

The issue of democratizing the party was another area where there was some progress made, but not enough to suit many delegates and party members. Voting had been made more efficient in keeping with the nation's technological progress. It was also made more democratic at the same time. However, rules for voting for the Central Standing Committee were unchanged in terms of the franchise among delegates. Likewise for the vice-chairmen. At the same time, procedural and other rules by which the party conducts its business were not changed significantly to make the party more democratic. Meanwhile there was too little progress made to suit many in terms of the representation of minority groups, women and disadvantaged in the top echelons of the party. Chairman Lee did not push for democratization of the party as he had done at times in the past and to the very credible degree he did at the last two congresses. Invidious comparisons were made with the DPP, which was seen as a paragon of progress in this realm.

Some party leaders offered a partial explanation: affirmative action had already gone too far, preferences were a dying thing in the United States and elsewhere, women were making it in politics without special advantages and giving them a pre-determined edge was insulting and divisive. Others, however, said that the party was too preoccupied with various problems and the party's declining popularity to focus on these matters. There was still another "second opinion": the KMT is a multi-ethnic, broadly based party in terms of its support; the other parties are not. Therefore, by its very nature it is a party that advances the causes of various groups of different strips and colors and does not need to focus specifically on certain ones. At the close of the congress and even weeks after, it was indeed uncertain if the KMT leadership had made a mistake or not in not pressing on affirmative action.

In terms of new personnel, the make-up of the Congress itself as well as its Central Committee and its Standing Committee and the Advisory Council and the vice-chairman, did not suggest any sea-change. Yet this can be justified by arguing that it was the will of the members of the party. Was this a problem? Clearly there was no loud outcry about the make-up of any of these groups, except for the complaint that James Soong should have been made a vice-chairman, that women should have been given a quota of seats in the party's decision making organs, and the fact that the parliamentary bodies were not well represented. Whether there will be any fallout from the dissatisfaction about personnel or not remains to be seen. After the congress was over it did seem to linger as a cause of some concern. The level of education, experience and ethnic make up of the top organs of the party did not evoke much controversy or criticism.

Changes in party policy were not divisive. Nor can it be said that much was accomplished in this realm. There was not much controversy because there were few policy changes that were terribly meaningful. In addition, most delegates were concerned more about personnel and other matters. Many were preoccupied with getting support for them-selves to be voted to the Central Committee or helping a friend get elected. To a sizeable number of delegates, winning on personnel matters meant winning on policy issues as changes would come in policy or not depending on who got elected to the Central Committee and the Central Standing Committee.

On the other hand, policy toward China was controversial and demanded attention. It was also seen as a barometer of which way Chairman Lee was leaning and which way the party was going in the future in a number of realms. President and party chairman Lee Teng-hui made several statements on this issue. Generally they were both tough and conciliatory. They were also somewhat ambiguous. This otherwise controversial issue did not become more divisive or more heated, probably because of the fact that KMT delegates saw relations with China getting better, yet did not expect anything major to happen before the congress of the Chinese Communist Party in September. They also were aware of pressure from the United States to pursue more amicable relations with China and did not know how to cope with this or felt it best left to the Ministry of Foreign Affairs.

There was much concern expressed during the congress by delegates and by party leaders, including, notably, Chairman Lee and General Secretary Wu Poh-hsiung about the party's image, its popularity and about how it would fare in the year-end local elections. Using these as standards for measuring the success of the congress, it could not be given high marks. Clearly the KMT's 15th Congress did not help the party get prepared for the elections coming in three months. The results of the November local elections certainly prove this.

On the other hand, the KMT could take credit for manifold accomplishments. It engineered the Taiwan economic miracle in the 1960s and the Taiwan political miracle in the 1980s. Chairman Lee said at the congress, KMT is the only party in the world that has led a "third wave" democratization and remains in power. There is certainly no cause to say that the KMT is soon to become a matter of historical record. It has weathered many storms and crises in the past. It has, almost as a rule, become a better party in the face of adversity. Given the difficulties faced at this congress and the election defeat in November, the KMT will have to employ its ability once again to adapt and to prove its resilience.

Appendix I: New KMT Central Standing Committee

Appointed:

Vincent Siew	Premier
Wu Poh-hsiung	KMT Secretary-General
Frederick Chien	National Assembly Speaker
Hsu Shui-teh	Examination Yuan President
Liu Sung-fan	Legislative Yuan President
Huang Kun-hui	Secretary-General to the President
Ting Mao-shih	National Security Council Secretary-General
Chiang Chung-ling	National Defense Minister
James Soong	Taiwan Provincial Governor
Koo Chen-fu	Straits Exchange Foundation Chairman
Li Huan	Senior Adviser to the President
Wu Den-yih	Kaohsiung City Mayor
Chen Tien-mao	Kaohsiung City Council Speaker
Liu Ping-wei	Taiwan Provincial Assembly Speaker
Chen Chien-chih	Taipei City Council Speaker
Chang Jen-hsiang	KMT legislator

Elected:

Lin Fong-cheng	Minister Without Portfolio
P.K. Chiang	Council for Economic Planning and Development Chairman
Yang Ting-yun	Veterans Affairs Commission, Chairman
John Chang	Vice Premier
Wang Jin-pyng	Legislative Yuan Vice Speaker
Lin Cheng-chi	Council for Cultural Affairs, Chairperson
Hsu Li-teh	Senior Advisor to the President
Chao Shou-po	Minister Without Portfolio
Kao Chin-yen	Chinese National Federation of Industries Chairman

Hsieh Lung-sheng	National Assembly Vice Speaker
Wang You-theng	ROC General Chamber of Commerce Chairman
Peng Tso-kwei	Council on Agriculture Chairman
Tai Tung-yuan	National Taiwan University Hospital President
James Chu	Overseas Chinese Affairs Commission Minister
Lee Cheng-chong	Chinese Federation of Labor President
Yeh Chin-feng	Interior Minister
Yao Eng-chi	KMT Policy Coordination Committee Executive Director

1. For details on these two congresses, see John F. Copper, "The KMT's 13th Party Congress: Reform, Democratization, New Blood," in Cynthia Chenault (ed.), *Modernizing East Asia: Economic and Cultural Dimensions of Political Change* (New York: St. Johns University Press, 1989) and John F. Copper, "The KMT's 14th Party Congress: Toward Unity or Disunity?" *American Journal of Chinese Studies,* October 1994.
2. See John F. Copper, "Taiwan's 1994 Gubernatorial and Mayoral Elections," *Asian Affairs,* Spring 1995 for further details.
3. For details on the conference, see Linda Chao, Ramon H., Myers and James A. Robinson, "Promoting Effective Democracy, Chinese Style: Taiwan's National Development Conference, *Asian Survey*, Vol. XXXVII, No. 7, July 1997, pp. 669–682. Also see James A. Robinson, "Consensus Forged," *Free China Review*, March 1997 and interviews conducted with a number of noted politicians in the same issue of that publication.
4. See Richard R. Vuysteke, "Thankfully, history does not repeat itself," *China News*, June 22, 1997, p. 4.
5. Julian Baum, "Perilous Politics," *Far Eastern Economic Review*, May 1, 1997, p. 18.
6. Ibid.
7. Julian Baum, "Fear and Loathing," *Far Eastern Economic Review*, May 15, 1997, p. 16.
8. Ibid.

9. Julian Baum, "Storm warning," *Far Eastern Economic Review*, May 22, 1997, p. 16.

10. Ibid.

11. Ibid.

12. Julian Baum, "Wishful Thinking," *Far Eastern Economic Review*, July 17, 1997, p. 20.

13. See Keng Bok-sui, "KMT goes on-line for congress," *China News*, August 13, 1997, p. 2.

14. This writer was on the scene before and during the Congress and observed delegates engaging in vote trading meetings. He also saw candidates' leaflets listing their qualifications, etc. passed out to other delegates and received a number under his hotel room door.

15. The debate about the degree or level of democracy in the KMT can be endless. Those who argue that it is not, cite its past, the use of party money (the KMT being the richest party in the world lending itself to such charges) to keep members in line and the view that Lee Teng-hui has not tried very much to democratize the party in recent years. Contrariwise, political parties in Western democracies are generally not very democratic in terms of their rules and procedures. In addition, it is no longer perceived that membership in the KMT is very relevant to getting ahead in life in Taiwan or that the other parties in Taiwan are significantly more democratic in their rules and procedures. Finally, President Lee's clout, which is seen as proof of undemocratic methods and attitudes, comes from the fact that he has a 90 percent approval rate among party delegates. (For this figure, see "Taiwan: Kyodo Previews KMT Party Congress," Foreign *Broadcasting Information Service–China*, August 24, 1997.

16. See "Lee seeks harsh penalties for party dissenters," *China News*, August 1, 1997, p. 1.

17. The provincial government has been estimated to cost taxpayers around U.S.$1.1 billion annually. See Todd Crowell and Laurie Underwood, "Plotting the Future: Discord Erupts Over Political Reform," *Asiaweek*, January 10, 1997, p. 20.

18. The views of both President Lee and Governor Soong about this issue were reported extensively in the Taiwan media during the weeks leading up to the 15th Party Congress.

19. "KMT pressures deputies on Constitutional reforms," *China Post*, July 9, 1997, p. 1.

20. "Lien presidency bid a mystery," *China Post*, July 6, 1997, p. 12.

21. See Virginia Sheng, "Lien, Soong gear up for presidential bids," *Free China Journal*, July 11, 1997, p. 2. Tien Tan had been created earlier, in 1994, as a vote-garnering organization for Soong during his election for governor.

22. "Soong challenges Lien to confirm resignation," *China News*, July 25, 1997, p. 1.

23. "Governor Soong's ultimatum to the Cabinet," *China Post*, July 25, 1997, p. 4.

24. "Government anxious to bury Soong controversy," *China News*, July 26, 1997, p. 1; "Lien, Soong ticket still too early to be decided: KMT," *China Post*, July 27, 1997, p. 1.

25. "Lee gives Soong cold shoulder," *China News*, August 4, 1997, p. 2.

26. "No meeting planned, says spokesman," *China News*, August 4, 1997, p. 2.

27. "Lee gives Soong the cold shoulder," *China News*, August 4, 1997, p. 2.

28. *United Daily News*, July 25, 1997, cited in "Lee turns Taiwan upside down," *China News*, July 26, 1997, p. 6.

29. "KMT and DPP may form new party: Shih Ming-teh," *China News*, August 6, 1997, p. 2.

30. "Soong gets committee nomination," *China Post*, August 12, 1997, p. 16.

31. Central News Agency, August 24, 1997 cited in *FBIS-China*, August 24, 1997.

32. "Taiwan: Kyodo Previews KMT Party Congress," *Foreign Broadcasting Information Service-China* (hereafter FBIS), August 24, 1997 (found on the internet). KMT Legislative Yuan members reportedly sought to increase their numbers from 32 to 46.

33. "Military denies officers sent to KMT Congress," *China News*, August 27, 1997, p. 2.

34. "Li Teng-hui Comments on Upcoming KMT National Congress," Central News Agency, August 16, 1997, cited in *FBIS*, August 16, 1997.

35. See, for example, Lee San Chouy, "Party unity the order of the day for KMT," *Straits Times* (Singapore), August 24, 1997, p. 14.

36. Lee San Chouy, "KMT set for next century with 15th party congress," *Straits Times*, August 25, 1997, p. 25.

37. Ibid.

38. See Teresa Poole, "Taiwan PM quits to have electoral makeover," *The Independent* (London), August 22, 1997, p. 13.

39. Some of these simply did not like Lee. Others opposed Lee serving another term, saying that this violated the Party constitution. (The Party constitution is, in fact, unclear on this matter because Lee served before the 13th Party Congress.) See "Party chairman has two more terms: a violation of party charter?" *World Journal* (Shih Chieh Jih Pao) August 26, 1997, p. A8.

40. Ibid.

41. William Ide, "Majority elects Lee chairman," *China News*, August 27, 1997, p. 1.

42. Susan Yu, "KMT congress elects new leadership lineup," *Free China Journal*, August 29, 1997, p. 1.

43. For further details, see "Lee re-elected as chairman of the ruling KMT," *China Post*, August 27, 1997, p. 4.

44. Ibid.

45. Yu, "KMT congress elects new leadership lineup." *Free China Journal*, August 29, 1997, p. 1.

46. Ibid.

47. The others were clearly more senior to Lien in terms of age. Lien, on the other hand, has had considerable experience in the party and the government. He was the youngest minister ever at age 45. He has served in a host of important positions in the government, gaining probably the broadest experience of any top official in the Republic of China.

48. "Lee re-elected as chairman of the ruling KMT," *China Post*, August 27, 1997, p. 4.

49. Some delegates at the Congress said this. So did observers present at the time.

50. "KMT Delegate Proposes Soong for KMT Deputy Chairman," Central News Agency, August 25, 1997, cited in *FBIS*, August 25, 1997.

51. "Lee Teng-hui's forthright talk: vice chairman is for me to propose, "*World Journal*, August 26, 1997, p. A2.

52. See Yu, "KMT congress elects new leadership lineup," *Free China Journal*, August 27, 1997, p. 1 for details on the numbers.

53. For the numbers, see Yu, "KMT congress elects new leadership lineup," *Free China Journal*, August 27, 1997, p. 1.

54. William Ide, "Soong's performance seen as a 'wake-up call,'" *China News*, August 29, 1997, p. 2.

55. These views were expressed to this writer by a number of KMT members as well as independent observers at the time of the 15th Congress.

56. Keng Bok-sui, "Soong grabs most votes," *China News*, August 28, 1997, p. 1.

57. "Party members give the strongest support to Song Chu-yu for first vice-chairman," *World Journal*, August 24, 1997, p. A6. Lien Chan ranked second it the poll, but there was a considerable gap, more than double regarding their choice for presidential candidates in 2000. Lien, however, ranked number one among party delegates.

58. Keng Bok-sui, "Siew tops 'Lee's list,'" *China News*, August 27, 1997, p. 2.

59. Keng Bok-sui, "Soong grams the most votes," *China News*, August 28, 1997, p. 1.

60. Yu, "KMT congress elects new leadership lineup," *Free China Journal*, August 29, 1997, p. 1.

61. The author heard this view expressed a number of times by observers at the congress.

62. Yu, "KMT congress elects new leadership lineup," *Free China Journal*, August 27, 1997, p. 1.

63. See William Ide, "Lawmakers scurry for support in KMT vote," *China Post*, August 27, 1997, p. 2. The writer suggests that National Assembly leaders hoped to get 78 seats on the Central Committee.

64. The new Central Committee elected at the 14th Party Congress found 19 women seated—nearly twice as many as at the 13th Congress. For details, see Copper, "The KMT's 14th Party Congress."

65. "Military denies officers sent to KMT Congress," *China News*, August 27, 1997, p. 2.

66. Julian Baum, "In the Party Mood," *Far Eastern Economic Review*, September 11, 1997, p. 25.

67. Central News Agency, August 27, 1997 cited in *FBIS*, August 27, 1997.

68. "Soong tops KMT committee race," *China Post*, August 28, 1997, p. 1.

69. Keng Bok-sui, "Siew tops 'Lee's list,'" *China News*, August 27, 1997, p. 2.

70. Yu, "KMT congress elects new leadership lineup," *Free China Journal*, August 29, 1997, p. 1.

71. William Ide, "no major surprises in the KMT's committee election," *China News*, August 29, 1997, p. 1. Former legislator and noted scholar Wei Yung attacked the party's leadership for an undemocratic spirit.

72. "Party Official—KMT at Critical Juncture, Needs Reform," Central News Agency, August 25, 1997, cited in *FBIS*, August 25, 1997.

73. By putting intimidation and kidnappings in one category, it appeared that kidnappings had declined in number, which was not the case.

74. Keng Bok-sui, "Lien lauds Cabinet's success," *China News*, August 26, 1997, p. 2.

75. "Lee defensive after Soong touted for KMT vice chairman," *China Post*, August 26, 1997, p. 1.

76. Keng Bok-sui and William Ide, "Whisper of dissent marks Congress," *China News*, August 26, 1997, p. 1.

77. Included are Chang Jen-syang, Aboriginal, Legislator; Lin Cheng-chih, Chair of Council for Cultural Affairs; and Yen Chin-fong, Minister of Interior.

78. Keng Bok-sui and William Ide, "Whisper of dissent marks congress," *China News*, August 26, 1997, p. 1.

79. The author heard about these issues from delegates and scholars at the time of the congress.

80. "KMT makes history and selects first aboriginal woman CSC member," *China News*, August 29, 1997, p. 2.

81. "KMT receives CCP's congratulations," *China Post*, August 27, 1997, p. 1. It is worthy of note that the message sent by the Chinese Communist Party went to the KMT's Central Committee, not to its chairman Lee Teng-hui, indicating that there remained strong hostility toward Lee.

82. Benjamin Kang Lim, "PRC throws cold water on Taipei's olive branch," *China Post*, August 27, 1997, p. 1.

83. Ibid.

84. Hong Kong, AFP, August 15, 1997 cited in *FBIS*, August 26, 1997.

85. "KMT National Congress Issues Declaration," China News Agency, August 28, 1997, cited in *FBIS*, August 28, 1997.

86. China New Agency, August 27, 1997 cited in *FBIS-China*, August 27, 1997.
87. Ibid.
88. China News Agency, August 28, 1997, cited in *FBIS*, August 28, 1997.

Chapter Five
U.S. China Policy and Taiwan
A U.S. Negotiating Role In Resolving
Beijing-Taipei Differences?

Introduction

During 1995 and 1996, China's military, the People's Liberation Army (PLA), conducted provocative missile tests in the Taiwan Strait, intimidating the government and population of the Republic of China (ROC). The first tests caused the stock market to drop precipitously while engendering widespread public fear (even to the extent of causing a rush on several embassies for visas). The tests conducted in 1996 were close to Taiwan's two major ports and live ammunition was used. They were aimed at influencing the ROC's first direct presidential election—the first and only such election among Chinese people in 5,000 years of Chinese history (or so proclaimed President Lee Teng-hui and others in Taiwan).

The reason for conducting the tests was said to be anger among leaders in the People's Republic of China (PRC) over Taiwan's President Lee Teng-hui's visit to the United States in the summer of 1995. The visit gave Lee positive global media exposure while according him a venue for promoting the ROC's status as a sovereign nation (which Beijing viewed rather as a renegade province of the PRC). President Lee was also able to promote his pragmatic diplomacy while justifying Taipei's efforts to obtain representation in the United Nations and other international organizations. Beijing took this as an affront and as portentous of Taiwan's becoming de facto independent. Chinese leaders were also irate that top U.S. officials had earlier promised that Lee would not be granted a visa.

Western scholars and other observers also linked the tests to the succession problem in the PRC, saying that Deng was very ill and was about to die (which he did in February 1997) and that in the context of a scramble for power the PLA gained added influence in the decision making process. The PLA had long espoused a very hostile attitude toward Taiwan, being much more a promoter of Chinese nationalism and being more concerned about China's "lost territory" than the government or the Chinese Communist Party. Thus PLA leaders pushed for an aggressive policy toward Taiwan.

The United States sent a warning to Beijing, ordering an aircraft carrier through the Taiwan Strait in December 1995 (for the first time in almost two decades) though Washington said nothing in conjunction with this action. In 1996, the Clinton Administration dispatched two aircraft carriers and an accompanying flotilla of ships to the area in an even bigger show of force at a time while the PRC's tests were in progress. On this occasion, U.S. officials talked about their mission and even about the likely results of a conflict with PRC forces (i.e. the destruction of a good portion of the PRC navy and air force). A leader, albeit not a top one, in Beijing declared in response that China may decide to nuke Los Angeles.

Military experts defined the Taiwan Strait in 1996 as the world's number one "flashpoint" or area where a major armed conflict was likely to occur. Clearly there was a face-off situation between Beijing and Washington, one that evoked serious concern about a broader confrontation and possibly a war in the area. The fact that U.S.-PRC relations had deteriorated over the past several years and were very strained at this time made the situation appear even more explosive and the prospects for conflict even greater.

Making the "Taiwan issue" an especially thorny or difficult one for U.S. policy makers was the fact that up to 1995 the United States had pursued a policy called "strategic ambiguity" in its relations with Beijing and Taipei. Beijing had cooperated by not pressing the U.S. too hard on Taiwan and by "negotiating" (i.e. holding talks) with Taipei to lay a foundation for improved contacts and eventually reunification (though Taipei had other objectives in mind). In 1995, because of the visit of President Lee to the U.S., Beijing reversed its "soft" or rapprochement policy toward Taipei and adopted (at least temporarily) a military or military-like stance thereby challenging the U.S. policy of strategic ambiguity.

This gave rise to calls from various quarters for the Clinton Administration to formulate a more lucid China policy to replace an ambiguous one, which now lacked support in the Congress, with the public, and to some extent the media, with a more clear policy. The fact that Beijing had become increasingly aggressive elsewhere in the region (as reflected by its seizure of Mischief Reef from the Philippines in early 1995 among other hostile or aggressive actions) and the fact its military power was growing exponentially, put pressure on the Clinton Administration to adopt new measures "to deal with China." Taiwan taking the final step to becoming a democracy, which the 1996 election underscored so vividly, meant that the U.S. could not turn its back on Taiwan or simply pursue a commercial China policy that favored Beijing. Thus events "boxed in" the White House regarding its formulating U.S. China-Taiwan policy.

At this juncture, observers began to expound on the idea that the U.S. had leverage over Beijing (because of the PRC's dependence on the U.S. markets for its exports—over 30 percent of which went to America) and over Taipei as well (because of arms sales—the ROC not being able to get the arms it needed to defend itself elsewhere). Furthermore, some opined that Washington could, and, in fact, had to, mediate between Beijing and Taipei. Their conflict was simply too threatening to world peace. Making a U.S. role both more realistic and palatable, the U.S. had the support of Japan and the Association of Southeast Asian Nations (ASEAN) to maintain a balance of power in the region while both as well as the rest of the world favored protecting the new democracy in the area—Taiwan.

Although the Clinton administration and the Department of State steadfastly denied that the U.S. would negotiate Beijing-Taipei differences (the U.S. having been down that road 50 years ago with the failed Marshall Mission, State Department officials quickly pointing out), there was reason to think, in fact, that the United States had been and was creating a situation to pressure, or at minimum would provide the negotiating framework, wherein Beijing and Taipei could mend their fences. Alternatively, the U.S. might actively negotiate with both to resolve their differences.

The U.S. had in place a law (the Taiwan Relations Act) which sets a framework for U.S. policy vis-a-vis the "Taiwan issue" and it has been respected (if not happily accepted) by both sides. Washington had also maintained a force balance in the Taiwan Strait area for some time and in recent years had been actively pursuing a balancing policy by providing Taipei with more and better arms at a time while Beijing was and is expanding its military capabilities. Finally, its past and present relationship with Beijing and Taipei suggest Washington was in a position to decide the fate of Beijing-Taipei relations, and perhaps would.

In the pages below the author examines the Taiwan Relations Act and United States military sales to Taiwan—the two main indicators of an expanded United States role in promoting better relations between Beijing and Taipei. Next the writer gives an account of past and present

U.S. diplomatic actions taken to resolve Beijing-Taipei tensions and recent initiatives that appear to suggest a more direct U.S. role. Conclusions follow.

The Taiwan Relations Act

In 1979, largely through bipartisan efforts in both houses, the U.S. Congress, by a huge majority, passed public law 96-98, better known as the Taiwan Relations Act (TRA). This was the first time in American history that Congress enacted legislation defining and setting the parameters of U.S. policy toward a specific nation or political entity, i.e. the Republic of China (referred to in the TRA as Taiwan). The circumstances were indeed unusual.[1]

Congress so acted because of the circumstances surrounding the Carter Administration's decision to break relations with the ROC and establish formal diplomatic ties with the PRC. President Carter negotiated the establishment of formal diplomatic ties with leaders in Beijing in 1978 in secret and in several senses in defiance of Congress, and in December signed the Normalization Agreement which defined, or more accurately redefined, U.S.-PRC relations.[2] This document clearly and unequivocally enunciated a one-sided policy—in contraposition to America's de facto China policy up to that point.

The U.S. officially espoused a one-China policy at this time, but it was shrouded in unclear language and did not represent the reality of Washington's relationship with Beijing and Taipei. The United States was, as a matter of fact, dealing with two Chinese governments and had on numerous occasions—in fact, almost daily—acted as though both possessed sovereignty (seldom acting or speaking in any other way). Most observers thus thought that indeed one-China referred to the historical China or a hope or expectation that Beijing and Taipei could someday reconcile their differences and the two parts of China, or Taiwan and China, would be unified or reunified.

By enacting the TRA, Congress turned Carter's unequivocal one-China policy (as stated in the Normalization Agreement) into one which pundits called "two China policies." The TRA treated the ROC as a sovereign nation-state, accorded U.S. security protection to Taipei, and asked Taiwan's government to respect human rights and democratize.[3] Congress, moreover, seemed prepared to defend cordial U.S.-Taiwan relations as well as its, (as opposed to the executive branch's view) policy that Taiwan was a sovereign nation.

However, for some years after the TRA was made law, there was
worry in some quarters that it would be marginalized or reduced in
status. Congress could not be constantly attentive to foreign policy
much less effectively oversee a specific tenet of foreign policy that the
Department of State was ill-disposed toward and the White House
sometimes disliked. Furthermore, Beijing steadfastly opposed the TRA
and railed against it at every opportunity.

Beijing indeed took both overt and covert measures to weaken or
damage the Taiwan Relations Act, efforts which some thought were
successful. For example, the TRA was regularly interpreted by the
Department of State and to a lesser extent by officials in the White
House as having equal status to the Shanghai Communiqué of 1972 and
the Normalization Agreement of 1978 (even though the TRA was a law
passed by Congress and the other two were simply executive
agreements). The executive branch also, on most occasions at least,
interpreted the language of the TRA narrowly, sometimes suggesting
that the Act did not commit the U.S. to defend Taiwan.[4] Finally, there
was talk of a fourth communiqué that would make further concessions
to Beijing on the "Taiwan issue."[5] Many saw all of this as the product
of Beijing's influence.

In 1982, it seemed the TRA was overtly and formally subverted
when the U.S. and the PRC negotiated the August Communiqué and
the U.S. promised to reduce and ultimately terminate arms sales to
Taipei. Critics in the United States and even PRC officials observed
that it contradicted an essential provision of the TRA which pledged the
United States would "provide Taiwan with arms of a defensive
character." Though the August Communiqué did not gain the stature of
the other two communiqués (because it was not signed and alleged
promises made by both sides relating to it were repudiated) it was
nevertheless seen as undermining the TRA.

Notwithstanding, the TRA gained status when, in 1992, the August
Communiqué was dealt a serious blow by President Bush announcing
the sale of high-performance F-16 fighter planes to Taipei. Candidate
Bill Clinton did not object to the decision while expressing hostility
toward Beijing on human rights and other grounds. In fact, he appeared
friendly toward Taiwan.[6] During the campaign Clinton gave no
indication that he did not support the Taiwan Relations Act or that he
sought it any way to alter or change it. In fact, Clinton appeared to be
more favorably disposed toward Taipei than Beijing.

In mid-1993, to ensure that Clinton pursued a China policy not
detrimental to Taipei (as there had appeared doubts about this) the

Senate Foreign Relations Committee adopted an amendment to the TRA proposed by Senator Murkowski of Alaska stating that the promise of arms sales to Taiwan in the TRA "shall supersede any provision of the August 17, 1982 Joint United States-China Communiqué...." The full Senate approved the amendment, though in conference with the House of Representatives a sense of the Congress declaration resulted instead.[7]

The following year, in April 1994, a conference bill, which included provisions from Congress's earlier declaration, was passed and subsequently signed into law by President Clinton. Before the president signed it, however, the Department of State registered its opposition and the word supersede (which the State Department argued would nullify all of the communiqués) was changed to assert simply the "primacy" of the TRA. Simultaneously Secretary of State Warren Christopher wrote a letter to Murkowski reaffirming the TRA's legal standing over the August Communiqué.[8] Clearly the TRA was strengthened by these actions.

Meanwhile the Clinton Administration ordered an interagency review of U.S. policy toward Taiwan, which was concluded in July 1994. There were strong feelings in Congress because the White House and the Department of State had not treated Taiwan with due respect especially considering its rapid democratization. Congress also reflected popular displeasure with Beijing over issues previously cited. The review made several policy changes in Taipei's favor. New Taiwan policies, which were formally announced in September, allowed U.S. officials to visit Taiwan and Taiwan's top leaders to transit the United States. The U.S. also acknowledged that Taiwan had a role to play in international organizations (though the U.S. would not support Taipei's entry into the United Nations). Taiwan's representative office in the U.S. was permitted to change its name from Coordination Council for North American Affairs (a nondescript title) to Taipei Economic and Cultural Representative Office in the United States. Last but not least, the U.S. pledged to continue to provide military material and training to Taiwan's armed forces.

However, Congress expected more. Its reaction to Clinton's Taiwan Policy Review ranged from luke-warm to negative. Most members of Congress concerned about Taiwan considered the policy review cosmetic rather than substantive.[9] Many said the Administration was still not abiding by the spirit of the TRA. In fact, there was speculation that Congress may seek to amend the TRA in ways advantageous to Taipei.

Meanwhile, trying to avoid a deterioration in relations with Beijing, the Clinton Administration adopted contradictory policy initiatives which appeared to violate the intent if not the letter of the TRA as it had been interpreted in recent years. In negotiating with Beijing on the Missile Technology Control Regime in 1994, it was reported that Washington agreed to discuss with Beijing the U.S. sale of F-16 fighter planes to Taiwan. This seemed a dangerous precedent, giving Beijing input into the U.S. decision making process relating to arms sales to Taiwan, some said even a veto. Indeed, this was something Chinese leaders had sought ever since the passage of the TRA. President Clinton also suggested in a letter to PRC President Jiang Zemin that the U.S. was committed to a "unified China." U.S. policy up to that point supported a peaceful resolution of the "Taiwan issue" but did not back any specific outcome. Finally, State Department spokesperson Michael McCurry used words that evoked some concern: saying that the U.S. "accepted" China's claim that Taiwan is part of China, rather than using the term "acknowledge" which had been in common usage.[10] All of this caused some members of Congress to see disturbing signs in the Clinton Administration's Taiwan policy.

After the Republican victory in the 1994 election and even more so following the missile tests in 1995 and 1996, U.S. Taiwan policy became the focus of attention in Congress and the foreign policy making community. In that context the TRA began to be perceived differently, meaning it became seen much more as a firm U.S. commitment to Taiwan. Although it was not amended and no serious attempts were made to do that (though there were some proposed amendments) it took on a renewed significance. For example, the TRA was invoked in statements about Taiwan and U.S. Taiwan policy many fold more often by Congress (and also the media) than it had been in previous years. Clearly, there was no possibility of it being marginalized. Furthermore, moves made by the Clinton White House and the Department of State to alter it through understandings with Beijing or changes in the language or provisions in U.S. China policy seemed to have been stopped in their tracks.

In December 1995, State Department spokesman Nicholas Burns said that, "according to the TRA the U.S. had committed itself to Taiwan's security," quoting directly from the Act to support his statement.[11] The Department of State in this instance veered from its usual stance of downplaying the TRA and promoting the communiqués. When the U.S. sent aircraft carriers to the Taiwan Strait in early 1996, Clinton Administration officials conveyed the impression that the

U.S. was indeed obligated (which is technically not the language of the TRA) under the Act to respond to the PRC threat. In fact, national security advisor Anthony Lake used the term "grave consequences" when warning the PRC—employing a term found in the TRA which declares: "to consider any attempt to resolve the Taiwan issue other than by peaceful means as a threat to the peace and security of the Western Pacific area and of *grave* (italics added) concern to the United States."[12]

Assistant Secretary of State for Asia and the Pacific, Winston Lord, in testimony before a House committee in early 1996 declared that the TRA "forms the legal basis of U.S. policy regarding the security of Taiwan." It is noteworthy that he did not mention the communiqués. Moreover, he stated: "Its premise is that an adequate defense of Taiwan is conducive to maintaining peace and security...."[13] Lord went on to say that he opposed ambiguity in U.S. China policy, thereby hinting that the TRA promised to protect Taiwan and that Taipei possessed sovereignty. This view contradicted the opinion of many in the executive branch of government and others in the Department of State regarding the breadth of the TRA's commitments.

Deputy Assistant Secretary of State for Asia and the Pacific Jeffrey Bader, also in testimony before Congress, said that the TRA "sets forth our abiding interest in the peace and security of Taiwan and the Western Pacific. He went on to say that U.S. arms sales to Taiwan have helped maintain a cross-strait military balance.[14] His statement again seemed to suggest, though he avoided saying this directly, that the U.S. has an obligation according to the TRA to defend Taiwan.

Congress shortly after this passed a joint sense of the Congress resolution which criticized the People's Republic of China for missile tests and declared that the United States is "committed to the military stability of the Taiwan Straits" (sic) and declared that the President should, "consistent with the Taiwan Relations Act, consult with the Congress on an appropriate U.S. response" (to the missile tests and the threat to the peace and stability of Taiwan).[15] Several members of Congress in their statements recalled that the TRA stated that U.S. policy is based on the expectation that the future relationship between Beijing and Taipei would be resolved peacefully and by mutual agreement. Congress also said that the People's Republic of China should engage in negotiations with Taipei and that Taipei should adhere to its commitment to negotiate.[16]

When House Speaker Newt Gingrich visited East Asia in early 1997, he said, during a stop in Hong Kong, that the TRA "being a law

passed by the Congress and signed by the president would take
precedence over a communiqué that was not in treaty form...."[17]
Gingrich also said in very clear words that the United States would
intervene militarily if Taiwan were attacked. The White House
responded, saying that Gingrich was "speaking for himself," but forthwith issued a statement saying that it is the policy of the United States
to "meet its obligations under the Taiwan Relations Act."[18]

One author, putting this apparent shift in U.S. policy in context,
asserted that the PRC's moves in the South China Sea caused Vietnam
to be admitted into the Association of Southeast Asian Nations
(ASEAN) and that its provocations in the Taiwan Strait repaired the
U.S.-Japan alliance and resuscitated the Taiwan Relations Act.[19] It
indeed appeared at this juncture that the TRA was very much less likely
to be downgraded, weakened or ignored; rather it seemed destined to
play a central role in U.S. China policy.

In terms of a U.S. role in negotiating differences between Beijing
and Taipei, the TRA was now seen by some as enunciating a different
U.S. policy toward both while declaring its expectations for talks or at
least amicable behavior on the part of the two sides. Importantly, the
TRA calls for a peaceful settlement only of the Taiwan issue. It thus
"restrains" the PRC from using military force against Taiwan, or
threatening such, or contemplating a blockade or quarantine. Finally,
unlike the communiqués, it does not suggest that the Taiwan issue is
for Chinese themselves to resolve (as the Department of State has often
said). In short, it may be seen as giving Washington a legal framework
and/or justification for initiating talks with the two protagonists.

U.S. Military Assistance to the ROC

The U.S. has a history of providing significant military as well as
economic assistance to Nationalist China in the past and to the
Republic of China on Taiwan more recently. America sent arms, aid,
and related support to the Nationalist Chinese government before and
during World War II and continuing this assistance after the war when
Nationalist forces were engaged in a civil war with Communist forces
from 1945 to 1949. When the Nationalists were defeated and fled to
Taiwan, that aid was discontinued and Washington delineated its
commitment to fight communism in Asia in the form of a "defense
perimeter" that did not include Taiwan. However, aid and support were
resumed to Chiang Kai-shek immediately after the onset of the Korean

War in 1950. President Truman also dispatched the Seventh Fleet to the Taiwan Strait to shield Taiwan from an invasion by Mao's forces.

U.S. military support proved critical during two Offshore Islands crises in the 1950s and in subsequent years during Taipei's protracted struggle with Beijing. In 1954, the U.S. military commitment was formalized in the U.S.-Republic of China Mutual Defense Treaty. Washington, however, also took the position that it did not want to be drawn into a conflict that Taipei might initiate with the PRC and thus provided the ROC with only limited amounts and only certain kinds of weapons.[20] The arms purveyed were categorized as "defensive only" and essentially precluded any effort by Taipei to successfully invade the mainland.

U.S. military assistance policy, in short, created a stalemate between Beijing and Taipei and established a kind of balance of power in the Taiwan Strait. This situation, in fact, put the U.S. in a position to negotiate differences between Beijing and Taipei—though for some time Beijing was America's arch-enemy and Washington had no interest in mediating or even suggesting negotiations except to prevent a conflict that might expand and involve the United States in a war with the Soviet Union.

Through the late 1960s, the U.S. regarded the ROC as a loyal ally, actively utilizing bases in Taiwan during the Vietnam War. The United States gave no indication of abandoning Taiwan or allowing the PRC to invade the island. Chinese leaders in Beijing clearly understood Washington's stance regarding its use of military force against Taiwan. On the other hand, Washington took calculated steps to ensure that the Vietnam conflict did not involve the PRC and warned Taipei not to initiate a conflict with Beijing knowing that it did have such an opportunity because of the Vietnam War and unrest in China caused by the Great Proletarian Cultural Revolution.[21]

During the period 1969-72, the United States and the People's Republic of China altered their policies vis-a-vis the other and ceased to regard each other as enemies. In fact, they became in the minds of some observers "allies" against Soviet expansionism and hegemonism. Commensurately they studiously ignored the "Taiwan issue." Beijing knew that the United States still regarded Taipei as a friend, that Taiwan had support in the U.S. both among the general populace and in Congress, and that Washington would continue to provide Taipei with military assistance. Beijing likewise realized that any feud over Taiwan would hurt the U.S.-PRC strategic relationship to Moscow's advantage.

Thus the stalemate between Beijing and Taipei persisted as did the military balance of forces on the two sides of the Taiwan Strait.

U.S. military aid to Taiwan, however, was not liked by Chinese leaders in Beijing, and it evoked domestic political tensions in China particularly after Mao's death. U.S. Taiwan policy, in fact, constituted the basis for a challenge to Deng's leadership. Leftist hard-liners increasingly attacked Deng on the "Taiwan issue." Having virtually abolished communism, substituting for it Chinese nationalism, China's "lost territory" (and Taiwan was the most salient case) was Deng's Achilles heel. The United States, favoring Deng, who was turning China into a capitalist country while helping the United States cope with the Soviet Union's massive arms building, sought to succor him and thus agreed to reduce and eventually terminate arms sales to Taiwan in the afore-mentioned August 1982 Communiqué.[22]

Deng subsequently reformulated China's external relations, in the form of an "independent" foreign policy (aligned with neither the U.S. nor the Soviet Union) allegedly to allow Beijing to play a "swing" role between Washington and Moscow. The effect (which Deng intended) was more to quell domestic opposition to China's close ties with the United States (which Deng's opponents contended guaranteed the PRC would never get Taiwan back) than to alter Sino-American ties. U.S.-China relations as a result remained "on track."

Washington, while it officially promised to cut arms aid to Taiwan, got around this pledge by reducing sales slowly (even arguing that it could increase them without violating the 1982 August Communiqué because of inflation). Meanwhile the U.S. provided Taiwan with critical military technology so that it could construct its own weapons, including a locally-built fighter plane (its most important weapon in deterring a PRC attack). The United States also sold Taiwan anti-submarine warfare equipment and helicopters to deal with the PRC naval threat against Taiwan, even while helping strengthen China's military with weapons and military technology transfers. In this way Washington continued to maintain a force level equilibrium between Beijing and Taipei (facilitated to some degree by the fact that Deng cut China's military budgets, justified by the need for investment capital to spur economic development).

The events of 1989 (the Tiananmen Massacre and the fall of the Berlin Wall, signaling the demise of the Soviet bloc), drastically changed U.S.-PRC relations. The "China card" or the strategic link with Beijing diminished in importance to the U.S., thereby affecting U.S. China policy. Meanwhile, Taipei had an important national election that sent the signal that it was becoming a democracy—in contrast to the PRC which was not. In short, Taipei's pariah image, if it still had one at this time, was "sent to Beijing." Military ties with the PRC in this milieu proved difficult for Washington to maintain, and strategic cooperation thus diminished.

At this same time, Beijing stopped regarding the Kremlin as a threat due both to internal difficulties in the Soviet Union which dramatically weakened Moscow's military capabilities, as well as a new more cordial relationship negotiated between them by General Secretary Gorbachev. Thus, the U.S. did not have the strategic importance (to offset alleged Soviet expansionism and hegemonism) to the PRC that it had before. As the Soviet threat diminished and Beijing-Moscow relations warmed, the Chinese People's Liberation Army (PLA) withdrew large numbers of its military units, including missile battalions, from the northern border and repositioned many in Fujian Province just across the Taiwan Strait from Taipei.

Meanwhile, U.S. criticism of China's human rights became more intense and less sufferable to Chinese leaders, especially PLA brass. U.S.-China relations, as a consequence, especially military relations (which were already on hold by the United States as a result of changes in U.S. policy after the Tiananmen massacre) deteriorated further.

The PRC's subsequent military expansion also became a serious concern to U.S. policy makers. American leaders questioned the purpose of China's growing military budgets as well as its weapons building and acquisitions at a time when other nations were cutting their military spending and when China no longer had to worry about the Soviet Union (its heretofore primary enemy). Washington began to see China's growing military power as aimed at Taiwan and as threatening to upset the military balance in the Taiwan Strait.[23]

This prompted the United States in 1992 to change or at least drastically alter its position on arms sales to Taiwan and offer F-16 aircraft (a high-performance U.S. fighter plane and a weapon Taipei had been wanting to buy for a number of years only to be regularly refused). The sale, from the point of view of U.S. military leaders, was needed to restore the balance of forces in the Strait and protect Taiwan.[24] Indeed that was true, especially in view of Beijing's recent purchase of top-of-the-line MiGs from Russia. One might also note, however, that the sales helped sustain Washington's capacity to mediate between Beijing and Taipei since it preserved the stalemated military situation between them.

As noted above, as a candidate for President, Bill Clinton did not oppose the sale of F-16s. Moreover, as president, Bill Clinton approved the delivery of the planes and other military equipment to Taipei. He obviously accepted the logic of maintaining a balance of military forces in the Taiwan Strait presented to him by military advisors. Sales of other weapons to Taiwan continued with deals allowing Taipei to purchase anti-ship Harpoon missiles and SuperCobra attack helicopters.[25] Incidentally, these sales came on the heels of Taiwan conducting military exercises at the time of the Hong Kong turnover to the PRC, exercises some observers called provocative.[26]

Not only has the U.S. recently provided weapons to Taiwan in increased amounts coinciding with the PRC's expanded military spending and its aggressive actions in East Asia, but Washington has also acted much more aggressively to challenge Beijing's policy toward Taiwan. As previously mentioned the Clinton Administration dispatched aircraft carriers to the region in 1995 and 1996 in response to Beijing's threatening missile tests. The first U.S. response was a subtle one. It was not reported to the media and when it was discovered U.S. leaders played it down saying that its naval movements were "weather-related." The second U.S. reaction was quite different; it constituted the biggest U.S. military deployment in Asia since the Vietnam War. It sent a clear signal that the United States was prepared to use its superior military forces to protect Taiwan.

In adopting this tough posture toward Beijing, the Clinton Administration had the support of the Pentagon, the Congress, the media and the American people. There was little dissent. In fact, this was quite unusual. It was thus likely an action that set a precedent. In many respects it could not but create a "mark in the sand." Contrariwise, not responding would have been interpreted as a U.S. retreat from its commitments, which would have severely damaged American's credibility in East Asia.

The U.S. action also represented decisions that accorded with the Taiwan Relations Act. The TRA declares that it is the policy of the United States "to maintain the capacity...to resist any resort to force or other forms of coercion that would jeopardize the security, or the social or economic system...of Taiwan." As a result of the missile tests and the subsequent U.S. actions to respond to this crisis, it is unlikely that there will be serious demands at home for the United States will cut its armed forces in East Asia any further. Recent statements from Pentagon officials, in fact, indicate the U.S. military position in the region may be strengthened if anything.

It is also noteworthy that the U.S. had the support, tacit or otherwise, of other East Asian countries in taking the aggressive actions it
did. U.S. moves, moreover, were seen by those nations as part of a
positive balancing effort. Indeed, U.S. operations were launched partly
from bases in Japan, without any opposition or negative comment of
significance from Tokyo. Subsequently Japan agreed formally to
update and upgrade the security relationship with the United States.
Singapore similarly expressed approval of the U.S. "balancing effort."
Other countries in the region noticeably did not oppose or complain
about Washington's show of force.[27]

In June 1997, Congress authorized the sale of Knox-class frigates to
Taiwan and in October, in the wake of the return of Hong Kong to the
People's Republic of China, declared that the United States should
assist in the defense of Taiwan in case of threats or military attack by
the People's Republic of China...."[28]

To offset or manage Congressional actions which favored Taipei in
terms of power balancing in the Taiwan Strait, the Clinton Administration adopted a new China policy, called "comprehensive engagement." However, this policy was poorly understood by Congress, the
U.S. media, and foreign leaders, including Chinese leaders. It was
portrayed as an alternative to American's earlier policy of containment.
Yet it was clearly not an alternative to a containment policy, which was
long discarded and reestablishing it was not feasible given China's new
presence in international politics and its impressive economic and
military growth. Nor did engagement explain U.S. objectives or intentions. In contrast, balancing did. One writer, describing the situation
quite succinctly, suggested that the United States not "trust in prayer,"
but rather "weave a net" in trying to deal with the People's Republic of
China.[29]

If, as it appears will be the case, the U.S. continues to pursue a
policy of balancing force levels in the Taiwan Strait area and in East
Asia generally, diplomacy will be an important tool of that policy (as it
has been in balance of power situations in the past). Washington will
want to involve or even negotiate with nations in the area, including the
PRC, to make the equilibrium understood and to make it work. This
may well entail a change of policy of not negotiating Beijing-Taipei
differences and leaving the "Taiwan issue" for the Chinese to resolve
themselves. Promoting negotiations seems to fit with the Clinton's
policy of engagement and may indeed be needed to give that policy
credibility. Negotiations may also dilute the administration's reputation

for responding quickly with force to events in 1996, too quickly in the minds of Chinese leaders in Beijing.

A U.S. Negotiating Role

In 1949, the United States abandoned any hope of bringing two antagonistic Chinese regimes to the negotiating table. A host of efforts had failed—mainly due to the fact that Washington had no leverage over Mao and the Chinese Communists and putting pressure on Chiang Kai-shek made Mao more confident and recalcitrant. Helping Chiang also made him less willing to talk. The failure of the well-known Marshall Mission underscored the futility of America's efforts at promoting a peaceful settlement. The only recourse was to abandon the Nationalist Chinese.

The next year, however, the United States abruptly ended its hands-off China policy. The U.S. became hostile toward the People's Republic of China for its mistreatment of U.S. diplomats in 1949, its alliance with the Soviet Union concluded in early 1950, and subsequently its participation in the Korean conflict (which cost the lives of more than fifty thousand American soldiers). Nationalist China in this context once again became a U.S. friend and ally.

The United States did not seek to start or even encourage negotiations between Beijing and Taipei; that was not considered to be in the U.S. national interest, nor feasible given the fact partisan blame casting over the "loss of China" in the 1950s and after seriously divided America. Also the failed Marshal Mission was still on the minds of many Americans, both policy makers and the public.

In ensuing years, Washington, however, sought aggressively to keep Beijing and Taipei from engaging in overt hostilities, especially of the sort that might escalate into a broader war that might involve the United States and the Soviet Union. After Korea Washington in particular wanted to avoid another "hot war" in Asia. America thus seemed reconciled to the reality of a divided China and close relations only with Taipei.

U.S. China policy shifted during the 1960s coinciding with the realization that the PRC government was unlikely to be overthrown and the fact the U.S. increasingly needed to deal with Beijing. This became even more obvious with the growing belief in Washington that the U.S. could not extricate itself from the Vietnam War and cope with the growing Soviet arms buildup without a new and different relationship with the People's Republic of China. Hence, with the announcement of the Nixon Doctrine in 1969, U.S. China policy headed on a new course.

Prior to Nixon making the breakthrough in relations with Beijing, the U.S. had adopted a policy of a "peaceful settlement only" of the Taiwan problem or issue. U.S. negotiators never won the PRC's acceptance of this policy, but there was some optimism in 1971 due to the PRC's acquiescence to the U.S. position on a negotiated settlement of the Taiwan matter: Mao had vowed never to allow a thaw in U.S.-PRC relations unless the Taiwan matter was resolved in Beijing's favor, but at this time scrapped this policy.[30]

In 1972, President Richard Nixon visited the PRC and signed the Shanghai Communiqué. In the communiqué, Nixon handled the sensitive "Taiwan issue" with ambiguous language and a declaration to the effect that both sides (meaning the governments in Beijing and Taipei) agreed there was only one China. Whether or not the U.S. at this point reversed a decade-long trend toward a two-China policy is debatable.[31] So too, whether the U.S. had any intention of trying to reconcile, mediate or negotiate differences between Beijing and Taipei must be left to speculation. Clearly one can make the argument that the United States did not reject the notion of serving as a negotiator based on the fact that Washington sought to pursue good relations with both and hoped the two sides would ameliorate their differences.

In any event the "Taiwan issue" was finessed (perhaps this can be called a special kind of negotiating). Washington and Beijing agreed to disagree and not allow the Taiwan problem to disturb the course of improving Sino-American relations. U.S.-PRC ties became closer even though the U.S. defeat in Vietnam evoked disappointment with the PRC (because Beijing was thought to be able and willing to help the U.S. withdraw with honor). Watergate and Mao's death also created problems, but neither were permitted to derail the U.S.-China rapprochement.

Nevertheless, when the issue subsequently arose of the U.S. helping to negotiate between Beijing and Taipei, Washington took the position that it was a "Chinese problem."[32] Most U.S. policy makers felt that the two would not negotiate, or, even if they did, there would be no meaningful results. However, they also understood that the U.S. held the key to improved relations across the Taiwan Strait. Washington concurrently realized that negotiations would be difficult and probably counterproductive for the U.S. to initiate. Most opined that more time was needed before anything could be accomplished in this realm.

After President Carter concluded the Normalization Agreement in 1978 (which he argued was a "follow-up" of the Shanghai Communiqué) and then established formal diplomatic relations with Beijing, Washington seemed to tilt toward Beijing. This was, as noted earlier, reversed or at least offset by the Taiwan Relations Act. The evidence, however, indicates President Carter expected and may indeed have wanted this so as to keep a balance in U.S. policy toward Beijing and Taipei (even though it appeared he did not).[33]

The PRC, now under Deng Xiaoping's leadership, for domestic political reasons, chose to interpret this apparent pro-PRC shift in U.S. China policy as giving it an advantage in negotiating with Taipei on the issue of reunification. Deng averred that Washington had put Taipei in an untenable position and had perforce to reach some understanding with Beijing.[34] Deng may have presumed the U.S. would help in promoting talks with Taipei, though he probably did not, but tried to give this impression. The U.S., in any case, due to the standoff between the executive and legislative branches of government, and for other reasons, did not, in fact, change its Taiwan policy. Washington continued to treat the "Taiwan issue" as a "Chinese problem" that the two sides should resolve themselves and one that the U.S. must not get directly involved in (though the United States continued to provide the ROC with arms and, some said, with favorable trade arrangements which gave Taipei the wherewithal to buy U.S. weapons and in other ways resist Beijing's overtures).

Outwardly, the Reagan Administration reversed course in terms of the United States favoring Beijing over Taipei. Some said that this evened the playing field, making it more likely that negotiations would take place since Taipei was recalcitrant before this and Beijing thought it could force Taipei into an agreement on its terms.[35] Deng, however, had not pressed hard for negotiations because of his concern with other matters—particularly China's economic development and its strategic cooperation with the U.S.(in the face of the Soviet Union's very rapid military buildup). He was also grateful for President Reagan's generous policies on technology transfers and trade, and perceived that Reagan would not force Taipei to the negotiating table. In fact, the U.S., in a declaration made by the Reagan Administration, formalized its policy of not pressuring Taiwan to negotiate.[36]

It was during the Reagan years, however, that progress was first made in the form of a rapprochement between Beijing and Taipei that served as the prelude to formal talks between them in 1993. U.S. firmness and its economic and other help to both Beijing and Taipei were apparently conducive to the two sides making serious efforts to reconcile their differences. Conditions also changed for both sides in terms of mutual economic (and political) advantages for leaders in Beijing and Taipei to deal with each other.

In 1981, then PRC President Ye Jianying issued a "nine-point" statement elucidating Beijing's policy toward Taiwan that was much more conciliatory than anything any top Chinese leader had said up to that point. In 1984, in what may be seen as a follow-up to Ye's proposal, Deng Xiaoping, in a formal address about China's unification, proposed the "one country, two systems" plan to bring Taiwan "back into the fold." Taipei responded with less hostile statements toward Beijing and, in 1987, legalized indirect trade and transportation links with the PRC and allowed its citizens to travel to the mainland.[37] This laid the groundwork for extensive economic ties across the Taiwan Strait. The shifts in policy by Beijing and Taipei were applauded by the Reagan Administration.

President Bush continued to pursue what he regarded as a "balanced policy" which would encourage better relations between the two erstwhile antagonists. And Beijing and Taipei proceeded further with their pursuit of ties. Economic growth in the PRC continued to change Beijing's perspective on Taiwan. So did, even more so, the opening of contacts as well as trade and investment by Taiwan in the mainland. The United States facilitated these ties by purchasing large amounts of goods made by companies in China which were started or invested by Taiwan businesses and in other ways encouraged the ties.

In June 1991, Wang Zhaoguo, director of the Taiwan Affairs Office in the State Council in Beijing, invited "all parties concerned" to discuss any issue relating to Taiwan. Chinese Communist Party General Secretary Jiang Zemin made essentially the same statement the next year. Meanwhile, in 1989, the ROC's President Lee Teng-hui established the Mainland Affairs Council to draft rules for formal contacts with the PRC and in 1990 set up the National Unification Council, which in March of the next year promulgated a three-phase program for the unification of China and Taiwan. That same year, the unofficial Straits Exchange Foundation provided an avenue whereby the two sides could engage in informal talks. All of this served as the groundwork for formal Beijing-Taipei "negotiations" called the Koo-Wang (or Wang-Koo) talks in April 1993.[38] The United States hailed these developments.

During these years, U.S. China policy in terms of relations and/or negotiations between Beijing and Taipei was comprised of two important elements. One, the unification of Taiwan with China, if there was to be one (U.S. policy did not, regardless of what was sometimes said, specify), was to be peaceful. Two, negotiations were to be between the two parties (or between the Chinese themselves) and would not involve the U.S. directly. The U.S. thus avoided a triangular situation and relations between Beijing and Taipei were bilateral with the United States, from the sidelines, supporting better relations between the two.[39]

Two major policy reversals dramatically damaged the credibility of the White House in making a cogent and consistent China policy.[40] In 1994, the Clinton Administration broke the linkage between granting the PRC most-favored-nation status and human rights. In 1995, as already mentioned, the Department of State acting on President Clinton's order, granted President Lee Teng-hui a visa to come to the U.S. after top State Department officials had promised Beijing this would not happen. Both actions hurt the Administration's image in foreign policy making and worsened relations between the White House and Congress. This, plus the perception that Clinton's foreign policy was almost solely a commercial one (i.e. exporting American products) and lacking in strategic vision, prompted Congress to become more active in foreign policy making in general and especially more assertive in the formulation of U.S. China policy.

However, it was not until Beijing responded so forcefully to the Lee visit and conducted missile tests in the Taiwan Strait in anger that the U.S. policy of promoting negotiations between Beijing and Taipei collapsed. Both Beijing and Taipei were blamed, but mostly Beijing. This crisis situation was also seen as in part as precipitated by strained relations between the executive and legislative branches of the U.S. government over China policy. It was the view of Congress that the Clinton Administration's China policy was both weak and confusing. Many in Congress also felt the White House did not take much interest in foreign policy, did not make strong appointments in that area, and unwisely diverted attention away from Asia with involvement in Haiti, Somalia, Bosnia and other places. Many also perceived Clinton had become hostile toward Taiwan.

Congressional opposition to White House China policy was further amplified by the Republican landslide victory and its takeover of Congress in 1994. The chasm thus widened even more between the legislative and executive branches of government and between Democrats and Republicans. In this context, the PRC showed favoritism toward the Democratic Party and apparently made monetary contributions that were aimed in part at engendering policies of greater restraint in selling weapons to Taiwan and in supporting Taiwan militarily.[41] This wrought even greater polarization in the making of China-Taiwan policy.

Beijing's aggressive actions—in grabbing Mischief Reef in the South China Sea in January 1995 and its subsequent provocative missile tests in the Taiwan Strait—helped rally pro-Taipei forces in the U.S. and weakened pro-PRC sentiment in the United States, especially in Congress. As a result, when Clinton sent an aircraft carrier thorough the Taiwan Strait in December 1995 as a warning, some said the decision was made in part to prevent Congress from demanding even more radical actions.[42] Clearly Congress expected and wanted stronger actions.

The same was said of Clinton's decision to dispatch two aircraft carriers to the Taiwan Strait in response to Beijing's missile tests in 1996. While the U.S. action seemed to reflect White House resolve, it was interpreted by many as having been compelled by Congress (just as the granting of a visa to President Lee Teng-hui in 1995 was) and done with the realization in mind that inaction would have spurred Congress to demand an even more hostile policy toward Beijing.[43]

In the wake of Hong Kong's return to the PRC on July 1, 1997, Congressional leaders joined together to propose a number of bills that would alter U.S. China policy drastically. These included proposals to promote individual freedom, democracy and free markets in China, ban Chinese leaders responsible for religious persecution in China from getting visas to visit the United States, and add enforcement measures to the 1992 Gore-McCain Act (that would impose sanctions on Beijing for selling cruise missiles to Iran). Another proposal would require the Central Intelligence Agency and the Federal Bureau of Investigation to prepare reports for Congress on the PRC's intelligence activities in the United States. Still another would deny normal trade status to PLA produced goods and products produced by prisoners (actually a tightening up of already existing legislation) while limiting the activities of PLA enterprises operating in the U.S. Last but not least proposals were introduced to sell theater missile defense systems to Taiwan and allow Taipei's admission to the World Trade Organization before Beijing.[44]

Given the impact Congress already had on the formulation of U.S. China policy and its growing concern over Taiwan together with charges against the Clinton Administration for receiving illegal campaign money from China by members of Congress and not being by the public as having formulated a credible China policy, the White

House began to see itself in a position of losing control over China policy and Congress taking over. Since relations with Taiwan are central to the friction between the two branches of government over China policy, it thus appeared wise for the president to get involved directly in negotiations between Beijing and Taipei to rectify this situation lest Congress take further initiatives.

Conclusions

U.S. policy regarding the mutual hostility between Beijing and Taipei has long been one of non-involvement. In 1947, the Marshall Mission returned to the U.S., having failed to get the two sides together. That failure hurt the Truman Administration's credibility. So did the subsequent U.S. "loss" of China. China's "falling" to communism evoked partisan blame casting (on communists in the Department of State and Chiang Kai-shek). It created bitterness in the United States and political polarization that lasted for years and made dealing with the matter of a divided China very difficult.

When the U.S. and the PRC became bitter enemies after the Korean War, efforts to bring about negotiations between Beijing and Taipei were out of the question. The U.S. had tilted toward Taipei. However, this carried with it some risk that Nationalist China might initiate a conflict with the PRC, knowing that the U.S. would fight the strategic part of the war and the Nationalist might once again govern China. So, Washington formulated a policy of preventing hostilities between the two sides that might draw the United States into a broader conflict. Washington accomplished this by signing a defense pact with Taipei and providing Taipei with military assistance to hold Beijing at bay, while at the same time limiting the arms it provided to only those that could be used for defense, not offense. This policy stalemated Beijing-Taipei relations.

The United States subsequently adopted two other policies that applied to the Beijing-Taipei conflict: a peaceful solution only to the "Taiwan issue" and a policy that negotiations should be by the "Chinese themselves." What role the U.S. played or might play behind the scenes in setting the stage for negotiations or pressuring both or either was never cited and was hinted at only infrequently.

President Nixon dramatically changed U.S. China policy but did not alter very much Washington's position on negotiating between Beijing and Taipei. Both sides perceived a mutual security benefit in ending

Washington-Beijing hostility in the face of a growing Soviet threat to both. The Taiwan matter was dealt with cautiously, generally by ignoring it. Nixon thus created deliberate ambiguity in U.S. China policy.

After the Carter Administration accorded diplomatic recognition to Beijing while withdrawing it from Taipei, the Taiwan Relations Act served as the framework for protecting the ROC. Ambiguity, though of a different sort, remained in U.S. China-Taiwan policy, with the White House and the Congress enunciating quite opposing policies regarding Taiwan. It was unclear, therefore, exactly what U.S. policy was. Many, in fact, saw this as advantageous. Flexibility was obviously needed and was desirable if the U.S. might eventually negotiate a resolution of Beijing-Taipei differences. At this time, however, it was clearly too difficult or too early to hold negotiations.

U.S. policy vis-a-vis Beijing-Taipei did not change fundamentally during subsequent administrations, though there were frequent efforts to resolve specific problems. More and more the U.S. played a balancing role while encouraging Beijing-Taipei to resolve their differences. And they did. It appeared, in fact, that the U.S. policies of a peaceful settlement of the Taiwan issue and the Chinese themselves resolving matters might succeed.

In 1995, however, U.S. China-Taiwan policy was thrown off course. President Lee's trip to the U.S. was the immediate cause. This happened at a time when the Congress (as well as most Asian governments) perceived a de-emphasis on foreign policy by the Clinton Administration, a lack of concern with Asia, and a decline in American power. The PRC's general aggressiveness, nationalistic statements and growing military budgets also had an impact.

When the PRC threatened Taiwan with missile tests, the U.S. intervened. The Clinton Administration was put in a dilemma: to not act would severely weaken U.S. credibility in East Asia, and perhaps throughout the world, and may have prompted Congress to become more assertive in foreign policy making. By sending aircraft carriers, the U.S. openly demonstrated it would protect the ROC. There had been some uncertainty about this. A revived Taiwan Relations Act, in the context of a more assertive Congress, strongly influenced the Administration's actions. Meanwhile, members of Congress as well as many independent observers suggested that due to the changed situation (meaning the PRC's increased military power and its aggressive policies) a policy of ambiguity was more dangerous than it was supportive of peace. Likewise, Washington's policy of non-involvement in Beijing-Taipei talks and its engagement (of the PRC) policy were seriously challenged.

The formulation of China policy meanwhile became more polarized between a Republican Congress that supported Taipei (more than Democrats) and a White House and State Department that supported Beijing more than Congress. With Congress increasingly asserting a role in foreign policy making, the White House ostensibly had more reason to promote negotiations between Beijing and Taipei. The TRA provided the legal or policy framework for this. U.S. military assistance to Taiwan provided the leverage. All of this added up to both motive and means for the United States to become more directly involved in and try to resolve Beijing-Taipei differences by negotiations.

Another factor that might have motivated the Clinton Administration to adopt a policy of pursuing negotiations was the fact that no other nation could possibly play a role in starting, sustaining or coercing negotiations between Beijing and Taipei. No other nation has ever tried. The former Soviet Union and Japan have been important players in East Asian politics, but they have never given any indication that they either will or are able to play such a role. The U.S., therefore, would face no competition if it were to decide to call for Beijing-Taipei talks and might improve its status internationally. On the contrary, Washington would have the support of other nations in the region.

The U.S. patently holds the key to Beijing-Taipei relations in several other respects. The two contenders were, and most likely will remain, unable to resolve their differences themselves even though prior to 1995 they seemed to be going in that direction. If Beijing were to try to resolve the "Taiwan issue" by force (and it says it will not renounce the military option) the United States could render such an attempt unsuccessful. If it did not, Taiwan would be invaded and would by force lose its sovereignty and would become part of the PRC. Consequently the U.S. is in a position to ultimately decide Taiwan's future (whether independent, a province of the People's Republic of China or something in between—such as an arrangement involving a commonwealth or some other "Greater China" plan).

The U.S. has also been, and is presently, instrumental in fostering trade and investment ties between the PRC and the ROC. America opening its market to the PRC in large measure prompted ROC investors to go there. This may eventually cement economic relations such that only a peaceful settlement is likely. If this doesn't work, and given the changed situation that makes a U.S. role in negotiating between Beijing and Taipei more desirable for the Clinton Administration, the White House may indeed reverse the policy of saying the problem is one for the Chinese to resolve and establish one of seeking negotiations.

This may indeed explain the flurry of activities in recent months, with a host of high-level U.S. officials travelling to Taipei, seemingly going there to persuade Taiwan's leaders, both government and opposition party, to dampen their comments and stance on Taiwan independence and to ensure that Taiwan does not alter its policy of negotiating with Beijing.

1. See John F. Copper, *China Diplomacy: The Washington-Taipei-Beijing Triangle* (Boulder, CO: Westview Press, 1992)
2. The Congress passed a sense of the Congress resolution in mid-1978 declaring that the president should not cancel a treaty passed by the Congress without consultations. (The U.S. Constitution does not state whether the executive branch of government has this power or not.) The Congress clearly had in mind the U.S.-Republic of China Defense Treaty. Congress also expressed its concern about Carter conducting negotiations with China in secret and without asking for Congressional input. President Carter's decision was announced just before Christmas when Congress had recessed for the holidays.
3. Copper, *China Diplomacy*, p. 135. It should be noted that Congress' call for democracy in Taiwan should have been seen as an obstacle to unification.
4. The language in the TRA (that certain actions are of "grave concern to the United States") allows two interpretations.
5. This was rumor for several months, though the source or sources and how serious such might have been considered is uncertain.
6. Dennis Van Vranken Hickey, *United States-Taiwan Security Ties: From Cold War to Beyond Containment* (Westport, CT: Praeger Publisher, 1994), pp. 82–83.
7. Martin L. Lasater, *The Changing of the Guard: President Clinton and the Security of Taiwan* (Boulder, CO: Westview Press, 1995), pp. 139–41.
8. Ibid., pp. 142–43.
9. Ibid. pp. 145–49.
10. Ibid., pp. 149–52.
11. *United Daily News* (Taipei), October 22, 1995, p. 2.
12. See *China Post* (Taipei), March 12, 1996, p. 1.

13. *Crisis in the Taiwan Strait: Implications for U.S. Foreign Policy* (Hearing before the Subcommittee on Asia and the Pacific, Committee on International Relations, House of Representatives held on March 14, 1996) (Washington, DC: U.S. Government Printing Office 1996), p. 6.

14. N.K. Han, "CNA on U.S. Official's Congressional Testimony on China," China News Agency, April 24, 1997 (from *FBIS* on internet).

15. This working is found in House Resolution H2342 of March 19, 1996 and Senate Resolution S2622 of March 21, 1996. A joint resolution came from these two resolutions. For the complete text, see the *Congressional Record* or, on the internet, www.policy. com (under Taiwan policy).

16. Ibid.

17. "Gingrich's Freedom to Disagree Eludes Ministry Spokesman," The *Nikkei Weekly*, April 14, 1997, p. 6.

18. Seth Faison, "Gingrich: U.S. Would Come to Aid of Taiwan," *Palm Beach Post*, March 31, 1997, p. lA.

19. See Peter W. Rodman, "Broken Triangle: China, Russia, and America After 25 Years" cited in "End of the Cold War has transformed the big powers' 'strategic triangle,'" *Washington Times*, May 19, 1997, p. A12.

20. See A. Doak Barnett, *Communist China and Asia: A Challenge to America* (New York: Vintage, 1960), p. 411.

21. Taipei may, in fact, have had its last good opportunity to "liberate" China during the Great Proletarian Cultural Revolution, especially its violent stage from 1966 to 1969. At this time, the U.S. warned ROC leaders on many occasions not to take any military actions against the mainland.

22. See Copper, *China Diplomacy*, pp. 50–51.

23. See, for example, David Shambaugh, "Containment or Engagement of China? Calculating Beijing's Response," *International Security*, Fall 1996, pp. 180–209.

24. See Dennis Van Vranken Hickey, *Taiwan's Security in a Changing International System* (Boulder, CO: Lynne Reinner Publishers, 1970), chapter 7.

25. "U.S.may sell Hellfire, SuperCobra to ROC," *China Post*, July 26, 19097, p. 1 and "Pentagon to sell Cobra helicopters to Taiwan," *China News*, July 26, 1997, p. 1.

26. Keng Bok-sui, "Military flexes new muscle," *China News*, June 25, 1997, p. 1.

27. For details, see Gerald Segal, "How insecure is Pacific Asia? *International Affairs*, April 1997, pp. 247–48.

28. See House Resolution HR 2035 of June 25, 1997 relative to the sale of ships and Resolution 178 of October 28, 1997 regarding the view of Congress regarding the transfer of Hong Kong and the possible threat it may bring t o Taiwan, in the Congressional Record and found on the internet: www.policy.com.

29. See James Shinn (ed.), Weaving the Net (New York: Council on Foreign Relations Press, 1996)

30. See Copper, China Diplomacy, p. 65.

31. Reflecting the difficulty with this issue, the phrase "one China but not now" was used. See Warren I. Cohen, America's Response to China (New York: Columbia University Press, 1990), p. 197.

32. It is uncertain when this position originated, but it became more widely cited after 1979.

33. See Copper, China Diplomacy, pp. 6–25. President Carter had, by this time, abandoned his "idealistic" views about world politics as a result of dealings with the Soviet Union.

34. Deng may well have thought that this was not the case but pretended it was in order to parry criticism from his opposition in the Party and the government. Deng was focused on economic development and the "Taiwan issue" was a distraction.

35. Taipei was quite tough on the issue of negotiations after the U.,S. broke diplomatic ties. See Copper, China Diplomacy, p. 88.

36. This was specifically stated by the Reagan Administration before the August 1982 Communiqué was negotiated.

37. For details, see Tse-kang Leng, The Taiwan-China Connection: Democracy and Development Across the Taiwan Straits (Boulder, CO: Westview Press, 1996), pp. 39 and 46.

38. For details, see Hungdah Chiu, Koo-Wang Talks and the Prospects of Building Stable Relations Across the Taiwan Straits (Baltimore: University of Maryland School of Law, 1993)

39. Ralph N. Clough, Reaching Across the Taiwan Strait: People to People Diplomacy (Boulder, CO: Westview Press, 1993), p. 82.

40. See Kim R. Holmes and James J. Przystup, Between Diplomacy and Deterrence: Strategies for U.S. Relations with China (Washington, DC: The Heritage Foundation, 1997), p. 4.

41. At the time of this writing, proof for evidence of this is tentative; however, there have been many accusations to this effect.

42. Reports about China's planned aggressive actions circulated in Washington, DC at this time. Pentagon analysts talked about it and some of these discussions reached Congress. This became sensational news in December when former assistant secretary of defense, Charles Freeman, told Anthony Lake, President Clinton's national security advisor, that top Chinese leaders told him of a plan to attack Taiwan after the March 23 presidential election. See Julian Baum and Matt Forney, "Strait of Uncertainty," Far Eastern Economic Review, February 8, 1996, p. 20.

43. A non-binding resolution was gaining support, even among Democrats, in the House of Representatives supporting Taiwan at this time. President Clinton was certainly made aware of this. He was also aware of a coming

election and that the fact that the Republican candidate might make issue of the PRC threats made against Taiwan. For further details, see Nigel Holloway, "Strait Talking," Far Eastern Economic Review, March 21, 1996, p. 16.
44. N.K. Han, "U.S. mulls new laws concerning ROC, PRC," China Post, July 19, 1997, p. 1.

Index

Aborigines, 26-27, 36, 134
Academica Sinica, 85, 92
Acer Sertek, Inc., 121
Adams, Gerry, 6
Advisory Council (of Nationalist Party), 130, 141, 143
Agriculture, 146
America, 6, 24, 31, 35, 48, 155-156, 161-162, 167, 175 (See also United States)
Ami, 83
Anti-Americanism, 5, 7
Anti-Communist sentiment, 136
Anti-independence sentiment, 136
Anti-Teng Hui Lee sentiment, 68-69, 118, 124
Army (of the Republic of China), 4, 1-3, 11, 21, 24, 74, 86-87, 89-90, 116, 153, 164
Asahi Shimbun, 96
Asia, 5, 7, 12, 17, 26-27, 48-49, 51-52, 73, 82, 88, 100-101, 155, 160-161, 165-167, 171, 174-175
Association of Southeast Asian Nations, 51, 155, 161
August Communique, 157-158, 163
Authoritarian, 4, 10, 66, 99, 121, 142
Bader, Jeffrey 160
Beijing, 4, 1, 3-17, 21-25, 27-28, 30-35, 37-51, 64, 71-77, 79-82, 84-93, 95-96, 100-101, 116, 118, 120-121, 127, 135, 138-

139, 153-165, 167-176. See also People's Republic of China
Bernstein, Richard, 12
Buddhists, 76, 103
Burns, Nicholas, 159
Bush, George, 4, 17, 157, 17
Business, 38, 49, 71, 74, 93, 98-99, 119, 129, 133-134, 137, 139, 142, 170
Campaigns (election), 44, 71, 94, 102-103, 120. See also Elections
Capitalism, 3, 42
Carter Administration, 156, 174
Carter, Jimmy, 16, 156, 169
Censorship, 66, 83
Central Advisory Committee (of Nationalist Party), 126, 130
Central Standing Committee (of the Nationalist Party), 121, 125-126, 134, 137-138, 141-142, 144-145
Chang Jen-syang, 138, 145
Chang Lung-sheng, 98
Chang, John 98, 131, 145
Chang, Parris, 87
Charismatic (leaders), 76, 115
Chen Cheng, 75
Chen Chen-sheng, 82
Chen Li-an, 70, 75-82, 84-85, 89, 91-94, 116, 118
Chen Shui-bian, 11, 80-81, 115, 124
Chen Tang-shan, 84
Chen Tzu-chin, 132
Chi Haotien, 24

ABOUT THE AUTHOR

John F. Copper is the Stanley J. Buckman Distinguished Professor of International Studies at Rhodes College in Memphis, Tennessee. He is the author of more than 20 books on China, Taiwan, and Asian affairs. His book *China's Global Role* (Stanford: Hoover Institution Press, 1980) won the Clarence Day Foundation Award for outstanding research and creative activity. Professor Copper's most recent books include *China Diplomacy: The Washington-Taipei-Beijing Triangle* (Boulder, CO: Westview Press, 1992); *Words across the Taiwan Strait: A Critique of Beijing's "White Paper" on China's Reunification* (Lanham, MD: University Press of America, 1995); *The Taiwan Political Miracle: Essays on Political Development, Elections and Foreign Relations* (Lanham, MD: University Press of America, 1997); *Taiwan's Mid-1990s Elections: Taking the Final Steps to Democracy* (Westport, CT: Praeger Publishers, 1998); *Taiwan: Nation-State or Province?* (3rd ed.) (Boulder, CO: Westview Press, 1999); *Taiwan Historical Dictionary* (second edition) (Lanham, MD: Scarecrow Press, 1999). Dr. Copper has also contributed to more than 40 other books and has published over 150 articles and pieces in scholarly journals and newspapers. Professor Copper has testified before the Senate Foreign Relations Committee and the House Foreign Affairs Committee. Dr. Copper received his B.A. degree from the University of Nebraska, his M.A. from the University of Hawaii, and his PhD degree from the University of South Carolina. He also studied at the University of California, Berkeley and at Taiwan Normal University in Taipei. He is the recipient of the 1997 International Communications Award. Dr. Copper speaks Chinese and has lived in Asia for 13 years.